TONGUES

BEYOND THE UPPER ROOM

Compiled from the teachings of

Kenneth E. Hagin

16 15 14 13 12 11 10   11 10 09 08 07 06 05

Tongues: Beyond the Upper Room
ISBN-13: 978-0-89276-538-6
ISBN-10: 0-89276-538-0

In the U.S. write:
Kenneth Hagin Ministries
P.O. Box 50126
Tulsa, OK 74150-0126
1-888-28-FAITH
www.rhema.org

In Canada write:
Kenneth Hagin Ministries
P.O. Box 335, Station D
Etobicoke (Toronto), Ontario
Canada, M9A 4X3
1-866-70-RHEMA
www.rhemacanada.org

TABLE OF CONTENTS

FOREWORD

I believe that my father, Rev. Kenneth E. Hagin, was one of the greatest men of God of this generation. I know I'm a little prejudiced, but I'd believe that even if I *weren't* his son. I certainly know a great number of other people who feel the same way I do.

Throughout my life, I listened attentively to Dad, trying to learn as much of his wisdom as I could. I always stood in awe of the revelations he received from God's Word over the years. In this book, Dad makes the statement that all those revelations came to him as a result of much prayer and studying the Word. I can personally attest to the truth of that statement.

I have vivid memories of my dad when I was six and seven years old and he was pastoring his last church before he went out on the field. Many times as I went to bed at night in that small, old parsonage, I'd look over at my dad—a tall, skinny young man of about 31 years old—as he sat bowed over his desk in the corner, studying the Bible by the light of a little desk lamp.

Sometimes I'd wake up and turn over in the middle of the night, and there that young man would be, still sitting at that desk. Mom would wake me up for school the next morning, and Dad would still be sitting there, with books and open Bibles lying all over the desk or spread out on the floor around him.

Dad would always get up from his desk and sit down at the kitchen table to eat breakfast with my sister Pat and me before we left for school. But many times when I came home from school in the afternoon, I'd see my dad still sitting at that same desk, surrounded by the same books and open Bibles.

I remember many mornings when I'd wake up and find out that my dad had prayed all night long. Without ever having gone to bed, he would take a shower and clean up; then he'd go out to take care of the business of the church all day long. Dad would simply say, "Well, the Holy Spirit will refresh me."

So if you have ever wondered how Kenneth E. Hagin learned all that he knew and all that he taught to so many people over his almost 70 years of ministry, now you know. He received that revelation knowledge by studying the Bible and other good books and by praying hours upon hours on end. Do you want to get to where my dad was in his spiritual walk? Well, that's the kind of price you have to be willing to pay.

During the Charismatic Renewal of the 1960s and 1970s, my father spoke into the lives of many, explaining the necessity of the power of the Holy Spirit. God used him in a profound way to touch that generation.

Then in the 1990s, it seemed that manifestations of that power waned. But now I sense in my spirit a greater move of the Holy Spirit on the horizon. Because tongues is so important, we have gathered transcripts of much of Dad's teaching on the subject and compiled a comprehensive study for these days. Dad spoke simply, and we believe his words will help others understand these vital truths.

I thank God for the heritage I have, and I am proud to introduce to you this powerful book that explores the profound value of speaking with other tongues. These pages contain the rich and timeless teachings of one of the foremost prophets of God given to this generation—my father, Kenneth E. Hagin.

He went home to be with the Lord in 2003, but his words and his prayers for the Body of Christ are still important and helpful, calling believers to come up higher in prayer and to live in the fullness of their inheritance in Christ.

The last days are upon us, and God is looking for those who are willing to pay the price in prayer. We've stopped short at the door to the supernatural far too long. For my father, the door was praying in tongues as provided to him through the infilling of the Holy Spirit. There are various evidences to the fullness of the Spirit in a person's life. But it's important that we begin with and not settle for less than what the Bible provides for us in tongues. As Dad stated so eloquently, "People are dying, and the end is coming. The end of all things is at hand, and what we do, we must do quickly."

So I urge you to let my father's teaching stir you to the depths of your being to begin praying in the Spirit like never before. It's time to step *through* the door and begin to walk in the power and revelation of the Holy Spirit on a daily basis. And as you make yourself available to God in prayer, He will begin to use you to bring about His purposes on this earth in ways that today you can't even imagine!

Kenneth W. Hagin

PREFACE

Over the centuries, there has been much misunderstanding in the Church concerning the matter of speaking with other tongues, not only among those who don't speak with tongues, but also among those who do.

First, there are those outside of Pentecostal and Charismatic circles who don't speak with tongues. They know nothing at all about the subject, or they have wrong ideas about tongues that cannot be born out in Scripture.

Then there are those in Pentecostal and Charismatic circles who also know very little about this subject, even though they themselves speak with tongues. These Christians don't realize the value derived from exercising that gift, nor do they understand the scope—the purpose and the use—of tongues. As a result, they often take tongues out of its proper setting in the Word, and their ignorance leads them into excess and unscriptural practices. They go too far, taking tongues beyond what the Word says.

In both cases, this lack of understanding about tongues has brought much damage to the cause of Christ and has robbed multitudes of the blessings God intended for them to have.

In the Church world as a whole, a wide variety of teaching exists on this subject of the Holy Spirit and speaking in tongues. But we need to examine what we believe in the light of God's Word, not in the light of our experience, nor in the light of what our particular church or denomination may teach.

We also need to remember what the Apostle Paul said in First Corinthians 12:1: *"Now concerning spiritual gifts, brethren,*

I would not have you ignorant." God doesn't want us to be ignorant of things pertaining to the Holy Spirit, yet the fact remains that misunderstandings abound when it comes to this subject of speaking with other tongues.

However, one thing is surely certain: This is not a subject to be cast lightly aside or considered to be unimportant to the Body of Christ. God does not fill His Book with things of minor importance, nor does He make unnecessary statements—and He has much to say about this matter in His Word. That is why I want us to do an in-depth study on speaking with other tongues.

Years ago the Lord told me that there are some areas of prayer and intercession that will be lost unless we who are experienced in prayer somehow get those truths over to this present generation. God needs more people of prayer to get the job done on this earth. I'm inviting you to be one of them— and to start by learning more about the true scope and value of praying in other tongues.

[This Preface was compiled from Kenneth E. Hagin's notes on the subject of tongues.—Ed.]

THE HOLY SPIRIT
AND TONGUES

PART 1

CHAPTER 1

FOUR COMMON OBJECTIONS TO SPEAKING IN TONGUES

Oftentimes our denominational friends who do not speak with tongues ask us, "Why do you folks give such prominence to speaking with other tongues?"

Well, the answer is that we don't! However, there are several reasons that make it seem like we do. One reason is the fact that those outside of Full Gospel circles are always asking us about the subject and compelling us to discuss it! Here are a few other reasons it seems like we give prominence to speaking in tongues:

1. Speaking with other tongues is always manifested when one is baptized with the Holy Ghost. It is the supernatural evidence of the Holy Spirit's infilling in a person's life. (We'll talk further about this later.)

2. The spiritual gifts of tongues and interpretation of tongues are distinctive of this dispensation in which we live (1 Cor. 12:1–11).

3. The Apostle Paul gave prominence to the subject of tongues. In fact, in his first letter to the Corinthian church, he wrote quite a bit about it. (See First Corinthians 14.) Why did Paul give so much prominence to tongues? Because then, as now, the subject was much misunderstood.

We're going to cover a lot of ground as we explore what God's Word says about the infilling of the Holy Spirit with the evidence of speaking in tongues. But first, I want to address some of the common objections people have against this subject of tongues.

Objection #1: 'Jesus didn't speak in tongues, so I don't have to either.'

It's true that although you will find all the other seven gifts of the Spirit manifested in the earthly ministry of Jesus, you won't find tongues and interpretation operating in His ministry. You also won't find speaking with other tongues or interpretation of tongues in demonstration in the Old Testament (although you will find this gift prophesied about in Isaiah 28:11–12). These two gifts of the Spirit are distinctive of this Holy Spirit Dispensation, or age, which began with the outpouring of the Holy Ghost on the Day of Pentecost as recorded in Acts 2.

Jesus mentioned this new gift that God would give to His people under the New Covenant. In Mark 16:17–18, Jesus declared that five supernatural signs are to follow believers, and one of them is that "... *they shall speak with new tongues*" (v. 17).

Some folks endeavor to explain that verse away by saying, "Well, that just means you used to curse and tell vulgar jokes before you were saved, but now you don't do that anymore. Or you used to lie, but now you don't lie anymore." It's true that you shouldn't be doing those things, especially once you're a child of God, but that is *not* what this scripture is talking about.

All five of these signs listed in Mark 16:17-18 are supernatural. Believers shall lay hands on the sick, and they shall recover—supernaturally. They will cast out devils—by the supernatural power of God. If they drink any deadly thing or take up a serpent, it will not harm them—because of God's supernatural protection.

Now, of course, that doesn't mean you can handle deadly serpents just to prove something. But you can be supernaturally protected like Paul was when he accidentally picked up a deadly viper along with an armful of wood on the island of Melita (Acts 28:3-5). The serpent bit Paul on the hand, but he just shook it off into the fire, and the poison had no effect on him.

If four of these five signs mentioned in Mark 16 are supernatural, does it make sense that God would add one more sign and make it natural? No! Besides, Jesus did *not* say, "*A few* believers will speak with other tongues." He clearly implied that *all* believers should do so.

Why is it, then, that most believers do *not* speak with other tongues? I'm sure we could find a number of reasons why this is true. Sometimes the reason is pertinent to the individual. In other words, some people have their own personal reasons for not speaking in tongues.

However, I'm also sure of the number-one reason: There has been very little sound, logical, and scriptural teaching as to the scope and the value of speaking with tongues. As a result, many folks are not cognizant of this gift that God has made available to them. They just don't realize the value of speaking in tongues—because if they did, they would all want to do it!

Objection #2: 'Tongues are of the devil.'

When I was just a young boy preacher, I would fellowship with the Pentecostals because they believed in divine healing. I had been healed and raised up from a deathbed by the power of God, and it strengthened my faith in healing to fellowship with others of like-precious faith. As a result, my denominational colleagues were deeply concerned about me, and they would warn me about "those Pentecostal people." They spoke in all sincerity and honesty, but with minds befuddled with unscriptural theological concepts.

I remember in particular the words of one Bible teacher, a graduate of a denominational seminary. He said to me, "I admit that almost everything those Full Gospel people teach and preach is fundamental and right. And I'll also admit that they live better lives than we do in our church. But that speaking in tongues is of the devil!"

I didn't answer this man right then, but I thought to myself, *How in the world can people get something from the devil that makes them better? I thought it was always the other way around! Isn't it the devil that tries to make people do bad things and the Holy Ghost who helps them to do right?*

That unscriptural thinking reminds me about something that happened to a fellow from east Texas who was *wild* before he got saved in his early thirties. As a boy, he had attended a denominational church, although he had never gotten saved. But once he hit his teenage years, the young man went wild and began to frequent bars every night.

Any sin you want to mention, this man did it in his younger years, from drinking and cussing to brawling and fighting. In fact, there were some nights when he'd whip everyone who challenged him and clear out the bar! They'd have to call in two or three squad cars to come and take him to jail. This young man was *tough!*

Years later, some Full Gospel people started witnessing to this man, and he got saved, baptized in the Holy Ghost, and spoke with other tongues. The church he'd attended as a child just left him alone during the more than 20 years he'd been so wild. The pastor hadn't bothered to visit him even once. But all of a sudden, the pastor who had ignored him for all those years came to visit the man with deep concern—because he'd "gotten something from the devil."

It would be funny if it weren't so pathetic!

That man told me personally what happened during the pastor's visit. He said, "I let the pastor talk for a while, but when he said, 'That speaking in tongues is of the devil,' I stopped him and said, 'Wait a minute, Pastor. I know that tongues isn't of the devil, because I had everything the devil could give me when I was a sinner. If tongues were of the devil, I would have had it long ago! But I didn't receive this gift until I turned my back on the devil and got saved and filled with the Holy Ghost!'"

No matter how much the pastor tried, he couldn't talk that man out of speaking in tongues. The man *knew* he had received that gift from God.

As for me, the moment I was filled with the Holy Ghost and began speaking with other tongues, I went looking for that Bible teacher who had told me that tongues were of the devil. In times past, he would always bring up the subject, but this time *I* brought it up because I wanted to get something over to him.

Once again, the Bible teacher warned me about "those Pentecostal folks." Again he told me, "That speaking with tongues is of the devil!"

I replied, "Now wait a minute—stop right there. You say that speaking with tongues is of the devil?"

"That's right!"

"Well," I said, "if tongues *is* of the devil, then so is our entire denomination!"

The man's eyes got as big as saucers. He looked like he'd seen a ghost! Finally he sputtered, "What are you talking about?"

I said, "You know I've been filled with the Holy Ghost and speak with other tongues. Well, the same Holy Spirit I got acquainted with in our denomination, the same Spirit who recreated my spirit and witnessed to my spirit that I am a child of God—that's the same Holy Spirit who gave me utterance in other tongues down at the Full Gospel church when I was filled with the Spirit!

"The Pentecostals don't have a different Holy Spirit than we have. He isn't twins or triplets or quadruplets or quintuplets. There is only one Holy Ghost! It's identically the same Spirit— just a different dimension."

"Oh no, no!" he protested. "That isn't right."

I said, "You're a Bible scholar, aren't you?"

"Oh yes, I'm a seminary graduate and have taught the Bible for 25 years."

"So let me ask you something," I said. "Have you ever spoken with other tongues?"

"No, of course not," the man said.

"Then how do you know what Spirit is behind it?" I asked. "You say you know the Bible. Then you must know the proverb that says a man who answers a matter before he hears it is a fool [Prov. 18:13]. According to that proverb, you're being foolish right now!

"I'm the only one qualified to speak on the subject of tongues in this conversation," I continued. "You're not qualified to comment unless you've spoken with tongues. If you had, you could tell me what Spirit gave you that utterance. But I can tell you right now that it's the same Holy Ghost. I didn't receive any strange or new spirit. He is identically the same Spirit I had all the time. When I got filled with the Spirit, I just experienced a greater measure of the Holy Ghost. So if speaking with tongues is of the devil, our entire denomination is of the devil!"

My words shocked this Bible teacher so much that he opened his mouth a time or two but couldn't think of anything to say!

Of course, that denomination is *not* of the devil, and neither is speaking with tongues! It's all of the Holy Ghost. Speaking in tongues just opens you up to a deeper dimension of the same Spirit. You can go deeper in God if you want to!

Your Father Will Give You
What You Ask For

Now, here's something I want to get over to you along this line: *If you're a child of God and ask to receive the infilling of the Holy Spirit, you're not going to get something else.*

I remember a Bible teacher from another church who had come to my meeting to get filled with the Holy Spirit. Before I prayed for him, he said to me, "Now, Brother Hagin, I'll just be honest with you ahead of time. I've been studying the Bible, and I've begun to see that tongues are not of the devil. But I'm still having trouble with it. I guess it's the way I've been taught against tongues for so long. Can you tell me how I can know that I won't receive the wrong spirit when we pray?"

This man had heard all kinds of stories about people receiving false spirits when they prayed for the baptism in the Holy Spirit. As a young denominational preacher, I had heard all those tales myself before I received the baptism in the Holy Ghost in 1937. But since then, in more than 65 years of preaching among Full Gospel people, I never once saw someone receive a wrong spirit when the person asked to be filled with the Holy Spirit—not one single time.

Now, don't misunderstand me. I've seen some Spirit-filled folks get in the flesh. But I'd rather have a little wildfire while God is moving than no fire at all! I'd rather have a little disorder than to have the order of a graveyard with nothing happening!

This man wanted to be sure he would receive the Holy Spirit and not some other spirit when we prayed, so I simply read Luke 11:11–13 to him.

LUKE 11:11-13

11 If a son shall ask bread of any of you that is a father, will he give him a stone? or if he ask a fish, will he for a fish give him a serpent?

12 Or if he shall ask an egg, will he offer him a scorpion?

13 If ye then, being evil, know how to give good gifts unto your children: how much more shall your heavenly Father GIVE THE HOLY SPIRIT TO THEM THAT ASK HIM?

I asked the man, "Do you have any children?"—to which he replied, "Yes." Then I asked him, "If your son asked you for a fish, would you give him a serpent? Or if he asked you for an egg, would you offer him a scorpion?"

The man replied, "No, of course not."

"Neither would God," I told him. "I want to show you what Jesus was actually talking about in this passage. We can find the answer one chapter earlier in Luke 10:19, where it says, *'Behold, I give unto you power to tread on serpents and scorpions, and over all the power of the enemy.'*"

I continued, "You see, Jesus wasn't talking about literal snakes or actual scorpions here. He was talking about the power of the enemy! He was talking about demons and evil spirits, and that's what He called serpents and scorpions."

This lets us know that Jesus was actually saying, "If a son asks for a fish, will his father give him a serpent (an evil spirit)? Or if he asks for an egg, will his father offer him a scorpion (an evil spirit)?"

Then I said to the man, "You're a child of God, and that means God is your Father, right?"

"Yes," he said.

"Well," I said, "Just as you would never give something evil to *your* children, do you think your Heavenly Father would give you, His child, an evil spirit when you ask Him for His Spirit?"

Do you know what that fellow did when I said that to him? He started laughing—and then he immediately began to speak in tongues! Once he was released from his fear, I didn't even have to pray with him to receive the Holy Spirit!

He said, "Brother Hagin, if I'd known what you just told me, I could have been talking in tongues long ago!"

That man had been bound up as a result of what he'd heard, missing out on the blessings God had for him. The devil had bombarded his mind with fearful thoughts that he might get the wrong spirit if he prayed for the Holy Spirit's infilling.

That never has to happen to you, friend. You never have to be afraid to receive the Holy Ghost. But here is what you must always keep in mind: The Word of God will *always* set you free!

JOHN 8:32

32 And ye shall know the truth, and the truth shall make you free.

Jesus didn't say the truth will bind you. He said the truth of God's Word will *make you free.*

There is absolutely no danger—none whatsoever—of a believer receiving the wrong spirit when he asks God to fill him with the Holy Spirit. In fact, I'll be even plainer about it and say this: If anyone claims he received the wrong spirit when he asked for the Holy Ghost, he lied about it!

To say that Christians can receive a wrong spirit when they ask for the Holy Spirit is saying that Jesus Christ is a partner to a lie. And I would much rather call a person a liar than to call *Jesus* a liar. As Romans 3:4 says, "*. . . Let God be true, but EVERY man a liar . . .*"!

Jesus said, "*. . . How much more shall your heavenly Father give the Holy Spirit to them that ask him?*" (Luke 11:13). In other words, if you ask for the infilling of the Holy Spirit, that is exactly what you will get!

Objection #3: 'Tongues have ceased.'

One time a person came to me and said, "Why, don't you know that the Bible said tongues have ceased?"

I answered, "No, I don't know that, and you don't either!"

"Oh, yes, I read it in the Bible!"

"All right," I replied, "if you can give me chapter and verse, I'll give you a thousand-dollar reward!" Now, I didn't have the thousand dollars, but I wasn't afraid. I knew I wouldn't have to pay the money, because I knew that person couldn't find any scripture in the Bible saying tongues have ceased!

The man looked and looked and looked, trying to find a verse that proved his point. Finally, he gave up searching, and I decided to help him out. I said, "The verse you're hunting for is First Corinthians 13:8."

"Oh, so I'm right that the Bible really does say tongues have ceased!"

I said, "Oh, no. Let's read it, and I'll show you what this verse really says."

1 CORINTHIANS 13:8

8 Charity never faileth: but whether there be prophecies, they shall fail; whether there be tongues, they shall cease; whether there be knowledge, it shall vanish away.

"When you read the whole verse," I told this man, "it gives a different understanding to it. You see, it says that tongues *shall* cease, not that they *have* ceased. It also says that prophecies *shall* fail and that knowledge *shall* vanish away. All of these things are future tense. So tongues haven't ceased yet anymore than knowledge has vanished away!"

Then I showed the man the next few verses so he could learn more about what Paul is actually saying about tongues in this passage.

1 CORINTHIANS 13:9–10

9 For we know in part, and we prophesy in part.

10 But when that which is perfect is come, then that which is in part shall be done away.

Some people use verse 10 to try to forbid tongues. In error they claim, "When Paul said, 'when that which is perfect is come,' he was talking about the Bible. So now that we have the

Bible in its complete form, we no longer need the supernatural gift of tongues!"

But that interpretation of verse 10 doesn't hold water when you combine it with verse 12.

1 CORINTHIANS 13:12

12 For now we see through a glass, darkly; but then face to face: now I know in part; but then shall I know even as also I am known.

It is obvious that we do not yet see face to face and that we still *do* see "through a glass, darkly." It is therefore also evident that prophecies have not failed, that knowledge has not vanished away, and that tongues have not ceased!

The people who try to forbid tongues based on this passage of Scripture would do well to also read First Corinthians 14:39: *"Wherefore, brethren, covet to prophesy, and FORBID NOT TO SPEAK WITH TONGUES."* The Apostle Paul and the Early Church certainly didn't forbid people to speak in tongues. In fact, Paul gave a number of reasons in this chapter to *encourage* people to speak with tongues, which is the subject of a later discussion.

Objection #4: 'Only the apostles could pray for people to receive the baptism in the Holy Spirit.'

Some people use Acts 8:14–17 to prove that the baptism in the Holy Spirit with the evidence of speaking in tongues was only available for the Early Church as long as the original apostles were still alive. These people mistakenly maintain that only the apostles could minister the baptism in the Holy Spirit to people.

However, this passage in Acts proves the contrary is true.

ACTS 8:14–17

14 Now when the apostles which were at Jerusalem heard that Samaria had received the word of God, they sent unto them Peter and John:

15 Who, when they were come down, prayed for them, that they might receive the Holy Ghost:

16 (For as yet he was fallen upon none of them: only they were baptized in the name of the Lord Jesus.)

17 Then laid they their hands on them, and they received the Holy Ghost.

People who hold to the argument that tongues ceased with the last apostle say, "The apostles received the Holy Ghost on the Day of Pentecost, and then they were able to pass on the Holy Ghost to others. But those folks in turn couldn't pass the Holy Ghost on to anyone else.

These people contend, "That's the reason Philip didn't try to pass the Holy Ghost on to the Samaritans after he got them saved. Philip couldn't minister the baptism in the Holy Spirit because he wasn't one of the original apostles. So Peter and John had to come down to Samaria to lay hands on the new believers to receive the Holy Ghost. But when the last apostle died, the ability to minister the baptism in the Holy Spirit to others ceased!"

But that argument just isn't in line with the Word. We are going to talk at length later about the five recorded instances in the Book of Acts where people were filled with the Holy Spirit. But I want to make this particular point here: In two of the five instances where believers received the Holy Ghost, they received without the laying on of hands. And on one of the other three occasions, the person who ministered the baptism in the Holy Spirit wasn't even an apostle! I'm talking about the "certain disciple at Damascus" named Ananias (Acts 9:10) who went to Saul of Tarsus (soon to be called Paul) and laid hands on him that he might be filled with the Holy Spirit (Acts 9:17).

Once after preaching at a meeting, I sat down on a chair on the platform and began laying hands on folks as they came by me in a line to be healed and to receive the Holy Spirit.

As I asked each person why he or she had come forward for prayer, a certain man in the line spoke up and asked, "Do you claim to be an apostle?" Everyone could hear this man's question over the microphone.

"No, I'm not an apostle," I replied, "and I don't claim to be one. I'm sure I don't have the qualifications."

"Well, then, what are you doing laying hands on folks to receive the Holy Ghost?" the man asked me.

Of course, the minute the man said that, I had him located. So I said, "Oh, I see that you really know your New Testament."

"Oh, yes! We speak where the New Testament speaks, and we are silent where it's silent."

"All right," I said. "Now, do you say that the New Testament teaches that no one but the original apostles could minister the infilling of the Holy Spirit to people? In other words, do you believe that only the 12 apostles received the Holy Ghost on the day of Pentecost, and not the 120?"

"Yes!" the man replied.

"And you also believe that these apostles had the power to pass the ability to minister the Holy Ghost on to someone else by laying on of hands—but that when the last apostle died, all of that ceased?"

"Yes, that's right."

"Well," I said, "the only difference between me and you is that you claim to speak where the New Testament speaks and to be silent where it is silent, but you're lying about it. On the other hand, I do speak where it speaks, and I'm silent where it is silent."

"What do you mean?" the man asked.

"What about Ananias in Acts 9?" I asked. "Ananias wasn't an apostle."

This man said, "I don't exactly know what you're talking about."

I opened my Bible to Acts 9 and read the following verses:

ACTS 9:10–12,17

10 And there was A CERTAIN DISCIPLE at Damascus, named Ananias; and to him said the Lord in a vision, Ananias. And he said, Behold, I am here, Lord.

11 And the Lord said unto him, Arise, and go into the street which is called Straight, and inquire in the house of Judas for one called Saul, of Tarsus: for, behold, he prayeth,

> **12** And hath seen in a vision a man named Ananias coming in, and PUTTING HIS HAND ON HIM, that he might receive his sight. . . .
>
> **17** And Ananias went his way, and entered into the house; and PUTTING HIS HANDS ON HIM said, Brother Saul, the Lord, even Jesus, that appeared unto thee in the way as thou camest, hath sent me, that thou mightest receive thy sight, and BE FILLED WITH THE HOLY GHOST.

"Now answer me please," I said to the man, "was Ananias an apostle?"

"I didn't know that was in there," the man said.

"You see, you'd better be careful when you say that you speak where the New Testament speaks! Nowhere in the Bible does it say that only apostles can minister the baptism in the Holy Spirit."

As the man started to walk away, I said, "Wait a minute! Before you leave, you asked me if I was an apostle and tried to prove that I had no right to lay hands on folks to receive the Holy Ghost because I am *not* an apostle. But I just proved to you from the Word that people who are not apostles can lay hands on others to receive the Holy Spirit."

I continued, "You wanted to know by what authority I minister by the laying on of hands, and I want to tell you. I lay hands on folks to receive the Holy Ghost by the same authority by which the 'certain disciple at Damascus' named Ananias laid hands on Saul of Tarsus. It says in verse 10: '. . . to him [Ananias] said the Lord in a vision. . . .'"

The word *disciple* just means "a follower of the Lord." This man Ananias was not an apostle. He was not a prophet. He was not an evangelist. He was not a pastor. He was not a teacher. He was just what you and I would call a "layperson," and he was directed by the Lord Jesus Himself, the Head of the Church, to go lay his hands on Saul to receive the Holy Ghost.

I believe God put this account in the Bible because He knew we'd face this argument from some folks—that only the apostles could minister the baptism in the Holy Spirit and that when the last apostle died, that was the end of it. People who argue that way are left speechless when they find out what the New Testament actually does say!

So I said to the man, "I lay hands on folks to receive the Holy Ghost because the same Jesus who appeared to Ananias in Damascus told me, 'I want you to go lay hands on believers to receive the Holy Ghost.'

"That is the authority by which I minister by the laying on of hands—the Lord Jesus, the Head of the Church! If you want to argue and fuss about it, I suggest that you go argue and fuss with Jesus, because He's the One who told me to do it." With that, I sent the man on his way.

I want to make one more point about what happened when Jesus told me that He had given me the ministry of laying on of hands for the infilling of the Holy Spirit.

I wasn't necessarily happy about that news. I said to Jesus, "Dear Lord, I get enough criticism just from folks getting filled with the Holy Spirit in my church. As sure as I start laying hands on people to receive the Holy Spirit, I'll get criticized even more!

Lord, I don't believe I want to do that. I just wish You'd give this ministry to someone else."

Well, Jesus sure did let me have it on that one! He asked me, "Who called you? Did I or did people?"

"Well," I said, "You did!"

Then He asked me, "To whom shall you give an account for your ministry—unto Me or unto people?"

"Why, unto You, Lord!" I said.

Then the Lord said, "It is written that all must stand before the Judgment Seat of Christ to give an account of the deeds done in the body [2 Cor. 5:10]. On that day, you will stand before Me and give an account unto *Me*! And all those who have criticized your ministry will also give an account unto Me for what they said about it. After all, it is *My* ministry, and when people criticize your ministry of laying on of hands, they are criticizing Me."

Jesus continued, "So you leave those people in My hands. They will have to give an account to Me for what they said. Meanwhile, I have given this ministry to you, and you're going to have to give an account unto *Me* as to whether you have or have not fulfilled this ministry I have given to you."

"Well, Lord, I guess I better do something about it then."

"Yes, you certainly had," Jesus replied.

"But what do I tell people?" I asked.

Jesus gave me the three instances in the Book of Acts where people received the Holy Ghost through the laying on of hands. Then He simply said to me, "Give people the scriptures."

So that's exactly what I've done! Thank God for the Word of God! It's so clear and concise and plain.

Don't Get in a Pentecostal 'Rut'

Before Jesus ever gave me the ministry of the laying on of hands, He was using me to get people filled with the Holy Spirit.

In 1939 I was ministering at another pastor's church, preaching a message on salvation—which, at the time, was the only message I knew how to preach. Right in the middle of my message, I suddenly began to speak with other tongues. I believe this was only the second or third time I'd ever given a message in tongues in the public assembly. I spoke with tongues three times in succession and interpreted each time.

All the interpretations were about the infilling of the Holy Ghost—an entirely different subject than what I was preaching about. God was trying to direct the service in another direction. (We ministers need to sense which way the Holy Spirit is going in our services and just flow with Him!)

Inspired by the Holy Spirit, I found myself doing something I'd never done before. I simply said, "Everyone who has not been filled with the Holy Ghost and wants to be filled, stand to your feet."

Immediately five people leapt to their feet.

Standing in the pulpit, I then said to those five people (and it startled me when I said it!), "Receive the Holy Ghost!" All but one of the five instantly began speaking in tongues. When one woman started speaking in tongues, she was so thrilled that she came out from between the pews and started dancing down the aisle!

The pastor looked at me startled and said, "My, my, my! Why, some of those people have been seeking the baptism in the Holy Spirit for years! They've tarried for hours on end! We've struggled with them and finally just given up on them— particularly this one woman who is so happy! We'd just given up on her as someone who couldn't receive the Holy Ghost. No one would even pray with her anymore."

No wonder this woman was dancing down the aisles! People had pulled and tugged and knocked and slapped and cried and hollered for years, trying to drag this woman into the baptism in the Holy Ghost—and God filled her in a split second!

After that service, the pastor asked me to start a week-long revival there—but the revival ended up lasting for a month! God gave us such a powerful revival that the pastor's Sunday school and church membership doubled and his finances tripled! I didn't do all of that—*God* did. I just let the Holy Spirit move.

I remember one night of that revival in particular. People were getting filled with the Holy Spirit every night, but on this one night, 12 people came forward to receive the Holy Ghost. That was the largest number to come up for prayer at one time. I wanted to get these 12 out of the spiritual rut they had been stuck in, so I wouldn't even let them kneel at the altar.

We can all get in certain spiritual ruts, even with scriptural acts such as kneeling to pray. That doesn't mean kneeling in prayer isn't good to do. After all, Paul said in Ephesians 3:14, "*. . . I bow my knees unto the Father of our Lord Jesus Christ*," and I myself like to kneel when I pray. But we can get in a rut where we seek God only in a certain way, until eventually we might find ourselves no longer making any spiritual progress.

That's what has happened with many in the Pentecostal and Charismatic circles. As people seek God to receive the Holy Spirit, they often get used to "doing it the way our church has always done it," such as kneeling at the altar to pray. Then too often they start praising God from their heads, parroting what they have heard others say rather than praising Him from their hearts—and that's as far as they ever get. I call it the "Pentecostal rut." It's a rut many people have a very difficult time getting out of!

So I instructed these 12 who came forward to receive the Holy Spirit to stand in front of the altar. Then I told them, "Receive the Holy Ghost!"—and every one of them started speaking in tongues all at the same time! It happened at the snap of a finger; they all received. I didn't touch them or lay hands on them at all.

Throughout the 1940s, this was the primary way the Holy Spirit used me to minister the baptism in the Holy Spirit (and He's continued to work with me that way at times throughout my ministry). Most of the time I wouldn't lay hands on the people. I'd just have them come and stand in front of the altar. Then I'd tell them to receive the Holy Ghost, and they would receive.

So you can see that biblically and spiritually, you don't have to be one of the early apostles to lead someone into the baptism in the Holy Spirit. You don't even have to be a minister. Today believers all over the world are helping people get filled with the Holy Spirit, just as a certain disciple named Ananias did long ago!

These are just four of the most common objections people use to oppose speaking with other tongues because they don't know what the Word says about it. As we go further in our discussion on this subject, we'll address other questions and misconceptions that commonly arise. But here is the bottom line to remember as we study this or any other area of our spiritual walk: *The closer we stay with the Word of God, the more correct we will be in whatever we do.*

CHAPTER 2

SALVATION AND THE INFILLING: TWO SEPARATE EXPERIENCES?

When I was a young denominational boy preacher, I began to see from the Word that although I was saved and I knew the Holy Spirit through His work in the New Birth, I hadn't yet experienced what the Pentecostals called "receiving the Holy Ghost." As I studied the New Testament, the Spirit of God helped me understand the passages on this subject.

Through the Scriptures I became convinced that if I received the same Holy Ghost the Pentecostals received, I'd have the same initial, supernatural sign—the evidence of speaking with tongues. I wasn't going to be satisfied with anything less!

I had been saved four years and raised up from a deathbed totally healed three years by that time. I knew I had the anointing of the Holy Ghost to preach. I also knew it was the Holy Spirit who healed people when I prayed for them. But eventually I came to see very clearly that I needed to receive the Holy Ghost as a separate experience from salvation.

Many people don't understand that truth, however. In fact, the distinction between the work of the Holy Spirit in the New Birth versus the infilling of the Holy Spirit is not clearly seen by the majority of the Church world. Yet the Scriptures thoroughly define these as two separate experiences.

Jesus' words about the Holy Spirit in John 14 refer to the New-Birth experience:

JOHN 14:17

17 . . . Ye know him; for he dwelleth with you, and shall be IN you.

Then in Acts 1:5 and 8, Jesus speaks of the Holy Ghost again, but His words clearly point to a different experience:

ACTS 1:5,8

5 For John truly baptized with water; but ye shall be baptized with the Holy Ghost not many days hence. . . .

8 But YE SHALL RECEIVE POWER, after that the Holy Ghost is come UPON you. . . .

So you can readily see that Jesus refers to two different experiences in these two separate verses: the Holy Ghost dwelling *in* you, and the Holy Ghost coming *upon* you in power.

'I already have all the Holy Spirit I can have.'

The denominational church I belonged to as a young preacher taught me that if you're born again, you have all the Holy Ghost there is to have—and that's the end of it. There is no other experience for you beyond the New Birth.

But although that teaching is partly true, it is mostly false. The first part is true because it is the Holy Spirit who imparts eternal life to our spirits. It is the Holy Spirit who through the Word makes the human spirit a new creature in Christ Jesus.

The problem is, people are actually more wrong than right when they say, "I'm a Christian, so I already have all the Holy Spirit I can have." A partial truth like that can do more damage than a lie.

You see, the Holy Spirit is present in the New Birth to bear witness with your spirit that you are a child of God (Rom. 8:14,16). The Bible calls that New-Birth experience *receiving Christ* (John 1:12), *receiving eternal life* (1 John 5:11), or *receiving forgiveness of sins* (Acts 26:18).

On the other hand, as you read the Book of Acts, you'll notice that it says people *receive* the Holy Ghost, *are filled with* the Holy Ghost, *are baptized with* the Holy Ghost, or *receive the gift* of the Holy Ghost. All four of those terms are used in the Acts of the Apostles concerning the same experience, and every time this experience comes *after* a person is born again.

The Witness of Jesus and the Apostle Peter

Let's take a look at Acts 8. I believe this passage helped me more than any other scripture to see this truth—that salvation and the baptism in the Holy Spirit are two separate experiences.

ACTS 8:12–17

12 But WHEN THEY BELIEVED Philip preaching the things concerning the kingdom of God, and THE NAME OF JESUS CHRIST, they were baptized, both men and women.

13 Then Simon himself believed also: and when he was baptized, he continued with Philip, and wondered, beholding the miracles and signs which were done.

14 Now when the apostles which were at Jerusalem heard that Samaria had RECEIVED THE WORD OF GOD, they sent unto them Peter and John:

15 Who, when they were come down, prayed for them, that they might RECEIVE THE HOLY GHOST:

16 (For as yet he was fallen upon none of them: only they were baptized in the name of the Lord Jesus.)

17 Then laid they their hands on them, and THEY RECEIVED THE HOLY GHOST.

As I said earlier, in my denominational church where I began as a young boy preacher, we were taught that if a person is saved, he has all the Holy Ghost there is. For instance, one prominent pastor in our denomination said, "When you're born again, you're born of the Spirit. If you receive Christ as Savior and confess Him as Lord, you have the Holy Ghost. That's all there is to it—period!"

Well, the first part of what that pastor said was a true statement. When you're born again, you're born of the Spirit

(John 3:3-8). But the rest of what he said was untrue! When you get saved, you *haven't* received all there is of the Holy Spirit. That's where folks get in trouble.

Many times when people give their opinion, they are just demonstrating their current state of spiritual growth. That's why it's important for us to understand that what man says is not the final authority. People can be wonderful folks and marvelous Christians, yet still be wrong about a given subject. The Word of God is always the final authority!

I learned that lesson early in my Christian walk, but I did get hung up for a while on what this pastor and other leaders in my denomination taught about the baptism in the Holy Ghost and speaking with tongues. Finally, I decided to just go to the Word and let *God* straighten me out.

That's when I read Acts 8:12-17 and realized that this pastor's teaching wasn't in line with the Bible. Those Samaritans got saved when Philip preached Christ to them, but the apostles Peter and John certainly didn't think the new converts had all the Holy Ghost they could have!

I said to myself, *Either the New Testament is wrong or that pastor is wrong. They both can't be right!*

I read Acts 8:12 again. Philip went to the city of Samaria and preached Christ unto the people. They *believed* his preaching concerning the Kingdom of God and the Name of Jesus Christ and *were baptized*, both men and women.

Right then I realized that not one minister in our entire denomination would insist that these people weren't saved! To do so would be to call the Lord Jesus Christ—the highest

Authority of all—a liar! After all, Jesus said in Mark 16:15–16: *"Go ye into all the world, and preach the gospel to every creature. He that BELIEVETH and is BAPTIZED shall be saved; but he that believeth not shall be damned."*

The Samaritans believed in Jesus and were baptized. So were they saved? According to the Lord Jesus, they were! Yet this was before Peter and John came down to pray for the Samaritans to receive the Holy Ghost.

Then I decided I'd just ask the Apostle Peter: "Peter, were those Samaritans saved? Were they born again before you and John went down there and laid hands on them to receive the Holy Ghost?" I mean, what better witness would there be than Peter, since he was actually sent to Samaria by the other apostles?

So Peter wrote me a letter in response to my question—and he wrote you one too! Were the Samaritans born again before Peter and John laid hands on them to receive the Holy Ghost? Peter answered this question in First Peter 1:

1 PETER 1:23

23 BEING BORN AGAIN, not of corruptible seed, but of incorruptible, by THE WORD OF GOD, which liveth and abideth for ever.

Compare Peter's words to what we read in Acts 8:14: *"Now when the apostles which were at Jerusalem heard that SAMARIA HAD RECEIVED THE WORD OF GOD, they sent unto them Peter and John."*

In John 1, Jesus is called "the Word of God."

JOHN 1:1,12,14

1 In the beginning was the Word, and the Word was with God, and the Word was God. . . .

12 But as many as received him, to them gave he power to become the sons of God, even to them that believe on his name. . . .

14 And the Word was made flesh, and dwelt among us, (and we beheld his glory, the glory as of the only begotten of the Father,) full of grace and truth.

The Samaritans received the Word of God, meaning they received Jesus, the living Word. So according to Peter, the people of Samaria *were* born again—not of corruptible seed, but of incorruptible, by the Word of God!

According to both Jesus and the Apostle Peter, then, the Samaritans were saved before Peter and John were ever sent to Samaria. Then when Peter and John came down, they prayed for the Samaritans—not that they would be saved or born again, but *that they would be filled with the Holy Ghost.*

The Witness of the Early Church

As you go back and read the entire context of Acts 8, you'll also notice this: Until Peter and John were sent to the Samaritans, the Holy Ghost isn't even mentioned in this chapter. Christ is mentioned. Water baptism is mentioned. Believing is mentioned. Miracles are mentioned. Healings are mentioned. Great joy in the city is mentioned. But the name of the Holy Ghost isn't there! Yet even though the Holy Ghost isn't mentioned, we can see His work throughout this passage.

Acts 8:5 says that Philip went down to Samaria and preached Christ unto them. We know that the Holy Ghost was present as Philip preached because of what we read in Acts 6:3–5. In this passage, it says that Philip was one of the seven men chosen to help serve the practical needs of the saints. These seven men were *". . . men of honest report, FULL OF THE HOLY GHOST and wisdom . . ."* (Acts 6:3). Then later on when Philip was called as an evangelist, we see the work of the Holy Spirit again as Philip was anointed to preach Christ to the people of Samaria (Acts 8:4–13).

It was the Holy Ghost through the Word who convicted those people and brought them to Christ. It was the Holy Ghost through the Word who recreated their spirits and imparted unto them eternal life. It was the Holy Ghost who bore witness with their spirits that they were children of God. It was the Holy Ghost operating in Philip's ministry through the gifts of the Spirit who healed people, worked miracles, and cast out demons.

So even though the Holy Spirit wasn't mentioned in those verses, He was the Agent in the Samaritans' New-Birth experience. Now let's look at Acts 8:14–15 where the Holy Spirit *is* mentioned.

ACTS 8:14–15

14 Now when the apostles which were at Jerusalem heard that Samaria had received the word of God, they sent unto them Peter and John:

> **15** Who, when they were come down, prayed
> for them, THAT THEY MIGHT RECEIVE THE
> HOLY GHOST.

Did Peter and John pray for the Samaritans that they might
be saved? No.

Did they pray for the Samaritans that they might accept
Christ? No.

Did Peter and John pray for them that they might be born
again? No.

Did they pray for the Samaritans that they might receive
eternal life? No.

The Samaritans were already believers, yet Peter and John
prayed for them *that they might receive the Holy Ghost.* Evidently
the apostles and the Early Church understood that being filled with
the Holy Ghost was a separate experience from the New Birth!

The Witness of Saul of Tarsus

The Apostle Paul was once called Saul of Tarsus, and his
testimony also bears witness to the truth that salvation and the
baptism with the Holy Ghost are two separate experiences.

Saul was converted on the road to Damascus when Jesus
appeared to him in a blinding light (see Acts 9:1–9). Saul asked
Jesus in verse 6, "... *Lord, what wilt thou have me to do? And the
Lord said unto him, Arise, and go into the city, and it shall be told
thee what thou must do.*"

Years later, Paul wrote a letter to the saints at Rome, and in
that letter, he said, "*That if thou shalt confess with thy mouth the*

Lord Jesus [the margin of my Bible says, 'or Jesus as Lord'], *and shalt believe in thine heart that God hath raised him from the dead, thou shalt be saved"* (Rom. 10:9). When Paul wrote that verse, I'm sure he looked back to that moment Jesus appeared to him in a vision on the Damascus road when he was still Saul of Tarsus and *he* believed that God had raised Jesus from the dead. After all, it was Jesus talking to him in that vision!

When Saul asked, "Lord, what wilt thou have me do?" notice that he confessed Jesus as his Lord. In other words, he put himself into the hands of Jesus, confessing Jesus' Lordship over his life!

Saul, who couldn't see after this vision, obeyed the Lord's instruction to go into the city, where he spent three sightless days in Damascus, praying and waiting on the Lord. Then the Lord appeared to a disciple named Ananias and instructed him to go to Saul and lay hands on him. Notice what Ananias said to Saul when he first met him:

ACTS 9:17

17 And Ananias went his way, and entered into the house; and putting his hands on him said, BROTHER SAUL, the Lord, even Jesus, that appeared unto thee in the way as thou camest, hath sent me, that thou mightest receive thy sight, AND BE FILLED WITH THE HOLY GHOST.

Ananias said to Saul, "The same Jesus who appeared to you on the way to Damascus appeared to me too." That indicates that Saul had already become acquainted with Jesus. He had met Jesus on the road to the city. Not only that, but Ananias addressed Saul as "brother," and people don't go around calling unregenerate murderers "brother"!

Ananias came in and said in essence, "You're my brother, Saul, because something happened to you out there on the road to Damascus. And now the same Jesus you met along the way has sent me to you!"

"Why did Jesus send you to me, Ananias?"

"Well, for one thing, that you might receive your sight."

"Is that the only reason He sent you to me?"

"No, Jesus also wanted me to come and lay hands on you so you'd be filled with the Holy Ghost!"

Notice that Ananias did *not* say, "Jesus sent me here to lay hands on you so you could get saved." After all, Saul had already gotten saved on the road to Damascus when he saw Jesus. And remember, Ananias had already addressed Saul as a Christian when he called him "Brother Saul"!

All of this is conclusive proof that Saul of Tarsus was born again on the road to Damascus and that later he was filled with the Holy Ghost when Ananias laid hands on him. So Saul adds his testimony to confirm that salvation and the baptism in the Holy Spirit are two separate experiences!

God's Gift to His Children

Let's go back to Acts 8 for a moment, because there's something else I want to point out. Notice in verse 5 that when

Philip went down to the city of Samaria, he preached *Christ* unto the Samaritans. He did *not* preach *the Holy Ghost* to them.

You see, you don't preach the Holy Ghost to the world; you preach *Christ* to the world so they can receive salvation. You *can* preach the Holy Ghost to *Christians*. Jesus confirms this in Luke 11.

LUKE 11:13

13 If ye then, being evil, know how to give good gifts unto your children: how much more shall YOUR HEAVENLY FATHER GIVE THE HOLY SPIRIT TO THEM THAT ASK HIM?

Jesus is telling us that the Holy Ghost is God's gift to His children—not to sinners!

On the other hand, we know from the Bible that the world *can* receive Christ and get saved.

JOHN 3:16

16 For God so loved the world that he gave his only begotten son that whosoever BELIEVETH ON HIM should not perish but have everlasting life.

So Jesus is God's gift to the world, and the Holy Ghost is God's gift to His children.

Nowadays you hear a lot about the brotherhood of man and the universal fatherhood of God. That all sounds good, but everyone is *not* a child of God, and although God is the *Creator* of all, He is not the *Father* of all. He is only the Father of those who have been born again. And the Holy Spirit is only God's gift to His children.

'The Spirit of Truth, Whom the World Cannot Receive'

John 14 is another passage of Scripture that tells us the baptism or the infilling with the Holy Ghost is not for sinners. A person has to be made a new creature first before he can receive the infilling of the Holy Ghost.

> **JOHN 14:16-17**
>
> **16** And I will pray the Father, and he shall give you another Comforter, that he may abide with you for ever;
>
> **17** EVEN THE SPIRIT OF TRUTH; WHOM THE WORLD CANNOT RECEIVE.

What is Jesus talking about here? He says that the world cannot receive the Spirit of truth. The "world" refers to sinners—to those who are outside of Christ. We've just seen in John 3:16 that the world *can* receive the New Birth: *"For God so loved the WORLD that He gave his only begotten son. . . ."* Jesus is sent to save the world!

So we know that the world *can* receive salvation and that the Holy Spirit is the One who recreates the human spirit in the New Birth. That means the experience in the Holy Ghost that Jesus refers to in this verse—receiving "the Spirit of truth"—has to be something different than salvation. Otherwise, if a person has all the Holy Ghost he can have when he's born again and there is no experience beyond salvation, you'd have to conclude that Jesus made a wrong statement.

But Jesus *didn't* make a wrong statement in John 14:17. The world *cannot* receive the Spirit of truth—that is, the Holy Spirit in His fullness. In fact, He makes the same point in Mark 2:22 that sinners cannot be baptized in the Holy Ghost. Jesus states, *". . . No man putteth new wine into old bottles: else the new wine doth burst the bottles, and the wine is spilled, and the bottles will be marred: but new wine must be put into new bottles."*

In this verse, wine is a type of Holy Ghost. In biblical times, wine was put in skin bottles. If new wine were put in old skin bottles, the wineskin wouldn't stretch as the wine expanded, and it would soon burst.

So in a sense, Jesus was saying that if a sinner were to be filled with the glory and power of the Holy Ghost, it would burst him wide open! No, the sinner has to be made a new creature in Christ *first* (2 Cor. 5:17).

That's the reason in the New Birth God recreates our human spirits—so He can fill us with the new wine of the Holy Spirit!

Understanding the Doctrine
of Baptisms

It has been my joy and privilege to get a great number of denominational ministers filled with the Holy Spirit over the years. When talking to ministers about whether the New Birth and the baptism with the Holy Ghost are two separate experiences, I have found that many get confused about that word "baptism." They think there is only one baptism available to the believer, so they confuse the baptism *with* the Holy Spirit (Acts 1:5) with being baptized *by* the Holy Spirit into the Body of Christ (1 Cor. 12:13).

ACTS 1:5

5 For John truly baptized with water; but ye shall be BAPTIZED WITH THE HOLY GHOST not many days hence.

1 CORINTHIANS 12:13

13 For by one Spirit are we all BAPTIZED INTO ONE BODY [in Christ], whether we be Jews or Gentiles, whether we be bond or free; and have been all made to drink into one Spirit.

People who believe there is only one baptism refer to Ephesians 4:4–5, where Paul says, *"There is one body, and one Spirit, even as ye are called in one hope of your calling; one Lord, one faith, ONE BAPTISM."* But in this context, Paul is talking about the one baptism that saves a person—the baptism into Christ in the New Birth. That's the same baptism into Christ we just read about in First Corinthians 12:13: ". . . we are all baptized into one body [in Christ]."

However, in Hebrews 6, the Bible talks about baptisms, *plural:*

HEBREWS 6:1–2

1 Therefore leaving the principles of the doctrine of Christ, let us go on unto perfection; not laying again the foundation of repentance from dead works, and of faith toward God,

2 Of THE DOCTRINE OF BAPTISMS. . . .

In this passage, the writer of Hebrews is talking about *all* the baptisms made available in the New Covenant. First, there is the baptism that saves. In other words, when a person is born again, he is *put into, baptized,* or *immersed* by the Holy Spirit into the Body of Christ. Then there is water baptism and the baptism with the Holy Ghost.

Well of Water vs. Rivers of Living Water

Because people get confused about this matter of "baptisms," I take them right to the Acts of the Apostles, and I use the illustration of water to show them there's more than one baptism. I tell them, "All right, you are born of the Spirit, so you have the Holy Spirit. You've had a drink of water, so to speak. But are you *full* of water? Is your heart hungry? Do you want to be *filled*?" I don't remember one time when that question didn't stir up a hunger for more of God in the heart of the people I was talking to!

Water is a type of the Holy Ghost in the Scriptures. There are two passages of Scripture where Jesus uses the image of water to beautifully picture both the Holy Spirit's indwelling Presence in the New Birth and the infilling of the Holy Ghost. These scriptures helped me immensely as I studied the Bible to understand God's perspective on this subject of baptisms.

First, there is the account in John 4 of Jesus' conversation with the woman at the well of Samaria.

JOHN 4:10,13-14

10 Jesus answered and said unto her, If thou knewest the gift of God, and who it is that saith to thee, Give me to drink; thou wouldest have asked of him, and he would have given thee LIVING WATER. . . .

13 . . . Whosoever drinketh of this water shall thirst again:

14 But whosoever drinketh of the water that I shall give him shall never thirst; but the water that I shall give him shall be IN him A WELL OF WATER springing up into everlasting life.

Jesus is talking here about receiving eternal life—the same thing He was talking about to Nicodemus in John 3:16. The experience Jesus called a well of water springing up *in* us is the work of the Holy Ghost in the New Birth, springing up into everlasting life. The well of salvation is for our individual benefit.

Then in John 7, Jesus speaks of another experience in the Holy Ghost:

JOHN 7:37–39

37 In the last day, that great day of the feast, Jesus stood and cried, saying, If any man thirst, let him come unto me, and drink.

38 He that believeth on me, as the scripture hath said, out of his belly shall flow RIVERS OF LIVING WATER.

39 (But this spake he of the SPIRIT, which they that believe on him should receive: for the Holy Ghost was not yet given; because that Jesus was not yet glorified.)

Jesus said, "Out of your belly shall flow *rivers* of living water." Notice He didn't just say *a river*, but *rivers*!

There is water in a well, and there is water in a river. The water in essence is the same, but the water in the well is for one purpose and the water in the river is for another purpose.

Since water in both of these passages represent the Holy Spirit, *Jesus is simply telling us that there are two experiences in the Holy Ghost.*

One experience in the Holy Ghost is to receive eternal life, whereby the Holy Spirit imparts eternal life into your spirit and bears witness with your spirit that you are a child of God (Rom. 8:16).

Then there is another experience, whereby out of your innermost being flows *rivers* of living water. The first experience, the New Birth, is primarily for your own good and your own personal blessing. But the other experience, being baptized with the Holy Ghost, enables God's power to flow out of you to bless *others.*

Later in Luke 24, Jesus called this second experience an *enduement of power from on High.*

LUKE 24:49

49 And, behold, I send the promise of my Father upon you: but tarry ye in the city of Jerusalem, until ye BE ENDUED WITH POWER FROM ON HIGH.

Notice Jesus didn't say, "Tarry in Jerusalem until ye *be converted* or *saved.*" No, this is a different experience; it's the baptism in the Holy Spirit. Actually, this is the same experience Jesus referred to in John 7 when He said *rivers* of living water would flow from the innermost being of those who believe in

Him. And on the Day of Pentecost, Jesus' words in John 7 were fulfilled.

ACTS 2:2-4

2 And suddenly there came a sound from heaven as of a rushing mighty wind, and it filled all the house where they were sitting.

3 And there appeared unto them cloven tongues like as of fire, and it sat upon each of them.

4 And THEY WERE ALL FILLED WITH THE HOLY GHOST, and began to speak with other tongues, as the Spirit gave them utterance.

At that moment, rivers of living water began to flow through believers—those who were born again—to make them a blessing to others. This is the infilling of the Holy Ghost, and it is the Father's gift to *every one* of His children!

CHAPTER 3

THE INITIAL EVIDENCE OF BEING FILLED WITH THE HOLY SPIRIT

If you study the Acts of the Apostles, you'll find out that when folks were filled with the Holy Ghost, they began to speak with other tongues. From this we can gather that tongues are the initial evidence of the baptism in the Holy Spirit. Of course, there are other evidences that follow. But this is the *initial* evidence or sign that someone has received the infilling of the Holy Spirit.

The Initial Outpouring

Let's look through the Book of Acts and study five instances where it is recorded that people were baptized in the Holy Spirit. We'll answer the question, "How many times do we find that speaking with tongues is the initial evidence for the infilling of the Holy Ghost?"

We'll start with the Day of Pentecost, when the Holy Spirit was first poured out on the Church.

ACTS 2:1–4

1 And when the day of Pentecost was fully come, they were all with one accord in one place.

2 And suddenly there came a sound from heaven as of a rushing mighty wind, and it filled all the house where they were sitting.

3 And there appeared unto them cloven tongues like as of fire, and it sat upon each of them.

4 And they were all FILLED WITH THE HOLY GHOST, and BEGAN TO SPEAK WITH OTHER TONGUES, as the Spirit gave them utterance.

Notice what happened at the very moment they were all filled with the Holy Ghost: They "*. . . began to speak with other tongues, as the Spirit gave them utterance*" (v. 4). Now, if that had happened just one time, we might think, *Well, that was just a phenomenon that happened at the very beginning when the Holy Spirit was first poured out on the Church!* But as you will see, this phenomenon did *not* just happen on the Day of Pentecost.

After Philip Preached Christ
to the Samaritans

Let's move on to Acts 8 and find out what happened after Philip the evangelist ministered to the people of Samaria:

ACTS 8:5–8,12,14–17

5 Then Philip went down to the city of Samaria, and PREACHED CHRIST unto them.

6 And the people with one accord gave heed unto those things which Philip spake, hearing and seeing the miracles which he did.

7 For unclean spirits, crying with loud voice, came out of many that were possessed with them: and many taken with palsies, and that were lame, were healed.

8 And there was great joy in that city. . . .

12 But when THEY BELIEVED Philip preaching the things concerning the kingdom of God, and THE NAME OF JESUS CHRIST [they were saved], they were baptized [in water], both men and women. . . .

14 Now when the apostles which were at Jerusalem heard that Samaria had received the word of God, they sent unto them Peter and John:

15 Who, when they were come down, PRAYED FOR THEM, THAT THEY MIGHT RECEIVE THE HOLY GHOST:

16 (For as yet he was fallen upon none of them: only they were baptized in the name of the Lord Jesus.)

17 Then LAID THEY THEIR HANDS ON THEM, and THEY RECEIVED THE HOLY GHOST.

Someone might say, "Well, it doesn't say in this passage that the Samaritans spoke with tongues, so that must mean a person can receive the infilling of the Holy Spirit without speaking with tongues."

But a person who makes that statement hasn't studied either the Scriptures or Church history very closely. First, a student of Church history knows that Early Church fathers agreed the believers of Samaria did speak with tongues. Second, if you go on reading in chapter 8, you'll learn something very significant about a fellow named Simon.

Once called "Simon the sorcerer," Simon had supposedly come to believe in Jesus under Philip's ministry in Samaria and had been baptized in water. Let's find out what happened next.

> **ACTS 8:18–19**
>
> **18** And when Simon SAW that through laying on of the apostle's hands THE HOLY GHOST WAS GIVEN, he offered them money,
>
> **19** Saying, Give me also this power, that on whomsoever I lay hands, he may RECEIVE THE HOLY GHOST.

If speaking in tongues did not accompany the baptism in the Holy Spirit, how would Simon have known that the Samaritans received the Holy Ghost? *No, Simon SAW something.* Verse 18 says, *"And when Simon SAW that through the laying on of the apostles' hands the Holy Ghost was given. . . ."* There had to be some outward evidence that registered on Simon's physical senses for him to know that the people had been filled with the Holy Spirit.

Well, Simon certainly didn't *see* the Holy Ghost. The Holy Spirit is a spirit being, unable to be seen by the physical eye. If there hadn't been some kind of supernatural manifestation that registered on his physical senses, Simon couldn't have *seen* that they had received the Holy Ghost.

One minister said to me, "Well, maybe the Samaritans were just full of joy. Maybe that is what Simon saw."

But that couldn't be the answer, because Simon had already seen joy manifested when the Samaritans had first gotten saved. Remember, verse 8 says, *"And there was great joy in that city."*

So what do you suppose happened in this instance? The most logical thing to conclude is that Simon saw the same thing that happened in Acts 2 when the 120 were filled with the Holy Spirit and spoke with other tongues. Acts 2:6 says, *"Now when this* [the 120 believers speaking in other tongues] *was noised abroad, the multitude came together. . . ."* Then Peter stood up and preached to them and said, ". . . *Having received of the Father the promise of the Holy Ghost, he* [Jesus] *hath shed forth THIS, which ye now SEE and HEAR"* (Acts 2:33). Notice those words *see* and *hear*!

The people who gathered together on the Day of Pentecost saw and heard the 120 newly Spirit-filled believers speak with other tongues. And evidently Simon saw the same thing!

Early Church fathers agree that the Samaritans spoke with tongues. And elsewhere in the New Testament, the Bible says that believers spoke with other tongues when they were filled with the Holy Spirit. So from all evidence, speaking with other tongues was the *sign* that convinced Simon that the Samaritans had received the Holy Ghost.

Notice what Simon did as soon as he saw this phenomenon: *He offered Peter and John money* because he wanted the same power to minister the Holy Ghost to people!

Some folks say, "Simon tried to buy the Holy Ghost." No, he didn't. He tried to buy the *authority* or the *power* to lay hands on people so they could receive the Holy Spirit.

Would Simon the sorcerer have tried to buy the power to give something to people if he couldn't discern whether or not they had received anything? Would he have tried to buy something if there was no supernatural manifestation in connection with it? Any sensible person would conclude that the answer is *no*.

So Simon offered Peter and John money, saying in effect, "Give me this power so I can lay hands on people and see them receive the Holy Ghost."

ACTS 8:20–21

20 But Peter said unto him, Thy money perish with thee, because thou hast thought that the gift of God may be purchased with money.

21 Thou hast neither part nor lot IN THIS MATTER: for thy heart is not right in the sight of God.

One Greek scholar points out that the root word of the Greek word translated "matter" in verse 21 is the same root of the word translated "utterance" in Acts 2:4, where it says, *"And they were all filled with the Holy Ghost, and began to speak with other tongues, as the Spirit gave them UTTERANCE."*

So when Peter said, "Thou hast neither part nor lot in this matter," he was literally saying, "Thou hast neither part nor lot in *this matter of supernatural utterance—this matter of speaking with other tongues.*" This proves conclusively that these Samaritans spoke with other tongues when they were filled with the Holy Spirit.

Saul of Tarsus

Now let's look in Acts 9 at what happened to Saul of Tarsus, soon to be called Paul, when he was saved and later in a separate experience received the Holy Spirit.

Saul was approaching the city of Damascus with letters in his possession that gave him the authority to put in prison any who were called Christians. Suddenly a light shone around about him, brighter than the noonday sun, and he fell to the earth, blinded by the light.

ACTS 9:4–6

4 And he fell to the earth, and heard a voice saying unto him, Saul, Saul, why persecutest thou me?

5 And he said, Who art thou, LORD? And the Lord said, I am Jesus whom thou persecutest: it is hard for thee to kick against the pricks.

6 And he trembling and astonished said, LORD, what wilt thou have me to do? And the Lord said unto him, Arise, and go into the city, and it shall be told thee what thou must do.

As we discussed earlier, Saul changed immediately when he saw Jesus in this vision and called Jesus *Lord*. Later the Apostle Paul may have had this personal experience in mind when he wrote to the Romans: *"That if thou shalt confess with thy mouth the Lord Jesus, and shalt believe in thine heart that God hath raised him from the dead, thou shalt be saved"* (Rom. 10:9).

We can therefore know that on the road to Damascus, Saul of Tarsus was born again. He confessed with his mouth that Jesus is Lord, and he certainly believed that God raised Jesus from the dead. After all, Saul was on that road to Damascus, talking to a resurrected Jesus Christ!

Then in verse 6, Saul asked, *". . . Lord, what wilt thou have me to do? . . ."*

Jesus answered, *". . . Arise, and go into the city, and it shall be told thee what thou must do."*

Now let's read further to find out what happened after Jesus told Ananias in a vision to go lay hands on Saul so that Saul could have his sight restored and be filled with the Holy Spirit.

ACTS 9:10–12,17–18

10 And there was a certain disciple of Damascus, named Ananias; and to him said the Lord in a vision, Ananias. And he said, Behold, I am here Lord.

11 And the Lord said unto him, Arise, and go into the street which is called Straight, and enquire in the house of Judas for one called Saul of Tarsus: for, behold, he prayeth,

12 And hath seen in a vision a man named Ananias coming in, and putting his hand on him, that he might receive his sight. . . .

17 And Ananias went his way, and entered into the house; and putting his hands on him said, Brother Saul, the Lord, even Jesus, that appeared unto thee in the way as thou camest, hath sent me, that thou mightest receive thy sight, and be filled with the Holy Ghost.

18 And immediately there fell from his eyes as it had been scales: and he received sight forthwith, and arose, and was baptized.

Notice that this passage doesn't say anything about Paul speaking with tongues. Yet later we read where Paul said, *"I thank my God, I speak with tongues more than ye all"* (1 Cor. 14:18).

When do you suppose Paul began to speak with tongues? The most logical thing to conclude is that Paul started speaking in tongues when he was filled with the Holy Ghost—just as the 120 believers did on the Day of Pentecost!

Cornelius and His Household

Ten years after the Day of Pentecost, the household of Cornelius, a devout Roman centurion, was saved and filled with the Holy Spirit.

Cornelius was praying one day when an angel appeared to him and told him to send someone to Joppa to inquire at the house of Simon the tanner for a man named Peter. Meanwhile in Joppa, Peter had gone out on the housetop to pray. During the time of prayer, Peter fell into a trance and had a vision. (Falling into a trance is one type of vision in which a person's physical senses are suspended as he or she receives revelation from God.)

In the vision, Peter saw a giant sheet let down from Heaven by its four corners. In the sheet were all kinds of beasts, both clean and unclean.

ACTS 10:13-15

13 And there came a voice to him, Rise, Peter; kill, and eat.

14 But Peter said, Not so, Lord; for I have never eaten any thing that is common or unclean.

15 And the voice spake unto him again the second time, What God hath cleansed, that call not thou common.

The Jews looked upon the Gentiles as being unclean and therefore wouldn't have anything to do with them. But God was getting Peter prepared for what Peter would soon witness: the Gospel being preached to the Gentiles. That's what the Lord meant when He said in the vision, "*. . . What God hath cleansed, that call not thou common.*"

While Peter pondered the meaning of this vision, the Holy Spirit spoke to him, saying that three men had come to see him and that he was to go with them. So Peter left with the three men for Cornelius' house, along with several Jewish brethren. When they arrived, Peter preached the Gospel to Cornelius and his entire household.

> **ACTS 10:44–46**
>
> **44** While Peter yet spake these words, THE HOLY GHOST FELL ON ALL THEM which heard the word.
>
> **45** And they of the circumcision which believed were astonished, as many as came with Peter, because that on the Gentiles also was poured out the gift of the Holy Ghost.
>
> **46** For they heard them speak with tongues, and magnify God. . . .

The believing Jews were astonished that the Holy Spirit had been poured out on the Gentiles. You see, up to that moment, it had been strictly a Jewish church. These Jewish believers didn't think anyone could get in on this New Covenant *except* the Jews.

So what convinced the Jewish brethren who were present that the door of salvation had opened to the Gentiles? How did they know that these folks had received the Holy Ghost? Verse 46 tells us: *"For they heard them SPEAK WITH TONGUES, and magnify God. . . ."* Hearing those Gentiles speak with tongues was the thing that convinced the Jewish brethren that Cornelius and his household had received the Holy Spirit just as they had.

The Disciples at Ephesus

The last recorded instance where folks received the Holy Spirit is found in Acts 19. This incident in the city of Ephesus happened about 20 years after the Day of Pentecost.

> **ACTS 19:1-2**
>
> **1** . . . [Paul and his company of believers] having passed through the upper coasts came to Ephesus: and finding certain disciples,
>
> **2** He said unto them, Have ye received the Holy Ghost since ye believed? And they said unto him, We have not so much as heard whether there be any Holy Ghost.

These were believers who were walking in all the light they had. They hadn't even heard that there *was* a Holy Spirit until they met Paul.

> **ACTS 19:3-4**
>
> **3** And he said unto them, Unto what then were ye baptized? And they said, Unto John's baptism.
>
> **4** Then said Paul, John verily baptized with the baptism of repentance, saying unto the people, that they should believe on him which should come after him, that is, on Christ Jesus.

You see, John the Baptist baptized in water, teaching people to believe on the One Who would come after him. But these Jewish believers lived in Ephesus, located in Asia Minor, and they didn't know all that had happened back in the land of Israel.

ACTS 19:5–6

5 When they heard this, they were baptized IN THE NAME OF THE LORD JESUS.

6 And when Paul had laid his hands upon them, THE HOLY GHOST CAME ON THEM; AND THEY SPAKE WITH TONGUES, and prophesied.

What happened the moment the Holy Ghost came on these believers? *". . . They spake with tongues, and prophesied."*

In Acts 2 the infilling of the Holy Spirit was accompanied by a rushing mighty wind and tongues of fire. In no other instance of believers receiving the baptism in the Holy Ghost do we read about either of these manifestations. For example, in Acts 10 the believers magnified God after receiving the Holy Spirit, and we just saw in Acts 19 that they prophesied.

Sometimes folks do receive something besides tongues at the time they are filled with the Holy Spirit, but remember—tongues always comes first. The Bible doesn't say that they prophesied and spoke with tongues. It said they *spoke with tongues and prophesied*!

We shouldn't expect any more when we initially receive the Holy Ghost than what the Word of God teaches. If another spiritual gift is added, well and good, but these other manifestations may or may not follow the baptism in the Holy Spirit.

On the other hand, in three out of five recorded instances in Acts where people received the Holy Ghost, the Bible definitely states that believers spoke with other tongues. These three instances occurred in the 20-year time period between the Day of Pentecost (Acts 2) and Paul's encounter with the Ephesian believers (Acts 19). The majority of evidence, then, would be on the side of tongues as the initial evidence of this experience. As for the other two instances, the Bible infers that believers spoke with tongues, as we already discussed.

So I believe it's safe to say we have proven conclusively that five times out of five recorded instances in the Book of Acts, believers who were filled with the Holy Ghost experienced the initial evidence of speaking with other tongues. This would lead us to believe that any person today who desires to be filled with the Holy Ghost will speak with other tongues as well!

CHAPTER 4

DO YOU HAVE TO TARRY TO RECEIVE THE HOLY SPIRIT?

In all the scriptural evidences we've examined so far, there is no suggestion that the people in the Early Church were ever taught to tarry to be filled with the Holy Ghost. And if we want to be thoroughly New Testament, we should never teach anyone to tarry for the baptism with the Holy Spirit either.

You might ask, "But what about the Day of Pentecost? Didn't those 120 believers tarry in an upper room in Jerusalem until they were endued with power from on High?" (See Luke 24:49; Acts 1 and 2.)

It's true that this is the only instance in the Book of Acts where people were baptized with the Holy Ghost after tarrying. But those 120 believers were waiting or tarrying for the *initial outpouring* of the Holy Spirit. Jesus had commanded them, ". . . *TARRY YE in the city of Jerusalem, until ye be endued with power from on high*" (Luke 24:49). They had to tarry because the Holy Ghost hadn't yet been poured out on the earth to carry on Jesus' ministry!

Then on the Day of Pentecost, the Holy Spirit came to this earth like a rushing mighty wind to carry on Jesus' ministry, and the Holy Spirit has been here ever since. From that day on, it's just a matter of *receiving* Him, not a matter of *waiting* for Him to come.

Tarrying for the Initial Outpouring

Just read back through those five instances of people being filled with the Holy Ghost in the Book of Acts, and you will notice that after the initial outpouring, people never again waited to be baptized in the Holy Ghost. Not one single time did they wait! After all, why should they wait? The Holy Spirit was already here!

Let's go back to what Jesus said to the disciples in John 14:

JOHN 14:16–17
16 And I will pray the Father, and he shall give you another Comforter, that he may abide with you for ever;
17 Even the Spirit of truth; whom the world cannot receive. . . .

Remember what we discussed earlier about this passage of Scripture. We know that the world *can* receive the work of the Holy Ghost in the New Birth. That means Jesus is not talking about the salvation experience here. He is saying that the world cannot receive the *infilling* of the Spirit of truth—the baptism in the Holy Spirit—because that is a gift reserved for believers.

Later in John 16:13, Jesus went on to say, *"Howbeit when he, the Spirit of truth, is come, he will guide you into all truth: for he shall not speak of himself; but whatsoever he shall hear, that shall he speak: and he will shew you things to come.*"

Notice those words, "*. . . when he, the Spirit of truth, is come. . . .*" The Holy Ghost in His fullness had not yet been manifested in the sense that Jesus was talking about here.

Jesus' words in this verse were fulfilled on the Day of Pentecost, when the Holy Ghost came like a rushing mighty wind to this earth and 120 believers in an upper room were suddenly baptized with the Holy Spirit and began to speak with other tongues.

We might experience supernatural manifestations when the Holy Ghost is moving, including something that seems like wind. But never do we experience the mighty outpouring of the Holy Ghost as those 120 believers experienced it on that first Day of Pentecost more than two thousand years ago.

What About the Other Four Instances in the Book of Acts?

As you move on to Acts 8, you won't find the least suggestion that the people of Samaria were taught to tarry for the Holy Ghost. These people believed in Jesus, got saved, and were baptized. Then the apostles who were in Jerusalem heard that the Samaritans had received the Word of God and sent unto them Peter and John. When Peter and John came down to Samaria, they laid hands on them and prayed for them, and the Samaritans received the Holy Ghost. There is no mention whatsoever that the Samaritan believers tarried before they were able to receive the free gift of the Holy Spirit.

The same is true for Saul of Tarsus, who later became the Apostle Paul. We already looked at what happened when Saul was filled with the Holy Ghost. But let's look again at Acts 9:17. We see Ananias arriving at the house where Saul had been waiting and praying for three days, ever since his conversion on the road to Damascus.

ACTS 9:17

17 And Ananias went his way, and entered into the house; and putting his hands on him said, Brother Saul, the Lord, even Jesus, that appeared unto thee in the way as thou camest, hath sent me, that thou mightest receive thy sight, and BE FILLED WITH THE HOLY GHOST.

Ananias knew nothing at all about Saul's spiritual condition other than the fact that Saul had been praying, because the Lord had told that to Ananias in a vision (Acts 9:11). Yet it seems that there was no doubt in Ananias' mind that Saul would receive the Holy Spirit at the moment he laid hands on Saul. There is no suggestion of Saul needing to tarry or wait to be filled with the Holy Ghost either, yet Saul probably didn't know a thing in the world about the Holy Ghost until Ananias came and laid hands on him!

Then in Acts 10, we see that Cornelius and his household didn't have to tarry at all to be filled with the Holy Ghost.

ACTS 10:44–46

44 WHILE Peter yet spake these words, THE HOLY GHOST FELL ON ALL THEM [in Cornelius' household] which heard the word.

> **45** And they of the circumcision which believed were astonished, as many as came with Peter, because that on the Gentiles also was poured out THE GIFT OF THE HOLY GHOST.
>
> **46** For they heard them SPEAK WITH TONGUES, and magnify God. . . .

Those in attendance at Cornelius' household were all Gentiles. They were not saved until Peter came and preached to them.

> ### ACTS 11:13–14
>
> **13** And he [Cornelius] shewed us [Peter and his Jewish companions] how he had seen an angel in his house, which stood and said unto him, Send men to Joppa, and call for Simon, whose surname is Peter;
>
> **14** Who shall tell thee words, WHEREBY THOU AND ALL THY HOUSE SHALL BE SAVED.

Cornelius and his household were saved *as* Peter preached to them. That means they received salvation and were baptized in the Holy Ghost almost simultaneously! When people first get saved is often the best and easiest time in the world to get them filled with the Holy Ghost.

No one laid hands on the people of Cornelius' household, yet they all received the Holy Ghost virtually at the same time. Not one in the room failed to receive.

As we noted earlier, it was these Gentiles' speaking with other tongues that fully convinced Peter's Jewish company that the Gentile believers had received the Holy Spirit. The Jewish brethren were astonished that the Holy Ghost had been poured on the Gentiles. But let me stress again: The fact that these Gentiles immediately began to speak with tongues and magnify God indicates that these people did not tarry or wait even for a moment to be filled with the Holy Ghost!

Finally, let's go on to Acts 19 and see if the believers Paul met in Ephesus had to tarry to receive the Holy Ghost.

ACTS 19:1-6

1 And it came to pass, that, while Apollos was at Corinth, Paul having passed through the upper coasts came to Ephesus: and finding certain disciples,

2 He said unto them, Have ye received the Holy Ghost since ye believed? And they said unto him, We have not so much as heard whether there be any Holy Ghost.

3 And he said unto them, Unto what then were ye baptized? And they said, Unto John's baptism.

4 Then said Paul, John verily baptized with the baptism of repentance, saying unto the people, that they should believe on him which should come after him, that is, on Christ Jesus.

5 When they heard this, they were baptized in the name of the Lord Jesus.

6 And WHEN PAUL HAD LAID HIS HANDS UPON THEM, the Holy Ghost came on them; and they spake with tongues, and prophesied.

As we saw earlier, these were Gentile believers who were walking in the little bit of spiritual light they had. Then Paul baptized them in the Name of the Lord Jesus. But Paul didn't stop there! He also got them filled with the Holy Ghost.

Here is the point I want you to see for this discussion: The moment Paul laid his hands upon these new converts, the Holy Ghost came upon them, and they spoke with tongues and prophesied. They all received the Holy Ghost without exception and without the slightest suggestion of tarrying!

Modern-Day Examples of Receiving Without Tarrying

In a certain meeting after I had taught along the line of faith, I invited folks to come and receive the Holy Spirit, and three people came forward. All three belonged to denominational churches that didn't believe in the baptism with the Holy Ghost and speaking in tongues.

I said to these three people, "You will receive the Holy Ghost right now as soon as I lay my hands on you."

Then I laid hands on them, and they were all immediately filled with the Holy Ghost and began to speak with other tongues.

After the service, a denominational minister who had recently been filled with the Holy Spirit came over to me and said, "Brother Hagin, that was amazing! I stood right there and listened to you say that three people would get filled with the Holy Spirit—and then they did in a matter of seconds! But I want to ask you a question, Brother Hagin. How did you *know* they were going to receive the Holy Ghost?"

"Well," I said, "I didn't actually know they were going to receive—but there wasn't any doubt in my mind that they *could* and that they *should* receive! So I just believed that since they had come forward with a desire to receive the Holy Ghost, they *would!*"

I continued, "The reason I could speak so definitely is that the Lord once appeared to me in a vision and said to me, 'Go lay hands on believers to receive the Holy Ghost!' And since Jesus is the One who sent me to lay hands on believers to receive the Holy Ghost, I *expect* them to receive. And, thank God, most of them do!"

Of course, once in a while someone doesn't receive the Holy Spirit. Sometimes it takes awhile for folks to get their minds renewed with the Word of God. That's particularly true if they've gotten confused with different ideas, such as the teaching that says it's necessary to tarry to receive the Holy Ghost with the evidence of speaking with other tongues.

It can take some time to reeducate these people and to help them get their thinking straightened out. It would be wonderful if all Christians were simply taught from the very beginning of their walk with God what the New Testament says about the Holy Spirit and praying in tongues. Then they wouldn't have such a struggle with it!

I remember holding a three-week meeting in a certain place. During those three weeks, we had 82 folks receive the Holy Ghost. In fact, everyone who came forward got filled with the Spirit. No one failed to receive.

Most of those 82 people instantly received the Holy Spirit. A few had to come two or three times to get their minds renewed by the Word before they were filled with the Holy Ghost. But no one came more than three times without receiving. And the only reason we didn't have more people get baptized in the Holy Ghost during that three-week meeting is that we ran out of people who hadn't received yet!

The Infilling of the Holy Ghost Is a Free Gift

Howard Carter was the general supervisor of the Assemblies of God in Great Britain for 19 years. He was also the founder of the oldest Pentecostal Bible school in the world and a leading teacher in Assembly of God circles worldwide. Carter said, *"To teach people to tarry to be filled with the Holy Ghost is nothing in the world but a combination of works and unbelief."* How true that is!

Throughout my almost 70 years of ministry, I have found that when people come in faith to receive the Holy Ghost, they *will* receive if they just cooperate with God. There isn't ever a doubt in my mind about it when I minister the baptism in the Holy Ghost because I learned long ago as a young denominational preacher what the Word says about it.

That revelation came as I was walking down the street in my town, praying about this issue of the baptism with the Holy Ghost, trying to understand what to believe about the matter. Suddenly the Lord spoke to my heart and asked me what Acts 2:39 said. I quoted the verse to Him: *"For the promise is unto you, and to your children, and to all that are afar off, even as many as the Lord our God shall call."*

Then the Lord asked me, "What promise is that?"

I said, "Well, the latter part of verse 38 says, '. . . *and ye shall receive the GIFT of the Holy Ghost.'*" Immediately I saw that the Holy Ghost is a *gift*. And since I saw no reason for waiting to receive a gift freely given to me by God, I just decided to immediately receive it!

I thought, *Well, I believe I'll just go down to the Full Gospel pastor's house and receive the Holy Ghost right now!* When I got to the pastor's house, the first thing he said was, "Brother Kenneth, why don't you wait until after the service is over tonight and seek the Holy Ghost at the altar?"

I said confidently, "Oh, it won't take me very long to receive"— and in eight minutes' time, I was speaking in other tongues! Why didn't I have to wait to receive? *Because we don't have to tarry for a gift God has freely given to all who believe!*

CHAPTER 5

HOW I WAS FILLED WITH THE HOLY SPIRIT

Let me tell you in more detail how I personally came to understand what God has to say about the baptism with the Holy Ghost and speaking with other tongues. I believe my story may help you or someone you know who has been struggling with this subject.

As I mentioned earlier, when I was a young denominational preacher, I fellowshipped with Full Gospel people because they preached divine healing, and they strengthened my faith in healing. When I first started preaching, I didn't know anyone else who believed in divine healing except me. I thought I'd found something in the Bible that no one else knew! I certainly knew that no one in *my* church knew about it!

What to Do With 'That Tongues Business'?

But then in 1935, someone came to our town and put up a tent to hold a Full Gospel revival. My grandmother went to the meetings, and she said to me, " Son, you ought to go to that Full Gospel revival."

"Why should I?" I asked.

"That Pentecostal fellow preaches like you believe, or else you believe like he preaches—one of the two. I never heard anyone sound so much like you in my life!"

So finally one night, I dropped by a meeting just as the preacher began preaching. I stood outside the tent listening, and I enjoyed every minute of it. I liked the way that man preached, because he preached like I believed! I needed folks like that to fellowship with so I could stay strong in faith.

But, of course, I found out that these Pentecostal folks didn't just believe in salvation and divine healing and the Second Coming like I did; they also believed in being baptized with the Holy Ghost and speaking with other tongues as the Spirit of God gives utterance. To tell the truth about it, I just closed my ears to that part. I really didn't listen to what they had to say about tongues. I let their words go in one ear and out the other because I thought my denomination was right on this subject and the Pentecostals were wrong.

I thought to myself, *I believe in the Holy Ghost, all right, and I'm sure I could be more full of the Holy Spirit than I am. But I don't believe in that tongues business! I'll just put up with that part in order to have fellowship with people who believe in healing.*

Meanwhile God was blessing me as much as He could in my ministry. I was laying hands on people and they were getting healed, because I was walking in all the light I had at the time. For instance, I saw one of my Sunday school teachers—who was scheduled for a major operation—get up out of bed instantly healed as I anointed him with oil, laid hands on him, and prayed.

But no matter how much I tried, I just couldn't seem to get away from "that tongues business"!

I Receive the Revelation: The Holy Ghost Is a *Gift*

I'll never forget that day I was filled with the Holy Spirit. It was Thursday, the eighth day of April, 1937. I mentioned earlier what happened that day as I walked down the street in my hometown, talking to the Lord in my heart. But now I want to go into more detail about what happened that day.

If you had been walking beside me along that street, you would have barely heard me talking to the Lord because I was praying in a whisper. I was getting ready to enroll in a denominational seminary in a few weeks, and I wanted to get this issue about the baptism with the Holy Ghost and tongues settled once and for all.

So I said, "Lord, who is right about this Holy Ghost business? One of the leaders in our denomination says that if a person is born again, he has all the Holy Ghost there is.

"Then there is another prominent pastor in our denomination who says, 'There is an experience subsequent to salvation called the baptism in the Holy Ghost, but I'm convinced that our dear Pentecostal friends are wrong in saying a person has to speak with other tongues. Acts 1:8 is our pattern, not Acts 2:4, and there is no mention of tongues in Acts 1:8.'"

ACTS 1:8

8 But ye shall receive power, after that the Holy Ghost is come upon you: and ye shall be witnesses unto me both in Jerusalem, and in all Judaea, and in Samaria, and unto the uttermost part of the earth.

"Lord," I continued, "This other prominent pastor went on to say, 'You don't need any manifestation or evidence of this subsequent experience called the baptism in the Holy Ghost. You just have to claim it by faith. Then the only outward result is that you go out to witness!'

"Lord," I continued, "those two preachers are both well-known pastors in my denomination, yet they're not saying the same thing about tongues. And then there's that noted elderly professor from our seminary who tells his graduating students: 'There is an experience subsequent to salvation called the baptism in the Holy Ghost. It is an enduement of power from on High, and don't you dare go out and preach without it!' But that's all this professor ever says about the subject!

"Finally, Lord, there are the Pentecostals, and they claim that Acts 2:4 *is* the spiritual pattern for getting filled with the Holy Ghost: *'And they were all filled with the Holy Ghost, and began to speak with other tongues, as the Spirit gave them utterance.'*

"So who is right about this, Lord?" I asked. "I'm prone to go the way I've been taught by my denomination. In fact, I'm thinking about going to their seminary this September, and that means I have to enroll this month."

I had told the Lord what all the other preachers had said. I had told Him what I thought about it. I thought I had finally made up my mind which direction to go.

Then as I related earlier, suddenly I heard the Lord speaking to me by His Spirit on the inside of me just as plain as can be. He asked me, "What does Acts 2:39 say?"

Well, the Holy Ghost knew that I knew what Acts 2:39 said or He wouldn't have asked me. I immediately answered, still walking down the street: "It says, *'For the promise is unto you, and to your children, and to all that are afar off, even as many as the Lord our God shall call.'*"

"What promise is that?" that inward Voice asked me.

I thought about verse 38—the verse I had used so many times to preach the message "repent, and be baptized." Then the inward Voice said, "What does the latter part of verse 38 say?"

I replied, "It says, *'. . . and ye shall receive the gift of the Holy Ghost.'* But, Lord, I do believe in the Holy Ghost, and I am born of the Spirit. I wouldn't say I'm *filled*, but at least I know the Holy Ghost. After all, it's the Holy Ghost talking to me right now. It's those tongues I don't know about, Lord!"

Then just as plain as anything, the inward Voice said, "What does Acts 2:4 say?"

I knew what Acts 2:4 said; I could quote it. But I didn't realize that the Holy Ghost was about to open up that verse to me in a way I had never seen before!

I answered, "Acts 2:4 says, *'And they were all filled with the Holy Ghost, and began to speak with other tongues. . . .'* Oh, oh, oh, I *see* it!" I exclaimed. "*This* was the gift of the Holy Ghost that was given! When the believers were all *filled*, they began to *speak*. So if I get full of the same Holy Ghost who got me born again, I'm going to begin to *speak*, just like they did! Well, I'll just go down to the Pentecostal preacher's house right now and get filled with the Holy Ghost!"

'It won't take me very long to receive.'

So I went to the home of the pastor of the Full Gospel Tabernacle and knocked on his door. The pastor and the visiting evangelist answered the door together. I told the pastor I wanted to be filled with the Holy Ghost. He replied, "Brother Kenneth, we're in revival right now with this evangelist. Why don't you wait until after the service is over tonight and seek the Holy Ghost at the altar?"

It was already 6:00 in the evening, and the revival service was going to start at 7:30. But I responded, "It won't take me very long to receive."

The pastor said, "Well, come on in then."

I went into the living room and knelt by a large chair. The pastor and the evangelist didn't tell me to do it; I just had an inner urge to do it. I could hear the sound of the two men's voices, but I don't know one word they said. I just shut my ears to all outside noise. Then I remembered that when I got healed, I had lifted my hands. So I closed my eyes, lifted up my hands, and started praying.

I said, "Now, Lord, I've come here to receive the Holy Ghost." I told the Lord again in prayer what the denominational pastors said, what the Pentecostal people said, and what the Bible says in Acts 2. Then I said, "By faith I was born again, and by faith I received healing. Now by faith I receive the Holy Ghost!

"I want to thank You, Heavenly Father, because I am now filled with the Holy Ghost. And now I *expect* to speak with other tongues as the Holy Ghost gives me utterance, and I'm not going to be satisfied until I do! I expect to speak with tongues just like the believers did on the Day of Pentecost and just as they did throughout the Book of Acts." Then I quoted to Him all the Bible evidence on speaking in tongues.

I continued, "Praise God, the Holy Spirit will give me utterance, and I'll speak with tongues and thank You for it!" Then I said, "Hallelujah" about eight or 10 times, never feeling so dry and dead in all my life. In fact, it seemed like I almost choked on those "hallelujahs." After all, we weren't used to saying that word in the church where I was raised! But I didn't stop just because I didn't feel anything.

To tell you the truth about the matter, I've never had much patience with folks who say, "Well, I don't feel anything, so I guess it isn't working for me." What do feelings have to do with anything!

What if someone gave you a cashier's check for a million dollars? Would you say, "No, no, I just don't feel like receiving this check. I don't feel like it will work if I try to cash it." Your feelings haven't a thing in the world to do with the validity of that cashier's check. It's the authority behind the cashier's check that counts!

Did you ever read in the Bible where it says, "We walk by feelings"? No, I guarantee that you never did read that. But you *can* read where it says, "*For we walk by faith, not by sight*"(2 Cor. 5:7). That means we walk by faith in what God has said in His Word!

So even though I never felt a thing as I said my "hallelujahs"— even though I never felt more dry in my whole life—I just kept thanking God for the Holy Ghost and for giving me utterance in tongues.

Now, I know everyone has his or her own experience in regard to receiving the Holy Ghost. Many have no supernatural manifestation at all other than the common experience of speaking with other tongues. I've had more than one preacher tell me that they were at the altar praying with their eyes shut when it seemed like the roof of the church came off and a huge ball of fire came down and burst over their heads—and they started speaking in tongues. I even heard someone say he saw a beam of light come down through the ceiling and strike him in his eyes—and at that moment, he started speaking in tongues.

Well, I never saw a beam of light or a ball of fire, but I'll tell you what did happen to me. Even though I had my eyes shut, suddenly it seemed like someone was building a blazing bonfire down on the inside of me. Well, I didn't know what to expect, so I prayed, "Lord, if that burning doesn't stop, I'm going to have to quit!"

Then it was as if I could see strange words boiling up inside. It seemed to me that I'd know what those words were if I just started speaking them out. So I did, and tongues just flowed out of me!

I opened my eyes and looked at my watch. (After all, the Bible says to watch and pray!) It was eight minutes past 6:00. I'd only been kneeling there in the Full Gospel pastor's home for eight minutes! But I kept on speaking with other tongues for an hour and a half and sang three songs in tongues. Oh, I could have quit if I had wanted to—but I didn't want to!

It doesn't take long to receive the Holy Ghost when you take God at His Word!

Should We Expect Other Spiritual Gifts Besides Just Tongues?

I was filled with the Holy Spirit after I saw what the Bible said and believed it. I started closely examining God's Word, and I saw in the Acts of the Apostles that whenever believers were filled with the Holy Spirit, they spoke with tongues.

What astounds me is that so many people have such little confidence in what the Bible says, even after they see it. That often includes Christian workers and preachers!

Sometimes people ask me, "So should we seek tongues?"

I tell them, "No, the Bible doesn't say we're to seek tongues. We're to seek the Giver—the Holy Spirit! In my case, I didn't *seek* tongues, but I *expected* to speak with tongues because that is the Bible evidence of receiving the Holy Ghost in His fullness!"

But even though I knew I had received the Holy Ghost because I spoke with tongues, I'll be perfectly honest with you—at the time I felt a little disappointed. After leaving the Full Gospel pastor's home, I said to myself as I walked down the street, *Well, all I did was talk in tongues. I've gotten a bigger blessing than that many times just praying the best I could as a denominational boy!* I'd heard some Pentecostal folks testify of *their* experiences of receiving the Holy Ghost that were just spectacular, so I guess I was expecting some kind of overwhelming, emotionally exhilarating experience.

I had yet to learn that the baptism in the Holy Ghost is much more than just receiving a blessing that affects us physically and emotionally, even though we can receive those kinds of blessings before, during, and after receiving the Holy Spirit. But I did know my Bible, so as I walked down the street, I said to myself, *I don't care what I feel or what I don't feel. I know I am filled with the Holy Ghost because I spoke with tongues. I have the Bible evidence!*

So I kept thanking and praising the Lord for filling me with His Spirit for the next three or four days, and after the fourth day, I never had another feeling of disappointment. In fact, later I came to realize that the same moment I received the Holy Ghost and spoke with other tongues, I also received another gift of the Spirit—the word of knowledge. And that spiritual gift began to manifest more and more in the weeks and months that followed.

Sometimes folks do receive other spiritual gifts in addition to speaking with other tongues when they are filled with the Holy Ghost. For instance, we saw earlier in Acts 19 that the disciples at Ephesus not only spoke with tongues when they received the Holy Ghost, but evidently some of them also prophesied.

Then many times other spiritual gifts are also added later as folks go on with God and learn to walk in the Spirit. The main thing to remember is that *speaking with tongues always comes first.* That is the one Bible evidence we should expect when we ask in faith to receive the Holy Ghost.

Walking in Wisdom With Those Who 'Tarried'

After I was filled with the Holy Spirit, I got the left foot of fellowship from my denomination and came over to the Pentecostals. But I had enough sense to know that it wasn't my place to start trying to straighten people out as soon as I joined them in fellowship. A person who does that is acting foolishly, and I'm not a fool!

So I became the pastor of a small Full Gospel church, and for two years I watched those Pentecostal folks come to the altar to tarry and pray for the infilling of the Holy Ghost. I'd invite the altar workers to come to the altar and let them pray with those who had come forward to get filled.

The altar workers would go on and on and on, praying and tarrying with the people who were seeking the baptism in the Holy Ghost, and eventually one or two would get filled. I knew the altar workers didn't need to do all that to get people to receive. But I knew better than to say anything at that moment, so I kept my mouth shut for the time being. After all, I knew it wasn't going to hurt them, since folks need to pray anyway.

The people would sing, "Come by here, Lord, come by here." But according to the Bible, the Holy Ghost is already here! We don't have to beg Him to come by. Or they'd sing, "Oh, Lord, send the power just now and baptize." But the Lord already sent the power—the Holy Ghost is already here! The Holy Spirit is the power source of God. He is present, just like the rain is already present in the clouds before it falls. The rain doesn't suddenly come out of nowhere; it's already there in the clouds!

I remember one night in 1940 when I started thinking about these songs the congregation would sing in our services. A visiting evangelist was holding a revival in our church at the time. My wife Oretha and I had gone to bed, and she was already asleep. But as I thought about the absurdity of it all, I started laughing and it woke her up.

My wife asked me, "What are you laughing about?"

I replied, "I'm laughing at us—at our whole church! Tonight we asked people who have gotten baptized in the Holy Ghost during this revival to testify. So the people testified and said, 'The Holy Ghost is here.' After they testified about the Holy Spirit's presence in our service, the preacher preached about the same thing. Then after his message, he invited people to come to the altar to be filled with the Spirit.

"So for an hour and half, people had been testifying and preaching about the Holy Ghost's power and presence. Why, the very atmosphere was charged with the power of God! A person who couldn't feel His presence must have been dead!

"But the minute we called the people who wanted to receive the Holy Ghost to the altar," I continued, "we changed our tune! Then we said, 'No, He isn't here yet.' And we started singing, 'Oh, Lord, send the power just now.'"

I said to my wife, "We fooled those people! We got them to the altar and then said, 'No, the Holy Ghost isn't here. We have to pray and sing that God will send Him and His power because the Holy Ghost isn't here yet!"

But that isn't true! The Holy Ghost is always present with us, and all we have to do is come and receive Him!

Nevertheless, I didn't tell those Pentecostal folks that it wasn't necessary to go through all that to receive the Holy Ghost. If I had, they would have risen up and kicked me out! You see, I would have been knocking down their spiritual sandcastles, and a person has to be careful about that.

So I just kept my mouth shut and let the altar workers pray with the people who wanted to receive the Holy Ghost. At times it was almost like a circus at that altar. One fellow would be on one side of a person, slapping him on the back and hollering, "Hold on, Brother, hold on!" Meanwhile, another fellow would be on the other side, hollering, "Turn loose, Brother, turn loose!"

Someone else would be right behind the person, yelling, "Holler louder so God will hear you!" And another fellow would be in front of the person, hollering, "Get your hands higher so God will hear you!" And every time the fellow in front hollered something, he'd give the poor person a spit-shower bath!

In spite of all this—not because of it, but in spite of it—some of these dear souls would actually get filled with the Holy Ghost! God would see their sincerity and honesty, and He'd honor their prayers and their eventual exercise of faith.

But the people who wanted to receive the Holy Ghost didn't have to go through all that, and I knew it. But for those first two years, I just kept my mouth shut. After all, who was going to listen to a 22-year-old boy preacher? Some of those Pentecostal folks had been filled with the Holy Ghost longer than I was old!

So what does a person do in a situation like that? He does what Aaron and Moses did in the Old Testament! Do you remember what happened when God told Aaron and Moses to lead Israel out of Egypt? Aaron threw down his rod, and it turned into a serpent. Then the Egyptian magicians threw down their rods, and they turned into serpents too. But in the end, Aaron's serpent swallowed up all the magicians' serpents (Exod. 7:8–12)!

So I just taught them the Bible evidence and gave them the testimony of my own experience, and that gradually swallowed up all the arguments about tarrying to receive the Holy Ghost. I didn't let anything deter me, and eventually I was able to lead most of those Pentecostal folks into understanding how to receive the Holy Spirit the Bible way!

CHAPTER 6

GOD WILL VISIT HUNGRY HEARTS

You'll never really begin to grow spiritually as you ought to grow until you are filled with the Holy Ghost and begin to speak with other tongues. That's absolutely the truth.

I know from personal experience that in the heart of every born-again man, woman, and child, there is a hunger that cannot be satisfied without the infilling with the Holy Spirit with the evidence of speaking in tongues.

In my case, I had already been preaching for four years before I received the Holy Ghost. I knew in my spirit I was a child of God. I had the witness of the Spirit that I was saved. I preached and saw others get saved. I prayed for the sick and saw them get healed. Nevertheless, there was a void in my spirit that was never filled until I received the Holy Ghost and spoke with other tongues.

'I Must Have *More*'

I remember a particular testimony I once heard that proves this point, shared by a denominational pastor at a Full Gospel

Businessmen's luncheon. Just a few days before the luncheon, this pastor had received the Holy Spirit in the sanctuary of his own church. As we all sat there eating our meal together, I looked over at this minister. I was drawn to him because his face was all lit up like a neon sign in the dark!

Later the minister stood up and shared his testimony with us. He said, "I'm so glad I'm here today. I heard a lot of negative rumors about you Full Gospel folks in the past and, I'm sorry to say, I believed it. But my heart was just so hungry, and nothing seemed to satisfy that hunger. There was a void and a vacancy within me, even though I've preached for a number of years and our church had just built a new church building. The more I read the New Testament, the more I was convinced in my own spirit that I didn't have what it takes to meet the people's spiritual needs."

The denominational pastor then related what had happened just a few days earlier as he walked up and down the aisles in his church sanctuary, praying. He prayed, "Lord, as I read the New Testament, I see that Your early disciples had something I don't have. You told Your disciples to tarry in the city of Jerusalem until they were endued with power from on High. Some way or another, there has to be an enduement of power that *I* can receive.

"I know I'm saved, but if I'm going on in the ministry, *I must have more*. I feel so inadequate. I just can't get behind the pulpit to preach again without receiving the 'something else' that I'm convinced You want to give me. I can't face the people feeling so empty!"

Then the pastor said to the Lord, "I've heard a lot about Pentecostal people and tongues, and I don't know what to think about that, Lord. But I want You to know this: If tongues are involved with this 'something else' that I need from You, then I want You to give me tongues!"

The pastor continued to walk up and down the aisles of his church, talking to the Lord. Suddenly he lifted up his hands and cried out in desperation, "Oh, God, hear me! Fill me with Your Spirit!" Just like that, the Holy Ghost fell on him, and he began to speak with other tongues!

The denominational minister related what he did next: "I thought, *Surely this is what those Pentecostal folks are always talking about!* Immediately I wanted to fellowship with someone else who'd had the same experience. I remembered that I'd once gone fishing with a Pentecostal pastor, although the pastor hadn't said a word about the Holy Ghost or tongues on the fishing trip. Our conversation had centered on Bible topics that weren't objectionable to either of us.

"So I rushed to my office, looked up the Full Gospel pastor's telephone number, and called him. When he answered, I reminded him of the fishing trip, and he remembered me."

Then this denominational minister blurted out to the Pentecostal pastor, "I think I just got what you folks have!"

"What do you mean?" the Full Gospel pastor asked.

"The baptism in the Holy Ghost!" replied the denominational pastor. Then he started speaking in tongues over the phone.

The Pentecostal pastor exclaimed, "That's it! You do have the baptism in the Holy Ghost! Praise the Lord!" And the two men rejoiced together.

This denominational minister's testimony is just like many other people's testimonies I've heard over the years. From these testimonies, from the Word, and from my own personal experience, I know for a fact that *God will visit hungry hearts,* wherever they may be.

A River of People With Hungry Hearts

I also want to relate to you a particular experience I had in the Spirit in 1962 that applies to what we're talking about here, because it convinced me that God wants His people to be filled with the Spirit. During a meeting in Texas, I was in the middle of relating to the congregation a particular vision the Lord had given me years earlier. Suddenly I realized that I'd misinterpreted part of that vision; I'd never received the whole interpretation until that moment. Overcome by that revelation, I immediately stopped speaking, knelt down behind the pulpit, and started praying. The congregation began to pray too.

Toward the end of that time of prayer, I fell into a trance, and my physical senses were suspended. In this trance, I suddenly seemed to be in a different place, walking toward a beautiful garden full of flowers in bloom. The garden had a white picket fence around it and many little paths running through it. Right in the middle of the garden was a little brush arbor, overflowing with vines and flowers, with a marble bench on either side of the arbor.

I came walking from the east to the gate of this garden, and Jesus stood by the gate. As I walked up to Him, we never said a word to each other. He just reached out His hand and took hold of my right hand. Then with His left hand, Jesus opened the gate, drew me inside, and shut the gate.

Jesus took my right hand in His hand and led me down the path to this little arbor in the middle of the garden. He sat down on the marble bench and drew me down to sit next to Him.

Then I looked to the west and saw a river flowing into the west side of the garden. The river was very narrow where it entered the garden. But as I looked at this river flowing toward us, it got wider and wider until it seemed to be 50 miles wide!

Suddenly the river was no longer a river of water but a river of many, many people. I could see them as they flowed toward us like a mighty army, coming faster than people could ever walk or march.

I asked Jesus, "Lord, what is this river I see? Who are these people?"

Jesus said, "This river flowing into the garden are those who shall be brought into the baptism in the Holy Ghost and the fullness of the Pentecostal message from other denominations and other churches.

"In these days," Jesus continued, "I am visiting and *will* visit every hungry heart, even in some religious areas where many might think I would not visit. Yet because people's hearts are open and hungry, I *will* visit them. And these you see flowing into the garden are those who shall come."

Thank God, since that vision so many years ago, we've been seeing countless multitudes of hungry hearts come into the fullness of the Holy Ghost—and there is no end to that river yet!

Then in the vision I asked, "Lord, what do all these flowers and that marvelous, fragrant aroma represent?"

Jesus responded, "The beautiful aroma of these flowers is the praise ascending to My throne as incense of the ones who will come into the fullness of My Spirit."

The Lord said to me, "You must play a part in this. You will work with these people in the various denominations. You will minister to Full Gospel people to help them be prepared for My coming. I will show you how and what to do."

A Little Deeper and Further

This truth was confirmed to me in the 1960s, during the move of God in the denominational churches that we call the Charismatic Movement. I was one of the speakers at a certain meeting, along with an Episcopal priest named Brother Patterson. While teaching on the baptism in the Holy Ghost, Brother Patterson related an incident that happened in one of his meetings when a man stood up in the back of the audience during his teaching and challenged him.

Since not everyone could hear the fellow in the audience, Brother Patterson, a very kind and soft-spoken man, said, "Brother, if you have something to say, come down here where everyone can hear it."

The man, who was obviously upset, came forward, and Brother Patterson handed him the microphone. The man said, "I was saying that I'm a pastor [and he mentioned his denomination], but I don't speak with tongues. But I'm just as much filled with the Holy Ghost as you are or anyone else is! I don't speak with tongues, and I don't *need* to speak with tongues!"

Brother Patterson then took back the microphone and said, "Dear Brother, if you're satisfied with what you have, that pleases us just fine. If you don't want any more of God or if you have all of God you need . . ."

"Oh, no!" the pastor interrupted. "I didn't say that I don't want more of God."

"Well," Brother Patterson said, "the way you talked, I thought you had all of God you ever wanted."

"Oh, no, no, no, no," the man said, "I'm still hungry. I'd like . . ."

Before the pastor could say more, Brother Patterson laid his hand on his head and said, "Lord, he's hungry. Just give him more." And that denominational pastor got filled with the Spirit and started speaking in tongues right then and there!

That happened because the man was hungry. He was open to going on with God—he just didn't realize that getting more of God would involve speaking with other tongues! This denominational pastor had already been introduced to the Holy Spirit in the New Birth, but that day he entered a new dimension in his walk with God—deeper and further than he had ever been before!

A Gift for the Hungry Heart

I read another testimony just after World War II of a denominational missionary to Africa. In 1946 this woman missionary returned to the United States for the first time after ministering without a break for 37 years in the bush country of Africa. When she first arrived in New York City, she was overwhelmed by all the noise, traffic, and crowds of people.

She said, "I just had to shut myself up in my hotel room, and I stayed there for five days away from everything. But I did listen to the radio, and I heard a broadcast from Glad Tidings Tabernacle, located there in New York City. I called the hotel desk and found out that the church was within two blocks of the hotel where I was staying. I thought, *Well, I believe I'll just get out and go to that church Sunday night. I believe I can do that. By then I'll have been in the city for seven days, so I think I'll be adjusted to city life enough to go out in public.*

"So I went to the Sunday night service. After the pastor's message, he gave an altar call and sent the people who came forward to a downstairs prayer room. Then when the service was over, I went over and introduced myself to the pastor's wife. I told her what denomination I belonged to and that I'd been a missionary in Africa for 37 years. She and her husband welcomed me and showed me around the church."

The pastor and his wife took the missionary downstairs to their large prayer room, where altar workers were praying with the people who had answered the altar call. Some were praying for salvation, while others were praying to be filled with the Holy Spirit. As the missionary observed, several believers in the prayer room burst out speaking with other tongues.

The pastor's wife explained to the woman, "Those folks are being filled with the Holy Ghost."

The missionary replied, "Well, I've never been around Pentecostal people, but I've heard folks talk about them. Is that strange language I hear those people speaking what you Pentecostals call the baptism in the Holy Ghost?"

"Well, you're hearing them speak in tongues, which is *the evidence* of the Holy Spirit's infilling," the pastor's wife said.

"Why, I've had that for the past 37 years!" the missionary woman exclaimed. "I knew that God had blessed me, but I didn't know what to call it!"

The missionary explained to the pastors: "When I first arrived in Africa years ago as a young single missionary woman, I had all these glamorous ideas about being a missionary. But when I got over there, I found out it was *tough*!

"After just a few months, I knelt down on my knees in my little thatched-roof grass hut and prayed, 'Lord, I believe You called me. I believe Your hand is on my life. But I just don't have what it takes. I need more of You, Lord!'

"I just kept praying that way whenever I could. But one day I felt desperate, and I cried out in prayer, 'Lord, I can't go on! I know You sent me, and I hate to disappoint the people who are supporting me. But unless I get more of You, I'm going to have to give up and go home!'"

The missionary continued, "Suddenly I started speaking strange-sounding words, just like these people here are speaking, and later I started singing those same strange words. I got so joyous and happy doing it that I thought, *God gave me something to help me along!* I didn't know it was a gift available to everyone! But every day since then for the past 37 years, I've gotten alone with God and communicated with Him in that strange language. And I often sing that way too! It just builds me up and blesses me so much!"

This missionary woman's testimony shows that it doesn't matter so much whether a person knows what to call the baptism in the Holy Spirit and speaking in tongues. The main thing is to receive this supernatural blessing!

I remember hearing another testimony along that line, this time from a Full Gospel missionary. He told me about a time when he was invited to preach at a denominational church in the capital city of an African nation. The elderly pastor of the church was an American who had been there for 35 years without ever returning to the United States. The Pentecostal missionary decided to preach a salvation message instead of a subject like the Holy Ghost that might be controversial.

This church had one of those old-time "mourner's benches" at the front of the sanctuary where people would gather around to pray. After the missionary's salvation message, seven people came forward to the altar to pray for salvation.

The Pentecostal missionary told me, "I didn't even pray with those seven individuals. The church altar workers gathered around them, and then the pastor invited all the Christians to come around the altar and pray as well. Then three of the seven who came to get saved suddenly began speaking with other tongues!

"I thought, *Dear Lord, I've messed up here!* So I ran over to the pastor and tried to apologize. I said, 'Brother, I didn't want to create any problems. I just preached a salvation message! I didn't mean to start something.'

"The pastor asked me, 'What are you talking about?'

"I replied, 'Well, those three believers are speaking with other tongues. They got filled with the Holy Ghost!'

"The denominational pastor exclaimed, 'Is that what you Pentecostal people call the baptism in the Holy Ghost? Why, for the past 35 years, all my converts have experienced that! We just call it "getting sanctified"!'"

Well, *whatever* people call the baptism in the Holy Ghost, God has made this precious gift available to all who call on His Name! Any believer anywhere just has to be hungry for more of God and get filled with the Spirit!

CHAPTER 7

GUIDELINES TO RECEIVING THE HOLY SPIRIT

Let's talk about why some folks have difficulty receiving the Holy Ghost, even when they are seeking to be filled. There are many opinions and ideas out there about how to get baptized in the Holy Spirit—but the Bible way is always the best way.

I want to start with an important truth that causes many who seek the infilling of the Spirit to stumble: *The Holy Spirit doesn't speak in tongues through you.*

Look at what Paul says in First Corinthians 14:14: *"For if I pray in an unknown tongue, my spirit prayeth, but my understanding is unfruitful."* Notice that phrase, "my spirit prayeth." The *Amplified* reads: ". . . My spirit [by the Holy Spirit within me] prays. . . ." God has provided a way for our spirits to pray apart from our understanding.

It isn't the Holy Ghost doing the praying; it is the Holy Ghost helping our spirits to pray. *He gives the utterance—we do the praying.* The miracle of tongues is not who is doing the speaking.

We are the ones doing the speaking. The miracle of tongues is *where the tongues are coming from* and *what is being said*.

That's where a lot of folks miss it. They sit around waiting for the Holy Ghost to do the talking. It is true that the Holy Ghost is the One Who gives the utterance. But it is *not* the Holy Ghost doing the talking. There is a difference.

Notice also what Acts 2:4 says about this: *"And they were all filled with the Holy Ghost, and began to speak with other tongues, as the Spirit gave them utterance."* On the Day of Pentecost, the Holy Ghost gave the utterance, but the believers did the talking.

'*They* Began To Speak'

I remember one conversation in particular that I had with someone who didn't understand this principle. I was holding a meeting at a church in Texas in December 1950, and a church member decided to write and tell her friend about the meetings. This friend lived further west in Texas and had been seeking the baptism in the Holy Spirit for many years. The church member wrote to her friend, "Everyone down here is receiving the Holy Spirit! Why don't you come visit for the weekend and attend the meetings with me?"

So this lady drove down for the Friday and Saturday night services, and both nights I laid hands on her to receive the Holy Ghost without any noticeable effect. That Sunday morning was to be the woman's last service before she headed back home that afternoon.

I preached that Sunday morning and then turned the service back over to the pastor. As he was making announcements, the church member who had written her friend lifted her hand and interrupted the pastor, saying, "Brother McMullen." The pastor stopped and acknowledged her.

The woman then related that she had written her friend, who was sitting next to her on the front row, and asked her to come to the meeting. The church member said, "Brother Hagin did lay hands on my friend, but I'm wondering if he would lay hands on her one more time. She has to go back now, and she's so disappointed that she has failed to receive the Holy Spirit."

The pastor turned to me for my answer, and I said, "Yes, I'll lay hands on her."

So the woman's friend came forward, and I laid hands on her again. I knew the Holy Ghost came on her, and I knew He gave her utterance, but she didn't speak with tongues. However, I didn't have time to preach her a sermon; it was already past twelve o'clock and the pastor was ready to end the service, so the women walked back to their pew.

A short time later I was walking through the church parking lot, and I walked by these women sitting in their car. As I passed the car, I could see the look of disappointment on this dear lady's face who had been seeking the Holy Ghost, and I felt so sorry for her. So I went back and knocked on her car window. The woman looked up at me, startled, and rolled down the window.

I knew exactly what this woman's problem was. I just hadn't had time to deal with it in front of everyone at the end of the service. So I asked her, "Sister, do you have your Bible there?" She nodded. I said, "Well, please open it to Acts 2:4."

Then before she could get her Bible, I opened mine and handed it to her. I said, "Would you read that verse out loud for me?"

The woman read the verse out loud: *"And they were all filled with the Holy Ghost, and began to speak with other tongues, as the Spirit gave them utterance."*

I asked, "According to that scripture, who did the speaking with tongues?"

"Why," she said, "the Holy Ghost did."

I already knew that this was the woman's problem. She was waiting for the Holy Ghost to speak with tongues for her, but the Holy Ghost doesn't speak with tongues!

So I said to her, "Read that verse again out loud." So she read it again: "It says, *'And they were all filled with the Holy Ghost, and began to speak with other tongues, as the Spirit gave them utterance.'"*

I said to her a second time, "Who did the speaking with tongues according to that scripture?"

She answered, "Why, it says that the Holy Ghost did!"

I said, "Would you read that verse again please?" The woman read it out loud a third time, and for the third time I asked her, "According to that scripture, who did the speaking with tongues?"

She said, "The Holy Ghost did."

I said, "Would you mind reading that verse again? Read it out loud."

For the fourth time, she read: "'*And they were all filled with the Holy Ghost, and began to speak . . .*'—wait a minute!" she exclaimed. "It says that *they* began to speak!"

She reached over for her own Bible and checked to see if the verse read any differently in hers. Then she said, "I thought for sure this verse said the *Holy Ghost* spoke in tongues! In fact, Brother Hagin, if I had been called on to witness in court and the judge had sworn me in and put me on the witness stand, I would have sworn that my Bible said the Holy Ghost did the speaking with tongues. And I would have been wrong!"

I said, "You sure would have. But wait a minute, Sister. We don't establish anything on one verse of Scripture. The Bible says, '*. . . In the mouth of two or three witnesses shall every word be established*' [2 Cor. 13:1]. Please turn in your Bible to Acts 10."

Then we read Acts 10:45–46 together: "*. . . On the Gentiles also was poured out the gift of the Holy Ghost. For THEY HEARD THEM SPEAK WITH TONGUES. . . .*" Peter and the Jewish believers who came with him heard Cornelius and his household—not the Holy Ghost—speak with tongues!

"Well," I said, "that's two witnesses; now let's read the third one. Turn over to Acts 19." I directed the woman to read verse 6: "*And when Paul had laid his hands upon them, the Holy Ghost came on them; and they spake with tongues, and prophesied.*"

"And *they* spake with tongues. Yes, I see that now!" she said.

Then I said, "I want you to notice that when Paul laid hands on those disciples in Ephesus, it says that '*. . . the Holy Ghost came on them, and they spake with tongues. . . .*' Now, may I ask you another question?"

The woman said, "Yes, you may."

"When I laid hands on you a moment ago in church, did the Holy Ghost come on you?"

The woman emphatically replied, "*Yes!*"

I asked, "Did your tongue seem to want to say something that wasn't English?"

"It was all I could do to keep from it!" the woman exclaimed.

"You're not supposed to keep yourself from it," I explained. "You're supposed to yield to that urge and *speak in tongues.* Now, if I'm wrong, tell me I'm wrong, but I sense that you have that same inner urge right now. You're having to hold back and almost swallow your tongue to keep from speaking!"

"Yes, you're right!" she replied.

I said, "Well, go ahead and yield to that urge and speak it out." Just like that, the woman started speaking fluently in other tongues!

That woman sat in her car with the window rolled down, speaking in other tongues and having a glorious time in the Lord. And as the other church members walked through the parking lot to their cars, they all heard this woman—who supposedly couldn't receive the Holy Ghost, no matter how hard she tried— suddenly speaking fluently in tongues and magnifying God!

Over the years, I've run into this kind of wrong thinking again and again when ministering the Holy Ghost to people. Some people seem to think the baptism in the Holy Ghost is like swallowing a little radio: When the Holy Ghost is ready to speak in other tongues through a person, He just "turns on the radio" on the inside and the tongues come out of the person's mouth automatically! But that isn't the way it works.

Wrong thinking in any area will defeat you. You have to learn to think in line with what God's Word says. And when it comes to speaking in tongues, you can't find the expression "the Holy Ghost spoke through them" or any similar expression anywhere in the New Testament. The expression the Bible uses every time is "*they* spoke."

There is another scripture that proves this point. It's found in First Corinthians 14:18, where Paul says, "*I thank my God, I speak with tongues more than ye all.*" Notice that Paul did *not* say, "I thank my God that the Holy Ghost speaks in tongues through me more than anyone else." No, he said, "I thank my God that *I* speak..."!

Speak as the Holy Spirit Prompts

Here's something else I want to point out. One day when I was studying Acts 2:4 in other translations, I noticed that *The Twentieth Century New Testament* translated that last phrase this way: "... [they] began to speak *with strange 'tongues' as the Spirit prompted their utterances.*" In other words, the believers had a *prompting* or an *urge* to speak.

That's the reason I said to that woman in the church parking lot, "Did your tongue seem to want to say something that wasn't English?" That was the Holy Ghost *prompting* her.

You see, the Holy Ghost never makes people do anything. If He did, He'd make everyone get saved today, and we'd all go together into the millennium tomorrow! No, the Holy Ghost leads. The Holy Ghost directs. The Holy Ghost gives a gentle push. The Holy Ghost prompts. The Holy Ghost urges. But devils and demons *drive* and *force* and *make* people do things.

Just as I told that woman, when you ask to receive the Holy Ghost and then sense the urge to speak words that are not your native language, you're not supposed to fight that urge. You're supposed to *yield* to the inner prompting of the Holy Spirit and begin to *speak*.

In 1951 while holding a meeting in east Texas, I was driving down the street with the pastor, and he pointed out a man who was the choir director of the largest Full Gospel church in that city. However, this pastor told me that the choir director had never been filled with the Holy Ghost, even though he'd attended a Pentecostal Bible college and had been the music director in that church for 21 years.

I thought no more about it, but the very next night, I saw this choir director and his wife sitting in the service. I preached about people getting filled with the Holy Spirit without tarrying, which was a new message for this congregation. After the message, I asked for those who wanted to be filled with the Holy Ghost to come forward.

I looked over at the music director. I could tell that his wife was trying to convince him to come forward and that he was saying, "Oh, there's no need for me to go. I've been seeking all these years without any success." Finally, the woman prevailed, and the man came forward. I could tell he came just to please her.

I went down the line and talked to each of the 13 individuals in the prayer line one by one before I laid hands on them. The first four or five immediately began to speak in tongues after I laid hands on them.

Then I came to this man, who stood there with eyes closed and hands lifted. When I laid hands on him, the word of knowledge began to operate. I knew immediately what part of his trouble was. I said to him, "Open your eyes and look at me." Then I stated to him, "Nothing in your life would keep you from being filled with the Holy Ghost. You have no secret sin that would hinder you from receiving the Holy Spirit."

The man's eyes opened wide as he said, "Oooohhh! Do you really think so?"

I said, "I don't think so—I *know* so."

Later I learned that the devil had so tormented this man's mind that sometimes he couldn't sleep at night and would be left with a bad headache for up to three days. Accusing thoughts bombarded his mind, such as, *You would already have the Holy Ghost if there wasn't something wrong with you—some secret sin you don't even know about.*

But there is no such thing as a secret sin you don't know about. The Holy Ghost or your own conscience will tell you. And if your conscience doesn't tell you anything, don't try to drag something up!

Then I said to the man, "I'll tell you something else while I'm at it. I will lay hands on you no more than three times, and you will be filled with the Holy Ghost."

Again the man asked, "Do you think so?"

I said, "No, I don't think so—I *know* so."

"Well, I'll be back tomorrow night!" he replied.

Sure enough, the next night the man was back. This time, his wife didn't have to encourage him to come forward. He was one of the first ones to get in the prayer line!

When I reached the man, he said to me, "Do you still think I'm going to receive the Holy Ghost?"

I said, "No, I've never thought it. I *know* it."

"Well, you said you wouldn't lay hands on me more than three times. Tonight is the second time."

"That's right," I said.

"The next time is it, then?"

"That's right," I replied.

The next morning, I was kneeling on the platform in prayer during our corporate prayer time. Suddenly I felt someone tap me on the shoulder. I looked up and saw the music director standing there. He stooped over and said, "Do you still think I'm going to receive the Holy Ghost?"

I said, "No, no, I don't *think* you're going to receive the Holy Ghost. I *know* it."

"You said you wouldn't lay hands on me more than three times without my getting filled. This will be the third time."

I said, "Yes, this is it."

Then he said, "Guess what? I just told my employees, 'Take over at work. I have to go see Brother Hagin. He said he wouldn't lay hands on me more than three times, so I've decided there's no use in my waiting for tonight. I'm going over there this morning!'"

I said, "Well, just kneel down here by my side." The man knelt down. I laid hands on him and said, "Receive the Holy Ghost in the Name of Jesus." The Holy Ghost came on him, and he began to stammer a little and speak a few words in other tongues. That was thoroughly scriptural, for the Bible says in Isaiah 28:11, *"For with stammering lips and another tongue will he speak to this people."*

I said to him, "Brother, that's it, that's it! That's the Holy Ghost giving you the utterance. Grab it like a dog grabs a bone, and run off with it!" What did I mean by that? I meant, "Just lift your voice and talk a blue streak in tongues!"

So the man lifted his voice and began to speak at the top of his voice in other tongues. Suddenly he could hear himself speaking with other tongues, and he got so thrilled that he danced all over the platform on his knees!

Later I asked the man, "What did I do or say that helped you more than anything else to be filled with the Spirit?"

"First, Brother Hagin, you said there's no secret sin that would keep me from being filled with the Holy Ghost." Then he told me that the devil had tormented him for more than 20 years along that line. (When a person doesn't know the Word, the devil will have a heyday with him!)

"What you said released me," the man said to me. "I went home and I had the best night's sleep I've had in years! And the second thing that helped me was the fact that you were so positive. You were so full of faith, you convinced me that I was going to receive the Holy Ghost!"

Then the man told me one other thing that helped him. He said, "When I began to stammer a little and say a few words in tongues, I had been to that place at least a thousand times in the 20-plus years I've been seeking the Holy Ghost. But someone would always say, 'Let the Holy Ghost talk,' and I'd stop to let Him talk—and that would be the end of it. But you didn't say that, Brother Hagin. You told me to go ahead and keep on speaking!"

I told the man that because the Holy Ghost wasn't the one speaking in tongues—he was!

You aren't supposed to stop and let the Holy Ghost speak. You are to speak the utterance He gives you! So if you've prayed to receive the baptism in the Holy Spirit and have had difficulty speaking with tongues, let this man's testimony help you. Realize that the Holy Spirit has already given you the utterance—now it's up to you to open your mouth and speak it out!

Drink Until You're Full!

We saw earlier in John 7 that Jesus likened *receiving the Holy Spirit to drinking water*:

JOHN 7:37–39

37 In the last day, that great day of the feast, Jesus stood and cried, saying, If any man thirst, LET HIM COME UNTO ME, AND DRINK.

38 He that believeth on me, as the scripture hath said, out of his belly shall flow RIVERS OF LIVING WATER.

39 (But THIS SPAKE HE OF THE SPIRIT, WHICH THEY THAT BELIEVE ON HIM SHOULD

RECEIVE: for the Holy Ghost was not yet given; because that Jesus was not yet glorified.)

Later in Acts 2:4, it says, *"And they were all FILLED with the Holy Ghost, and began to speak with other tongues. . . ."* Well, how do you get full of water? By drinking! How do you get full of the Holy Ghost? By drinking! Jesus invites you to "come and drink." That means to speak freely with other tongues until your spirit is satisfied!

In First Corinthians 12:13, Paul uses this same analogy of water: *"For by one Spirit are we all baptized into one body* [that's the New Birth], *whether we be Jews or Gentiles, whether we be bond or free; and have been all made to DRINK INTO ONE SPIRIT."*

Just because you've had one drink of water is no sign you are *full* of water! You have water in you, but that doesn't mean you're *full.* In the same way, it's one thing to be born of the Spirit, but it's another thing to be *filled* with the Spirit.

The Bible doesn't tell you to be *half-filled* or *two-thirds filled* with the Holy Ghost. It says to *be filled.* So if you aren't full of the Holy Ghost, drink in the Holy Spirit until you get full! How can you tell when you're full? The one clear answer I know of is found in Acts 2:4: When they were filled with the Holy Ghost, they began to *speak*! While there are other evidences, the one consistently found in Scripture is speaking in tongues as the Spirit gives utterance.

Jesus' invitation is simple: *Come and drink*—and keep drinking until you get full. But can you drink with your mouth shut? No, just as you can't drink water with your mouth shut, you also can't "drink" of the Holy Spirit with your mouth shut. You have to open your mouth and drink till you're full.

Then when you get full, you'll start speaking with other tongues, for that is the initial sign or evidence of the Spirit's infilling. And you can continue to drink a full measure of the Holy Spirit by praying in tongues every day of your life!

Hindrances to Receiving the Holy Ghost

There are some things that can keep a person from being filled with the Holy Ghost with the evidence of speaking in tongues, such as *a lack of faith* or *a lack of yieldedness*. Remember, the Holy Ghost gives the utterance, but the person must do the talking. That means the person must open his mouth and use his own voice to start speaking.

After a believer asks Jesus to baptize him with the Holy Ghost, he needs to quiet his mind and see if he senses the Holy Spirit giving him syllables or words on the inside. If he doesn't sense anything, the problem may be a lack of faith. Why? Because a person must first *receive* the gift of the Holy Spirit he's asked for by opening his heart to the Spirit and drinking Him in. When he *receives* the Holy Ghost, the Holy Ghost *will* give him utterance.

In this case, it would behoove that believer to go back and study the five recorded instances in the Book of Acts where people got filled with the Holy Ghost (see Acts chapters 2, 8, 9, 10, 19). He should read those verses very carefully, for faith comes by hearing, and hearing by the Word of God (Rom. 10:17).

On the other hand, if that believer does speak out an utterance in tongues—even if he speaks only a few syllables—he needs to hold on to that utterance and refuse to give up on it. However, he should also expect more to come! The problem in this case is a lack of yieldedness. Therefore, when he's alone and undistracted, the believer should pray in other tongues. He should start with the utterance he has already received but should determine to yield more and more to the Holy Ghost.

Once when I was holding a meeting in a certain church, a young businessman came forward one night to receive the Holy Ghost. When I laid hands on the man, the Holy Ghost came on him, but all I heard him speak were two words in tongues.

The next night when the pastor asked for testimonies from folks who'd been saved, healed, or filled with the Holy Ghost during the meetings, this young man got up and said, "I want to praise God for filling me with the Holy Ghost last night." Then he sat down.

The next night the pastor once more asked for testimonies. Once again this young man got up and testified, "I want to thank God that two nights ago when Brother Hagin laid hands on me, I received the Holy Ghost and spoke with other tongues."

At the next evening service, the pastor once again asked for testimonies, and once again the young man jumped up to testify. But this time when he jumped up, I thought he would go through the ceiling! He said, "Folks, three nights ago the Lord baptized me with the Holy Ghost, but I spoke only two words.

"Because my family has been staying up late every night to attend the services, I've been coming home from my business at lunchtime to take a 30-minute nap every day at noon. But these last two days, I haven't been able to take my nap."

The young man went on to explain why he hadn't been able to take his midday nap. The day after I ministered to him, he was trying to go to sleep when the devil started whispering to his mind over and over again, "*You didn't get anything last night when you asked to be filled with the Holy Spirit.*"

The man said out loud in reply, "Yes, I did."

The enemy answered, "*But you didn't speak with tongues.*"

So the young man rose up, got his Bible, and opened it to Acts 2:4. Then he said, "Mr. Devil, in case you can't read, I'll read it for you. It says here, '*And they were all filled with the Holy Ghost, and began to speak with other tongues, as the Spirit gave them utterance.*' Last night I began to speak with other tongues, so I have received the Holy Ghost. I spoke two words, and that is a beginning!"

The next day this young businessman came home at noon again and ate a little lunch. Then he went to his room to lay down for a nap. But once again, he couldn't sleep because the devil kept saying to his mind, "*Now you've testified about being filled with the Holy Ghost, but you're NOT filled! Let's hear you talk in tongues.*"

The man couldn't speak more than those two words in tongues. Then the devil said to his mind, "*See? You didn't get anything!*"

But once again the young man rose up and opened his Bible. He said, "Mr. Devil, in case you can't read, I'll read it to you!" Then after reading Acts 2:4 to the devil again, the man said, "I know I spoke only two words, but that's a beginning. I began to speak with other tongues, so I'm filled with the Holy Spirit!"

Then the young man said to us, "At noon today, I tried to take a nap again, and the devil started saying the same thing he'd been saying to me for the past two days. So I got up and opened my Bible and read Acts 2:4 to him again. I said again, 'Three nights ago, I began to speak with other tongues, so that means I'm filled.' Immediately after I said that, I started laughing at the devil. And before I knew what I was doing, I was speaking fluently in other tongues! So I spent the rest of the time praying in the Holy Ghost!"

You see, this young man had *received* the Holy Ghost. It was just a matter of his learning how to *yield* to the Holy Ghost. So, you see, when he yielded to the Holy Ghost's prompting to laugh at the devil in faith, that helped him yield to the Holy Ghost to pray in other tongues!

It's so important for a person to stay in faith as he learns to yield to the Holy Spirit. Otherwise, he'll fall back into unbelief and think, *Well, I just spoke a couple words, so I didn't really receive anything.* The devil likes to use doubt-filled arguments like that to bind up a believer so he can't enjoy the benefits of the infilling he's already received.

I'm telling you, you're going to have to learn how to answer the devil with the Word if you're ever going to amount to anything in the Lord!

Someone might say, "Why, I can't rebuke the devil! I'm scared of him!"

But if that's what *you're* saying, you've already let the devil take you captive. You've already played into his hands, for the spirit of fear is of the enemy.

The devil will always bring up the same old arguments because he doesn't know any new ones. He will try to talk you out of what God's given you, but you can *always* whip him with the Word!

So if you've only spoken a few words in tongues, hold on to that utterance in faith and *keep speaking out those words you've received*. Certainly that's the Holy Ghost, for He said, *"For with stammering lips and another tongue will he speak to this people"* (Isa. 28:11).

I like what Donald Gee, the famous British preacher, said about people who stammer a word or two of tongues when they first get filled with the Holy Ghost. He likened this situation to a whistling teakettle. As the water in a teakettle starts to get hot, every now and then the teakettle will let out a little whistle. But you don't take the teakettle off the stove when it just starts to whistle. You keep it on the burner until it's whistling long and loudly and giving off a steady stream of steam. Only then do you pour out the hot water to make tea!

In the same way, if you've spoken only a few words in tongues, it's important that you don't stop there. Keep speaking with tongues until out of your innermost being a steady stream is flowing out of your mouth and you enter into the fullness of God's blessing!

Don't Look for Outward Actions

Too often we try to judge spiritual things by fleshly standards, deciding what a person has or has not received from God according to how they act outwardly. Let's say three people come forward to receive the Holy Ghost. One of them receives and just stands there speaking very quietly with other tongues. Another receives and also speaks with tongues, but he gets so happy he runs up and down the aisle. The third one speaks with tongues and dances a little jig for joy. Then he cries and hugs the people around him.

The next day someone asks those who were present, "What happened at the service last night?"

"Well," someone says, "three received the Holy Ghost, but two of them *really* received!"

But the truth is, the two who showed more outward emotion didn't receive any more of the Holy Ghost than the person who only spoke quietly in other tongues.

I learned a long time ago that you can't tell what is in a book by looking at the cover. You also can't tell whether a person has received the Holy Ghost by his outside actions at the moment— unless it's speaking in other tongues.

Sometimes people just get stirred up emotionally, shouting and carrying on and making a lot of noise, and it doesn't mean a thing in the world. Of course, other times a display of outward emotion is a result of a true spiritual experience. But whether or not a person has truly received from the Lord is not determined by his outward emotions; it is determined by his *heart*.

Are You 'Good Enough' to Receive the Holy Ghost?

Years ago I was holding a meeting at Brother and Sister Goodwin's church, who were also our close friends and fellow ministers. After one of the morning services, a denominational woman came over to Brother Goodwin and me and said, "I want you to pray for me. I've come to understand that I need to be filled with the Holy Ghost."

Brother Goodwin replied, "Well, there's never a better time than now!"

She said, "Oh, no, I just want you all to pray for me, but I couldn't receive right now. I have some more digging to do." She meant that she had more praying and preparing to do before she could be ready to receive the Holy Ghost.

Brother John Osteen was also present at the meeting and was standing nearby. Brother Osteen came from the same denominational background as this woman, and he knew where she was missing it in her thinking.

"Well, now, Sister," Brother Osteen said, "aren't you saved?"

"Oh, yes."

"Aren't you a blood-washed, born-again child of God?"

"Yes."

"Do you believe that if you were to die this minute, you'd go to Heaven?"

"Why, yes!" she replied. "I know I would."

Brother Osteen said, "Well, then, Sister, *if you're good enough to go to Heaven, you're good enough to have a little more Heaven in you!* You don't have to do any more praying. It's the blood of Jesus Christ that cleanses you from all sin. It's the blood that made you worthy to receive the Holy Ghost. It isn't anything you did! It's the blood of Jesus that made you a new creature!"

Well, this woman saw what Brother Osteen was saying to her. Then Brother Osteen, Brother Goodwin, and I prayed for that dear lady, and she almost instantly received the Holy Ghost and began to speak in other tongues!

Too often Christians make the same mistake this woman made, thinking there is something *they* have to do to be worthy enough to receive what God already promised to give them. Or they get on the negative side of being filled with tongues and talk themselves out of what they already have.

This is what you have to get established in your heart: When a child of God asks in faith to be filled with the Holy Ghost, our Heavenly Father is not going to refuse his request. And when someone receives the Holy Ghost, he *will* receive the Bible evidence of that gift. All he has to do is yield to the Holy Spirit and begin to speak in faith, not allowing himself to speak in his own native language. As he does, he *will* speak with other tongues as the Spirit gives him utterance!

So open your mouth, and drink deeply of the Spirit. Keep drinking until you're full. Then speak out the utterance He gives you. Don't let the devil or anyone else—including yourself—talk you out of what God has already given you. There is a whole new dimension in God to explore after you receive the Holy Spirit!

CHAPTER 8

MORE THAN AN INITIAL EXPERIENCE

Receiving the Holy Ghost is so much more than just an initial spiritual experience. I believe this is the whole crux of the matter—the point where so many believers miss it. They keep looking back to the day when they got filled with the Holy Spirit. But the baptism in the Holy Ghost is so much more than a one-time experience. The third Person of the Godhead actually comes to fill believers with divine power that enables them to live their lives supernaturally from that moment forward!

I told you how I was filled with the Holy Ghost in 1937 at the Full Gospel pastor's house. On that day, I spoke with tongues for an hour and a half and sang three songs in other tongues. But I want you to know this too: That experience was just the beginning for me!

Some believers make a big deal about their initial experience of being baptized in the Holy Ghost. To hear them talk, the day they were filled with the Holy Ghost was the greatest thing that ever happened in their lives. The trouble is, they never talk about any subsequent experiences in the Spirit. They never go on to develop themselves further spiritually. Or they keep trying to have another infilling experience just like their first one.

Certainly the initial experience of receiving the Holy Ghost is important, but it's just the beginning. We shouldn't have to look back to some experience we had at the altar years ago as our only contact with the Holy Spirit. The Holy Ghost should become more real to us every single day. He ought to be more real to us now than He ever was on the first day we received Him. If He isn't, then we haven't been walking in close fellowship with Him. We haven't remained conscious every waking moment of His indwelling presence.

Your greatest experience in the Lord should be that of walking in close fellowship with Him *today*. Every single day you should be conscious of the Greater One living in you and empowering you to come through every situation you encounter victoriously. As you live each day like that, the Holy Spirit will become more and more real to you, and you will begin to fully enjoy His empowering Presence in your life.

You Can Dwell on the Mountaintop

I remember preaching at a particular camp meeting in the mountains of California in 1955. Then in the summer of 1956, I returned again to preach at the same annual camp meeting. During the second year I was there, a lady got up and testified about her experience at the previous year's camp meeting. She said, "Last year when I came up here on the mountain, I didn't know about the baptism in the Holy Ghost, but before I left, I was filled with the Spirit!

"Then after camp meeting was over, I went back to my home in the valley and started having a hard time of it. Life got really busy—getting the kids ready for school, sewing clothes for my children, taking care of church responsibilities, and so forth. I started feeling spiritually dry and powerless. In fact, since last summer, I haven't had another blessing like the one I experienced when I received the Holy Ghost. So I could hardly wait to get back up here to receive another blessing!"

When I heard that, I thought, *That dear woman missed the whole thing! She's been dry and bereft of power for 12 months, yet she had the Powerhouse, the Greater One, on the inside of her all the time!*

This woman hadn't been rightly taught, so she thought, *I feel helpless, powerless, and spiritually dry. If I could just go back up the mountain and get blessed again like I was last year, it sure would help me!*

That's the way a lot of folks think—and that is what defeats them.

If the Holy Ghost has come upon you and you're filled with His power, you can enjoy experiences with Him every day. You shouldn't have just one experience and then that's the end of it. You don't have to wait until you can get back to a mountaintop experience. You can be up on the mountaintop spiritually every single day of your life!

What Does It Mean to Receive 'Power'?

If you'll remember, I said I was actually a little disappointed in my initial experience of getting baptized in the Holy Spirit. I was quite conservative and reserved before I got baptized in the Holy Ghost. So I was just sure that when I received the Holy Ghost, I'd have a loud, emotional, boisterous time in the Lord. But as it turned out, I didn't do a thing except speak with other tongues. (Of course, that's all the 120 believers did on the Day of Pentecost too!)

So I felt a little deflated. I'd seen others get boisterous and shout with joy when they were filled with the Spirit, and part of me wished I could have that kind of emotional experience when *I* got filled. I prayed, "Lord, Pentecostal people keep saying that when the Holy Ghost comes upon a person, he shall receive power [Acts 1:8]. So where's the power? If I have any more power than I had before, I don't know it!"

Many times we don't know what power is. We think power is something we feel, and that isn't always so. Jesus didn't promise an emotional experience; He promised an enduement of supernatural ability when the Holy Spirit comes upon us.

ACTS 1:8

8 But ye shall receive power, after that the Holy Ghost is come upon you: and ye shall be witnesses unto me both in Jerusalem, and in all Judaea, and in Samaria, and unto the uttermost part of the earth.

Even though I felt disappointed, I had enough Bible in me to accept my experience of the baptism in the Holy Ghost for what it was. I said to myself, *Well, getting filled with the Spirit wasn't like I thought it would be, but it was scriptural, so I'll stay with it. As far as I am concerned, I'm filled with the Holy Ghost!*

Nevertheless, I didn't say anything about it to anyone, nor did I preach about that experience to my congregation. I was still a young denominational pastor of a little community church, so I decided I was going to wait until I had some kind of power explosion before I talked to anyone about it. I thought, *I want people to be able to see the proof of the power without my having to say anything!* Besides that, some way or another, I had a sense in my spirit—an inward intuition more or less—that I shouldn't say anything about it.

Well, there was a man in our congregation named Mr. Curry. He and his wife had been away on a trip to Europe for three months, and just before they returned, I got filled with the Holy Ghost.

Not long before Mr. Curry left for Europe, some Pentecostal folks began to attend our church because it was the only church in that little country community. These families would have had to travel for miles to find a Pentecostal church to attend, so they came to our church instead.

Even though people from all kinds of denominations attended our church, Mr. Curry was *not* happy when he learned Pentecostal families were starting to come. So he went to see Mr. Cox, another church member, and said, "I don't know whether we ought to let those Pentecostal folks come or not."

Of course, it was a public meeting, so even if we'd wanted to, we couldn't have kept them from coming!

Mr. Curry went on to say to Mr. Cox, "If that speaking in tongues gets in here, I'm going to pull my family out of this church! I won't keep going here."

Then Mr. Curry and his wife left for Europe, and while they were gone, I received the Holy Ghost with the evidence of speaking with tongues. As I said, I didn't share this news with the congregation at that time because I was a little disappointed about it and didn't "feel the power" the way I thought I ought to feel it.

However, I did talk to one person privately about my infilling experience, and that was Mr. Cox. Actually, Mr. Cox was a very spiritual and biblical man, and he figured out what had happened to me before I said anything. He and his family were the ones who graciously allowed me to stay with them whenever I traveled out into the country to preach on weekends.

Mr. Cox told me what Mr. Curry had said before he left about the Pentecostal folks coming to our church. Later after Mr. Curry had been back for a while, Mr. Cox told me of another conversation he'd had with him.

Mr. Curry said to Mr. Cox, "Something has happened to our little preacher while I was gone!"

Mr. Cox thought, *Who told Mr. Curry what happened to our preacher? I know I didn't tell him! Maybe Brother Kenneth told someone else, and it leaked out somehow.* Then Mr. Cox said, "What do you mean, something happened to him?"

"Well," Mr. Curry said, "he's a better preacher than he was before."

Mr. Cox replied, "Well, Mr. Curry, I always thought Brother Kenneth was a pretty powerful preacher."

"Oh, I did to!" Mr. Curry answered. "But I'm telling you, he has something he didn't used to have!"

By then, Mr. Cox realized that no one had told Mr. Curry anything. So to encourage Mr. Curry to keep talking, Mr. Cox said, "Oh, sure enough. Well, what is it that our preacher has?"

"Well," Mr. Curry said, "I don't know what it is. But nowadays when he preaches, you can feel it! When he talks, he has a power he didn't used to have!"

The church members were sensing the extra power in my life, even if I wasn't!

"I've always enjoyed Brother Kenneth's preaching," Mr. Curry continued. "But I'll tell you, when he preaches now, it *hits* you. His message has a *punch* to it! His words have authority behind them they didn't have before."

Mr. Cox thought, *Well, I better tell Mr. Curry what really happened to Brother Kenneth before he hears it from someone else in a negative context.* So Mr. Cox said, "Do you want to know what happened to our little preacher while you were gone?"

"Yes!" Mr. Curry replied.

"He was baptized with the Holy Ghost and spoke with other tongues."

Mr. Cox told me later, "When I said that to Mr. Curry, he dropped his head and didn't say anything for a long time. I didn't know if he was going to look up and say, 'Well, that's it! I'm pulling my family out even if it creates division in the church.' I didn't know *what* he was going to say!

"But when Mr. Curry looked up, he had tears in his eyes," Mr. Cox told me. "And he said, 'Well, I'll tell you one thing about it—it makes a believer out of me. I heard Brother Kenneth preach before, and I've heard him preach since. There is a power, a depth of spirituality he didn't have before."

When I heard what Mr. Curry said, I started repenting. I prayed, "Dear God, I had that power all the time, but I doubted it. Now I understand that this power wasn't given to me just for my individual benefit. It was given to bless others. That's why my congregation can tell something has happened to me, even if I can't!"

Then I began to notice the difference, too, even in my personal life. I'd come up against tests, trials, and temptations that used to take everything I had to barely squeak through them. But since I received the Holy Ghost, I noticed I had an extra "something" that helped me come through trials and temptations with a new sense of victory!

I prayed, "Dear Lord, I had this wrong idea in my mind about power. I thought that some way or another, power would be something I'd be able to feel physically. I thought I'd feel like I was about to blow up like a ton of dynamite! And because I haven't felt that way physically, I thought I didn't have any power.

"But *You* said that out of my innermost being would flow rivers of living water and that those rivers would flow out to bless others [John 7:37–39]. *That's* the purpose of the power I received from the Holy Ghost, and my congregation can tell the difference!"

Soon it wasn't just Mr. Curry who was talking about the difference in my preaching. Everyone in the church was talking about it as well! They said to each other, "What has happened to our preacher? He's got power! What's his secret? Whatever it is, I want it!"

Finally, I decided it was time to tell the congregation what had happened to me. I said, "All I know is that I got filled with the Holy Ghost and started speaking in tongues. You'll receive power, too, when you receive the Holy Ghost and speak with tongues."

That divine power wasn't evident in my life until I was filled with the Spirit, and my congregation knew it! After all, they had been hearing me preach for the previous two years and hadn't noticed that kind of power in my preaching!

Praise God, my testimony made such an impression on the people that almost every single one of them eventually got filled with the Holy Ghost. And it wasn't long before we'd turned that church into a Full Gospel church! We never lost a family. Everyone kept coming. In fact, the church grew even bigger in the years that followed!

After that experience, I never again doubted the benefits I'd received when I was filled with the Holy Ghost. I understood that it wasn't a matter of "feeling" power. It was a matter of yielding to the Holy Spirit. It was a matter of releasing the power of the Greater One Who lives within me.

The Fruit of Listening to the Holy Spirit

Before I was ever filled with the Holy Spirit, I enjoyed many blessed hours in prayer and communion with the Lord. Many times I prayed most of the night in English, and a few times I prayed all night long.

But even though I'd spent hours in God's presence, some way or another I'd leave that place of prayer feeling dissatisfied. It always seemed like I hadn't said what I wanted to say to the Lord. I'd use every descriptive adjective at my command to tell the Lord how wonderful He is, but I'd still go away from my prayer time feeling like my heart hadn't truly expressed itself.

But after I was filled with the Holy Spirit and began to pray in other tongues, my prayer life changed dramatically. Finally, my spirit could express itself, and I found myself leaving my time of prayer feeling satisfied in my spirit.

Of course, I already received the Holy Spirit *in a measure* through the New Birth (John 3:3–8). He had borne witness with my spirit that I was a child of God (Rom. 8:16). And as I lay on the bed of affliction as a teenager with two serious organic heart problems and an incurable blood disease, the Holy Spirit spoke to my heart, trying to direct me to the subject of divine healing in the Word.

I desperately needed the Word and the Holy Spirit to guide me into healing, because all I'd ever heard preached was the salvation message. I'd gone to Sunday school and church all my life—never missing until I became bedfast—yet I'd never received any training at all in listening to the Holy Spirit and following Him.

But as a 16-year-old boy on the bed of affliction, I began to hear an inward Voice as the Holy Spirit spoke to my spirit. No one told me to listen, but I finally just said, "Well, I can't be any worse off by listening than I am right now. After all, the doctor says I'm going to die, and I can't do anything more than that! So I think I'm going to start listening here on the inside of me."

And as I listened to the Holy Ghost Whom I knew in a measure through the New Birth, He led me right into divine healing!

The day came when the Holy Spirit spoke to my heart and said, "Now you believe you're well."

"I sure do!" I said.

"Get up then," the Holy Spirit said. "Well people ought to be up by ten o'clock in the morning."

So there in the bedroom, all by myself, I struggled to a seated position and twisted my body around on the bed so I could push my feet off the bed onto the floor. Then I grabbed ahold of the bedpost and pulled myself up. Draped over that bedpost, I declared, "I want to announce in the Presence of Almighty God, the holy angels, the Holy Spirit, the devil, and all his cohorts that according to the Word of God, I am healed and I believe it!"

Suddenly I felt a warm glow of God's healing Presence come down all over me like warm honey, and I stood up straight and started walking around that room healed!

How did I get to that moment of healing after being paralyzed on the bed of affliction with a terminal heart condition for 16 months? *I listened to the Holy Spirit with Whom I'd become acquainted in the New Birth.* Then later I listened to the same Voice of the Holy Spirit, and He led me into the baptism in the Holy Ghost (Acts 1:5)!

Think back to the analogy of drinking water. When I was born again on that sickbed, I had one drink of water—my

New-Birth experience. But the same Holy Ghost Who made me a new creature in Christ also led me into divine healing. Then I received the Holy Spirit, and I drank until I was full. From then on, His ministry *to* me and *through* me and His dealings *with* me were amplified many fold!

Maintaining the 'Greater Measure' of the Holy Spirit

The Holy Spirit guides Christians who know Him through the New Birth as much as He can. But for those who are filled with the Holy Ghost and pray with other tongues, the Holy Spirit's guidance is available in a far greater measure.

However, I have found that this extra measure of the Holy Spirit operates in my life only if I follow the practice of continually praying daily in tongues.

I'm not talking about rattling off a few words in tongues. If that's all you do, the ministry of the Holy Ghost in your life won't differ much from what it was before you were filled with the Spirit. I'm talking about taking the time to really pray in tongues and spend time with God on a daily basis. If you'll make an effort to maintain a Spirit-filled life by praying much in other tongues, the Holy Spirit *will* communicate with you through your own spirit.

First Corinthians 14:14 says, *"For if I pray in an unknown tongue, my spirit prayeth, but my understanding is unfruitful."* It's the Holy Spirit Who gives your spirit the ability to pray to God. The Holy Ghost supernaturally directs your prayer as He gives you the utterance. He prays through you about things before they ever happen.

I've found out over the years that there's never been a sickness or a death in my family that I haven't known about and prayed about ahead of time—sometimes even two years ahead of time. This kind of revelation knowledge doesn't just come through the revelation gifts of the prophet. I also operate in that ministry. But the Bible says the Holy Spirit will show any believer things to come.

JOHN 16:13

13 Howbeit when he, the Spirit of truth, is come, he will guide you into all truth: for he shall not speak of himself; but whatsoever he shall hear, that shall he speak: and HE WILL SHEW YOU THINGS TO COME.

Any believer can know by the Spirit about something ahead of time as he presses into God. Many times things will be revealed as believers pray in tongues.

Ever since I was baptized in the Holy Ghost, I've often had this experience as I've prayed in other tongues. The Holy Spirit showed me things to come before they ever happened so I could pray through on them. It was simply a matter of praying in tongues and sensing in my spirit what I was praying about.

Praying Out Mysteries

Let me give you an illustration from my own life about the Holy Spirit alerting me to pray about things in tongues before they happened. I was holding a meeting in St. Louis in 1958, and I'd gone back to my hotel room after the service. I tried to read a book, but within me I kept having an uneasy feeling. So finally I put the book down and began to pray. I asked, "Lord, what is it?"

Remember, Jesus said that the Holy Spirit will not speak of Himself, but whatever He hears, that shall He speak (John 16:13). That means you can expect the Holy Spirit to speak to you. Certainly He will speak through the Word, because He is the Author of the Word. But He will also speak on the inside of you as you pray in tongues.

I kept asking the Lord, "What is it?" as I prayed out mysteries in the Spirit.

1 CORINTHIANS 14:2

2 For he that speaketh in an unknown tongue speaketh not unto men, but unto God: for no man understandeth him; howbeit IN THE SPIRIT HE SPEAKETH MYSTERIES [divine secrets].

After a while, I got the sense that someone in my family was in physical danger, like an attack of sickness. I immediately thought of my wife Oretha since I was out ministering in another city and she was at home. But as I kept praying in tongues, I knew on the inside of me it wasn't my wife.

Then I thought of my two children, Ken and Pat. I prayed for each one of them in tongues, and as I prayed, I knew it wasn't either of them in physical danger.

Then I thought of my mother. As I began to pray in other tongues about her, I knew she was the one I was praying for.

About that time, the telephone rang. It was my wife, and she said, "Ken, your mother is in the hospital."

I replied, "That's all right. I know it. I've already been alerted, and I have the answer. The Holy Spirit told me that she'll be fine!" It's good to be on top of a situation, isn't it?

It is of great benefit for us to know the Holy Ghost through the New Birth, but the baptism in the Holy Spirit is an addition to this blessing. God has also given us the opportunity to experience a greater measure of the Spirit through the baptism in the Holy Ghost with the evidence of speaking in tongues.

You see, the New Birth is God's introduction of His life and nature to the sinner. But the baptism in the Holy Ghost is God's introduction of His supernatural power to His children.

The Great Adventure Has Just Begun

Let me stress again: Although the initial infilling is the beginning of something great, it shouldn't be the greatest experience you ever have with the Lord. *In fact, the greatest things that ever happened to me in my walk with God came as a result of praying with other tongues.*

As I said, I knew the Holy Spirit in the New Birth. Of course, even before I was filled with the Spirit, I knew the Holy Spirit as a young denominational boy preacher. The Holy Spirit would come on me and anoint me to preach. And although I didn't hold any public healing services, I would publicly preach on healing, and privately I'd lay hands on folks and get them healed.

Thank God for the healings and conversions that happened in my ministry those first four years after I was born again. But I never had supernatural manifestations until I was filled with the Holy Ghost in the second week of April 1937—and I'd already been preaching four years!

After I was filled with the Holy Spirit, I learned to pray much in other tongues, and that made all the difference. No one told me to do it. We didn't have much teaching on the subject back then. I didn't even know whether or not I was supposed to pray in tongues whenever I wanted to. But I found out that it was easier to pray in tongues than it was to pray in English. I also learned I could get further spiritually in tongues than I could any other way, so I just did it.

For instance, the greatest healings I've ever seen in my ministry came after a time of praying in other tongues. As I prayed, I saw in the Spirit what I was praying about. (You see, we can pray in the Spirit about physical things as well as about spiritual things.) And then as I just obeyed and did what I saw in the Spirit, the person would be healed!

Yes, the initial infilling of the Holy Ghost is wonderful. But that initial experience is only meant to be the beginning. God has an entire lifetime of supernatural adventures in store for us as we learn how to operate in the realm of His Spirit.

That's why I want to take you further in our discussion about speaking with other tongues. Once you realize the true value and the infinite scope of communicating supernaturally with God, I believe you'll want to take advantage of this gift more than ever before!

THE VALUE OF SPEAKING WITH TONGUES

PART 2

CHAPTER 9

PAUL GAVE PROMINENCE
TO SPEAKING IN TONGUES

Much ignorance exists in the Church today about the value of speaking with other tongues. Many Christians don't know a thing about the subject. Others know that tongues are the initial evidence of the baptism in the Holy Ghost, but they don't understand the many other scriptural purposes for speaking in tongues.

We're going to discuss at length the many reasons God gave us this supernatural gift to benefit and bless us. But first, I want to ask this question: What value did the Apostle Paul put on speaking in tongues?

As you study Paul's Epistles, you find that he wrote much about the subject of tongues, and apparently he practiced what he preached. After all, he declared to the Corinthian church, *"I thank my God, I speak with tongues more than ye all"* (1 Cor. 14:18)!

A well-known Christian leader once wrote a negative letter regarding tongues to one of his "star" converts who had gotten filled with the Holy Ghost. I was allowed to read excerpts of that letter. In his letter, this Christian leader stated that Paul took a very dim view of speaking in tongues and that the apostle tried to discourage and forbid the Corinthians from speaking in tongues. And although this man never gave chapter or verse for his statement, he tried to prove his point by claiming that Paul said, "I'd rather speak five words with my own understanding than ten thousand words in an unknown tongue."

Did Paul Take a Dim View of Tongues?

But Paul didn't say that. That Christian leader took part of a verse out of context to make it say what he wanted it to say.

Let's see what Paul really said. First, he made the statement we already mentioned: *"I thank my God, I speak with tongues more than ye all"* (1 Cor. 14:18).

Let's say you got up one morning and declared at the breakfast table: "This is the day the Lord has made. It's a good day, and I thank God for it!" You're making a positive statement, but according to this fellow, you would be taking a very dim view of the day!

That doesn't make much sense, does it? Yet this Bible scholar followed the same kind of logic when he said Paul took a dim view of tongues. After all, Paul said he thanked God that he spoke with tongues more than the entire church at Corinth!

If Paul spoke with tongues more than this Corinthian bunch did, then he must have done a tremendous amount of speaking in tongues. As you read the rest of chapter 14, you'll find that speaking in tongues was about all the Corinthians wanted to do! Paul even had to correct the church in Corinth along that line because many of the people were speaking with tongues in the wrong place in worship, and in the wrong manner.

1 CORINTHIANS 14:22–23

22 Wherefore tongues are for a sign, not to them that believe, but to them that believe not: but prophesying serveth not for them that believe not, but for them which believe.

23 If therefore the whole church be come together into one place, and all speak with tongues, and there come in those that are unlearned, or unbelievers, will they not say that ye are mad?

Paul plainly said in verse 23 that it wasn't good for the whole church to come together into one place and all speak in tongues at the same time. If Paul had to say that, it must mean that the Corinthian believers spent much of their time in church speaking with tongues all at the same time. If that was going on and someone who was unlearned in spiritual things came to church, that person might think those believers had lost their minds!

So Paul wasn't telling these Corinthians that speaking in tongues was wrong, nor was he forbidding them to speak with tongues. He didn't say, "You have the wrong thing!" Certainly not! They had the right thing, but they were just so thrilled and exuberant with that supernatural gift that they would all start speaking in tongues at once!

Paul was just telling these believers that in the church service, everything should be done to edify or build up those who hear. Then later in the chapter he gave further instructions about speaking in tongues in the public assembly:

1 CORINTHIANS 14:27–28

27 If any man speak IN AN UNKNOWN TONGUE, let it be by two, or at the most by three, and that by course; and let one interpret.

28 But if there be no interpreter, let him keep silence in the church; and LET HIM SPEAK TO HIMSELF, AND TO GOD.

Thank God, a believer can sit in a church service and hear everything that is being said and still talk quietly to himself and to God in tongues. And in doing so, he will be getting edified in two different ways. One, he'll be edified by the preaching of the Word. And two, he'll be edified by speaking quietly to God in other tongues!

Different in Purpose and Use

This is what Paul was talking about in First Corinthians 14:19, when he said, *"Yet in the church I had rather speak five words with my understanding, that by my voice I might teach others also, than ten thousand words in an unknown tongue."*

Paul thanked God that he spoke in tongues more than all the Corinthian believers, even though there was a super-abundance of speaking in tongues. *Yet in the church,* Paul said he'd rather speak five words with his understanding than ten thousand words in tongues. Why? *So that by his voice, he might teach others.*

In other words, Paul was saying that the purpose of tongues isn't for teaching or preaching. *Tongues is primarily for a believer's own personal spiritual edification.* It's his own personal way to communicate with God.

1 CORINTHIANS 14:4

4 HE THAT SPEAKETH IN AN UNKNOWN TONGUE EDIFIETH HIMSELF; but he that prophesieth edifieth the church.

This means that Paul primarily spoke in tongues in his private prayer life, not in church. Apparently, Paul must have gotten up in the morning speaking in tongues. He must have spoken in tongues between meals and gone to bed at night speaking in tongues.

It also means that Paul valued speaking with tongues. After all, a person doesn't thank God for something he doesn't value, for something of little importance, or for something he is opposed to!

So we see that tongues is primarily a gift for us to use in our private devotions to pray and fellowship with God our Father. Of course, there is the operation of tongues with interpretation. These two spiritual gifts are given for the church's benefit (and, at times, for an individual's benefit) and used together are equivalent to the gift of prophecy. We'll talk about that later.

But this is what we need to understand now: *All tongues are the same in essence because it's the Holy Spirit giving the utterance in every case. But they are different in purpose and use.*

Now, if believers are all praising God together in church, it's perfectly acceptable for them to praise God in tongues all at once. But it certainly would be wrong for them to all start speaking in tongues out loud while the preacher is trying to teach the Word! And it certainly wouldn't be right for the preacher to spend an hour teaching the people in tongues with no interpretation! In that case, the preacher would be edified, but the people wouldn't get anything out of it. This is what Paul is talking about in this passage.

Learning the Value of Tongues

The Word of God is so simple and plain! Some folks have made a mountain out of a molehill, claiming that Paul was teaching the Church that believers shouldn't speak with tongues at all. Paul wasn't teaching any such thing. His wish and desire was that *every* believer would speak with other tongues (1 Cor. 14:5). He thanked God that he spoke in tongues more than anyone else because he understood the full scope and value of this supernatural gift.

Paul knew from personal experience that there is a blessing and a source of power for everyday life found only in speaking in other tongues. So let's explore further what Paul knew about this subject. In the process, we'll find out what the Bible says about the value and purpose of speaking with other tongues. The more we know *why* we should speak with tongues, the more our testimony can stand with Paul's as we declare in faith, "I thank God that I speak *much* with other tongues!"

CHAPTER 10

A SUPERNATURAL MEANS OF SPEAKING TO GOD

We have already covered at length the first scriptural purpose of speaking in tongues—that tongues are the initial evidence of the baptism in the Holy Ghost. Now let's talk about the other benefits that are ours when we make a practice of praying in other tongues on a regular basis.

The second purpose of speaking in tongues is found in First Corinthians 14:2:

1 CORINTHIANS 14:2

2 For he that speaketh in an unknown tongue SPEAKETH NOT UNTO MEN, BUT UNTO GOD: for no man understandeth him; howbeit in the spirit he speaketh mysteries.

Notice, we are not talking to men when we speak in an unknown tongue; we are talking to *God*. In other words, God has given us a divine means by which we can speak to Him supernaturally.

Sadly, most Christians are not taking advantage of this gift like they should. Some even ask, "But is that form of communication necessary?" It must be necessary—after all, God provided it for us!

Paul goes on to say, ". . . *In the spirit he speaketh mysteries.*" I like the *Moffatt* translation, which says, ". . . He speaketh *divine secrets.*"

That's the reason no man can understand you when you pray in tongues—you're talking divine secrets with the Father! And I want to add something else: I'm thoroughly convinced that Satan can't understand you either! I believe that's the primary reason the devil fights tongues so hard—because he can't get in on the conversation! He can't know what you are praying about when you're praying mysteries with the Father, so he fights it every way he can.

Is there any value in speaking divine secrets with God? Emphatically yes! Otherwise, God would not have given to the Church this divine, supernatural means of communication with Himself!

Talking to God, Not to Man

My father-in-law, Mr. Rooker, was a denominational man, a farmer in the blacklands of northcentral Texas near the little town of Tom Bean. I came along in 1938 to pastor a small Full Gospel church in town—and then began to court his daughter!

I remember Mr. Rooker telling me about the preacher who came to hold an open-air revival meeting in Tom Bean a few years before I arrived. (After the revival, the minister built the very church I was pastoring.)

My father-in-law related that in the beginning of the revival, the preacher preached only about the New Birth. A few hundred farmers and their families from all around Tom Bean would come in to hear this preacher, and many came forward to pray at the altar and get saved. The entire community was stirred by what was happening in those tent meetings.

After the revival had been running for several weeks, the preacher began to preach about the baptism in the Holy Ghost and speaking with other tongues—and people began to receive! As you might imagine, that created quite a furor in the little town of Tom Bean.

People had their theories about what was happening to the local people who spoke in strange languages at those tent meetings. For instance, some decided it had something to do with the gasoline lanterns that were lit and hung on poles to give light in the tent meetings! (Remember, these were Depression days, and there often wasn't any electricity in country open-air meetings.)

Someone said, "Those gas lanterns throw out circles of light. I'm telling you, the preacher must be putting something in the lantern light that gets on you and makes you speak with tongues!" You can see the ignorance about spiritual things that was common back then.

There was also the theory about the anointing oil that the preacher used when he prayed for the sick. The concept of healing and anointing the sick with oil was new to the people. So some speculated, "The preacher must put something from that bottle on people that causes them to speak in those strange languages. Don't get too close to the preacher, or whatever it is will get on you!"

People had all kinds of foolish ideas! But they needn't have worried. The Holy Spirit won't "get on" a person if that person doesn't want Him. He is a perfect Gentleman.

My father-in-law told me, "The whole community was divided on one side or the other of this issue of the baptism in the Holy Ghost and speaking in tongues. Everyone was talking about it, and many people went to the tent meetings just to see what would happen. The curious onlookers would stand back in the shadows away from the lantern light. After all, they certainly didn't want whatever it was that caused people to act strangely to get on them!"

Then a neighboring farmer got saved, and Mr. Rooker said to me, "I knew that man. He was an upright citizen, a truthful man. So another farmer friend and I said to each other, 'There's one thing we know—if that neighbor gets that experience, we'll know it is real because we know *him*. He won't go in for anything fake or false.'"

Mr. Rooker continued, "All that people knew to do in those days was to come to the altar and seek to be filled with the Holy Ghost. So my friend and I would stand back in the shadows and get as close as we dared to the altar so we could watch what happened to this man.

"One night this neighboring farmer was praying all by himself at the altar. Everyone else had left, and my friend and I were closer to him than anyone else. We watched carefully as our neighbor knelt there at the altar praying. Suddenly he lifted both hands, looked up to Heaven, and started speaking in this strange language—and it happened without anyone shining the lantern light on him or putting any oil on him!

"My friend who was watching from the shadows with me turned to me and asked, 'What's he saying? What's he saying? What's he saying?'

"I replied, 'I don't know—he's not talking to me!'"

My father-in-law didn't know how scriptural that statement was! Mr. Rooker was speaking right in line with First Corinthians 14:2, which says, *"For he that speaketh in an unknown tongue speaketh not unto men, but unto God: for no man understandeth him. . . ."* This neighboring farmer wasn't talking to Mr. Rooker or the other man. He was speaking divine secrets to *God!*

Prayer Apart From Our Understanding

I want you to notice verse 14 in connection with supernaturally communicating with God.

1 CORINTHIANS 14:14

14 For if I pray in an unknown tongue, my spirit prayeth, but my understanding [mind] is unfruitful.

Once again, the *Amplified* translation reads, ". . . My spirit [by the Holy Spirit within me] prays. . . ." Keep in mind that the Holy Spirit isn't the one praying. He is helping *you* pray by giving you utterance in your spirit.

Paul is telling us that God has given us a means whereby our spirit man can pray apart from our understanding. Our understanding doesn't have anything to do with praying in the Spirit. Is that kind of prayer necessary? It must be, because God made the supernatural provision for it!

Someone once asked me, "What good is prayer when you have no idea what you're saying?"

I replied, "But I'm not talking to myself—I'm talking to God!"

So once again, we see that the Holy Spirit is the One helping us pray in tongues, but we are the ones doing the praying. With that thought in mind, let's look again at First Corinthians 14:2.

1 CORINTHIANS 14:2

2 For he that speaketh in a tongue speaketh not unto men, but unto God: for no man understandeth him; howbeit IN THE SPIRIT he speaketh MYSTERIES.

What does Paul mean when he uses the phrase "in the Spirit"? We know in this verse that he is talking about speaking in tongues. But we don't have to put our interpretation on what Paul meant. The Bible defines what he means by that phrase, as does Paul himself!

Let's go to the letter that Paul wrote to the Ephesians, where he said, *"Praying always with all prayer and supplication IN THE SPIRIT, and watching thereunto with all perseverance and supplication for all saints"* (Eph. 6:18). If praying in the Spirit in First Corinthians 14:2 refers to praying with tongues, we have every reason to conclude that praying in the Spirit in Ephesians 6:18 refers to praying with tongues as well.

Now let's go back to First Corinthians 14 to get a better idea of what Paul means by the phrase "in the Spirit."

1 CORINTHIANS 14:14-15

14 For if I pray in an UNKNOWN TONGUE, MY SPIRIT PRAYETH, but my understanding is unfruitful.

15 What is it then? I will pray WITH THE SPIRIT, and I will pray with the UNDERSTANDING [mind] also. . . .

Notice the phrase "with the spirit" in verse 15. Most prayers that people pray are mental prayers and don't have a lot to do with the Holy Spirit. But Paul said here that he prayed both ways—with the spirit *and* with his understanding or mind.

As a young denominational boy pastor before I was ever filled with the Holy Ghost, I saw these different scriptures about praying *with* the spirit and praying *in* the Spirit. I asked different ministers in my denomination, "What does it mean to pray *with* the spirit or to pray *in* the Spirit?"

"Well," some of the ministers said, "that just means to pray with a little extra 'spizzerinktum.'" (Do you know what they meant by that? They meant "to pray with a little extra energy or punch"!)

Sometimes we'd be singing a hymn from the church hymnal, and the song leader would say, "Now let's sing this next verse with the spirit *and* with the understanding." But all he meant by that was, "Let's sing the next verse with a little bit more energy—a little more 'spizzerinktum'!"

But that isn't what this passage in First Corinthians 14 is talking about at all. If your spirit were praying in English, your mind would understand what you said. Therefore, your mind wouldn't be unfruitful. But Paul is plainly talking about praying in tongues in this case, because he said, *"For if I pray in an unknown tongue, my spirit prayeth . . ."*(v. 14).

Paul wrote both of these letters—one to the Corinthians and one to the Ephesians. In both letters, he uses the phrase, "in the spirit." And in First Corinthians 14:15, he also uses the phrase "with the spirit." As you follow Paul's writings wherever he uses these terms, you find that he is either referring to praying with other tongues or he is at least implying praying in other tongues.

Now, of course, you could also pray "in the Spirit" by the spirit of prophecy. Praying by the spirit of prophecy occurs when the Holy Ghost takes hold together with you as you pray in tongues and you begin to pray by inspiration in your known language.

At times I've prayed with my understanding in English for an hour or more by the spirit of prophecy. I knew what I was saying, but my mind didn't have a thing in the world to do with it. The words just came rolling out of my spirit.

You can see examples of this kind of prayer in the Book of Psalms. The prayers of David, Moses, and other psalmists were given by the Spirit of God. No one spoke in tongues under the Old Covenant. As we saw earlier, tongues and interpretation of tongues are exclusive to the New Covenant. Yet these men prayed "in the Spirit," or by the Holy Spirit in the spirit of prophecy.

When you pray by the spirit of prophecy, you get your tongue hooked up with your spirit and pray by Holy Ghost inspiration in your own language, yet your mind has nothing to do with it. Your prayers are not something you're thinking up on your own. Instead, they come out of your spirit, inspired entirely by the Holy Ghost. This is not mental praying, or praying out of your understanding, even though you understand what you are saying. Rather, this is another way to pray in the Spirit.

Let's go back to what Paul said in Ephesians 6:18 and notice one more thing:

EPHESIANS 6:18

18 Praying always with all prayer and supplication IN THE SPIRIT, and watching thereunto with all perseverance and supplication FOR ALL SAINTS.

When we pray with other tongues, we are able to not only build ourselves up, but also to fulfill God's command to pray for all the saints. There is no way we could pray for all saints with our understanding because in the natural we don't know all the saints. But God has provided this means of supernatural communication, apart from our understanding, to enable us to do just that.

If Only I Had Understood

It would be good to just stop here for a moment and think about the amazing thing God has done for us: He has provided a way for us whereby our spirits may pray *apart* from our minds:

"For if I pray in an unknown tongue, MY SPIRIT PRAYETH . . ." (1 Cor. 14:14). Through this gift of speaking with tongues, our spirits can now communicate directly with God, Who is a spirit being.

You see, once you get filled with the Spirit, for the first time your own spirit can talk directly to God. Before that, you could talk to God with your mind and, of course, your emotions were involved. But speaking in tongues is a means of spirit-to-Spirit communication.

You may remember what Jesus said to the woman at the well of Samaria (John 4:4–26). The woman said to Jesus, "Our forefathers worshiped God in this mountain, but the Jews say we have to worship God in Jerusalem. What do *You* say about it?"

When Jesus answered, He didn't say that either of those views was right. Instead, He said, *"God is a Spirit: and they that worship him must worship him in spirit and in truth"* (v. 24). We don't have to worship God on a mountain in Samaria, and we don't have to worship Him in Jerusalem. God is a spirit being, and we can worship Him anywhere!

However, Jesus said that the time has come when you must worship God in spirit and in truth because *He* is Spirit. This gives you another indication of the value of speaking in tongues. When you pray in tongues, your spirit man is in direct contact with God, Who is a Spirit. Remember, Paul said that when you're praying in an unknown tongue, your *spirit* prays (1 Cor. 14:14). You're talking directly to God in a divine, supernatural way.

I know from my own experience the great difference between praying only with the understanding and praying with the spirit.

I remember what my prayer times were like as a young denominational boy pastor. At the time, I was born again, thoroughly saved, healed by the power of God, raised up from a deathbed, and the pastor of a little church. I was still living with my grandparents, my mom, my two brothers, and my sisters, where I'd lived ever since I was nine years old.

Sometimes I'd go down to Grandpa's barn and climb up among the hay bales where I could be alone with God and pray for an hour or so. During those times of prayer, I'd pray the only way I knew how—with my understanding.

I remember the times I'd try so hard to tell the Lord in English how much I loved Him and how wonderful He is. But even though I would stay in that place of prayer for an hour or two, it seemed like I never left feeling satisfied on the inside. How could I be satisfied? My spirit hadn't really had the chance to express itself. But after being filled with the Holy Ghost and speaking with other tongues, I noticed that I never left that place of prayer dissatisfied again because my spirit was finally able to communicate with God!

Before I was filled with the Spirit, I remember something else that happened in my prayer life. It happened on more than one occasion, but one incident stands out in particular. As I was praying and endeavoring to tell the Lord how much I loved Him—using all the words in my vocabulary to try to describe all He meant to me—it seemed like my lips and tongue were having certain sensations. It was almost as if I could hardly make them speak English without slurring my words!

Now, it hadn't been that long since I'd been bedfast and partially paralyzed for more than a year. At one point when I was bedfast, my throat and tongue had been partially paralyzed and I wasn't able to speak clearly. So up in Grandpa's hayloft that day as I endeavored to pray and my tongue felt thick and wobbly, it reminded me of the time my tongue was partially paralyzed. I got scared, so I got up and left!

After that, I never stayed long enough for my tongue to feel that way again. As soon as I started sensing anything, I'd just stop praying and get up and leave! Then my tongue would go back to feeling normal again.

It was only after I got filled with the Spirit that I realized what was happening during those times of prayer in Grandpa's barn. The Holy Ghost was trying to give me utterance, but I didn't know that back then. No one had ever taught me about the Pentecostal experience. And since I had no one to talk to about what was happening to me during those times of prayer, I wouldn't yield to the Holy Spirit. I just got up and ran out of that place!

Later when I did get filled with the Holy Ghost and spoke with other tongues, I realized that if I'd yielded to the Holy Spirit back then, I could have spoken with tongues long before I did. You see, the Holy Ghost was in me all the time, and He was trying to fill me to overflowing!

I said to myself, *Dear Lord, if I'd only understood, I could have been praying this way all along! I could have been edifying myself all this time. I could have been building myself up. I could have been talking to God supernaturally!* But, thank God, I've taken advantage of that gift ever since then!

Feeling Cheated

Back when all I could do was pray with my understanding, I'd use every adjective at my command to try to praise the Lord and tell Him how wonderful He is. But some way or another, deep down on the inside of me, I felt cheated.

I sort of describe it like this sometimes: After my wife and I left our last church in 1949, I traveled by automobile for more than two decades to hold meetings all over the United States and Canada. It's no exaggeration to say that I actually traveled almost two million miles by automobile during that time period, traveling many thousands of miles every year.

Many times when I was traveling, I didn't know where to stop to eat when I was in an unfamiliar town. But if I'd driven through the noon hour and was hungry, I'd settle for a restaurant that looked good and stop there to eat.

Now, I didn't mind paying for a meal if I *got* something for my money. But I hated it when I marched up to the cash register to lay down hard-earned money and all the while my stomach was hollering, "You cheated me!" (I imagine you know what I'm talking about!)

Well, that's very similar to what happened every time I left that place of prayer in Grandpa's barn. My spirit was telling me, "You cheated me! You cheated me!" But at that time I didn't know how to yield to the Holy Spirit. I didn't know my spirit could pray, so I just talked to God with my understanding as best I could.

But ever since I got filled with the Holy Ghost and began to speak in other tongues, I've never left that place of prayer without my spirit being satisfied. Why? Because my spirit is now able to say what it wants to under the inspiration of the Holy Ghost!

We Need Both Kinds of Prayer

You can readily see how the Church as a whole has fallen so far short and so far behind in prayer. Many Christians have tried to get by on just mental praying, so it's no wonder they haven't gotten any further in their spiritual progress. They're trying to get by on one kind of praying when God has given His children the ability to pray with the spirit *and* pray with the understanding!

Praying only one way is like trying to ride a two-wheeled bicycle with just one wheel. If you do that, I guarantee you're going to have a problem going very far!

We can apply that illustration to "the two wheels" (or two kinds) of prayer—praying with the understanding and praying with tongues. These are the two wheels that propel prayer forward and produce long-lasting, spiritual results.

When the majority of the Church decided that praying in tongues (the "front wheel") died with the apostles, believers were left with only one wheel of prayer and could no longer get very far spiritually. So most Christians put their one-wheeled bicycle (praying with the understanding) on a stationary bicycle stand

and started pedaling. And as a result, those Christians have stayed in the same spot for years, never making much progress. They may think they are moving forward, but compared to the destination God intended for them to reach, they haven't gotten very far at all!

That's why Paul said, *"What is it then? I will pray WITH THE SPIRIT, and I will pray with the UNDERSTANDING also . . ."* (1 Cor. 14:15). We need *both* "wheels" of prayer so we can fulfill God's highest and best in our lives!

Many folks haven't been taught what the Word says about this issue. Some will still try to tell you speaking with tongues is not for believers nowadays. But if it was necessary for believers to pray to God with their spirits apart from their understanding back then, it stands to reason it's also necessary for us to do so *now*!

We need to pray with our understanding, but we can't get by with only that kind of prayer for the simple reason that we wouldn't know how to pray as we ought.

ROMANS 8:26

26 Likewise the Spirit also helpeth our infirmities: FOR WE KNOW NOT WHAT WE SHOULD PRAY FOR AS WE OUGHT: but the Spirit itself maketh intercession for us with groanings which cannot be uttered.

On the other hand, we could say the same thing about praying with the spirit. We also can't get by with praying in tongues alone. Sometimes we need to articulate our needs to God in our known language. Therefore, we need *both* kinds of prayer.

So learn how to develop your prayer life with the help of the Holy Spirit. By all means, pray with your understanding. But if you're not filled with the Holy Ghost, ask for that priceless gift, and then learn how to communicate with your Heavenly Father by His divine, supernatural means.

CHAPTER 11

A MEANS OF SPIRITUAL EDIFICATION

In writing to the church at Corinth and other churches where he preached, Paul encouraged believers to continue to speak with other tongues. In First Corinthians 14:4, Paul explained why praying this way is so vital: *Tongues is a divine means of spiritual edification.*

1 CORINTHIANS 14:4
4 He that speaketh in an unknown tongue EDIFIETH HIMSELF [builds himself up]; but he that prophesieth edifieth the church.

Paul encouraged the Corinthian believers to continue the practice of speaking with other tongues in their private worship and in their prayer life as a means of spiritual edification.

In studying along this line, I noted a number of years ago what Greek scholars tell us about the word "edify." They say we have a word in our modern vernacular that is closer to the original Greek meaning. That word is "charge." The word "charge" is often used in connection with a battery. If the battery in an automobile runs down, we hook it up to a power source and charge it up. In other words, we build up the battery until it has the power to do what it was made to do!

So we could paraphrase First Corinthians 14:4 like this: "He that speaketh in an unknown tongue *edifies himself, builds himself up*, or *charges himself up like a battery*." In other words, as we pray in tongues, we are charging up our spirits by the power of the Holy Spirit!

The word "edification" isn't talking about mental or physical edification. No, this verse is talking about a wonderful, supernatural means of *spiritual* edification, and it is available to every single believer. Of course, whatever edifies or builds up a person spiritually will also help him mentally and physically.

Paul knew something about the fact that speaking in tongues charges up and strengthens a believer. After all, he said, "*I thank my God, I speak with tongues more than ye all*" (1 Cor. 14:18). In other words, Paul was saying, "I build myself up and charge myself like a battery by speaking in tongues more than all of you do!"

I want to get more than one scriptural witness, so let's look at what Jude said.

JUDE 20

20 But ye, beloved, BUILDING UP YOURSELVES on your most holy faith, praying in the Holy Ghost.

If your spiritual battery runs down, this scripture tells you how to get it charged: You *pray* in the Holy Ghost.

Notice that phrase "building up *yourselves*." When you pray in tongues, are you building up your neighbor? No. Are you building up your fellow Christian? No. Tongues are a dynamic means of spiritual edification that works for *you!*

Notice also that Jude didn't say, "Praying in the Holy Ghost will *give* you faith." No, faith comes by hearing, and hearing by the Word of God (Rom. 10:17). But praying in tongues will build you up in your most holy faith.

So speaking with tongues is primarily for your own personal, spiritual edification. It benefits *you* as it builds you up and strengthens you in your spirit man!

Smith Wigglesworth was an English preacher who experienced revival—outstanding moves of the Holy Spirit—on every inhabited continent of the earth. Marvelous things happened in Wigglesworth's ministry. For example, an elderly Pentecostal minister from England once told me that he personally knew a number of people who had been raised from the dead under the ministry of this mighty man of God.

Wigglesworth went to work pulling turnips in England when he was just six years old. Later he worked in a factory in the days before child labor laws were enacted. He was a grown adult before someone taught him how to sign his own name! Wigglesworth never read a thing in his life until after he was filled with the Spirit and spoke in tongues. Then the Holy Ghost taught him to read the Bible.

In his biography of Wigglesworth, Stanley Howard Frodsham wrote the following: "The gift of tongues was a priceless treasure to him and many times every day his heart went out in love and adoration to God, not in the defiled languages of earth, but in the Holy-Spirit-given language of love that God had graciously given him. He found that this speaking in tongues was always a source of spiritual edification. He lived that verse in Jude 20, 'Beloved, building up yourselves in your most holy faith, *praying in the Holy Ghost*. . . .'"[1]

You can't edify the people unless you've been edified yourself. But once you've been built up spiritually, you can then help others.

Too many times folks want to experience the success of people like Wigglesworth, but they don't want to pay the price these great men and women of God paid. They want a shortcut—an instant "fast-food" type of solution. But God doesn't deal in "instant pudding"! He works the same way He's always worked—according to the truths He's set forth in His Word.

One of those truths is found in First Corinthians 14:4 and Jude 20. God provided us with a divine, supernatural means of spiritual edification. Now it's up to us to build ourselves up on our most holy faith by praying much every day in the Holy Ghost!

A Personal Example of 'Charging Myself Up'

When I first read that the word "edifies" carries the meaning of "charging yourself up like a battery," I realized that in the past I'd prayed without really understanding everything I was doing. I had "charged myself up" by praying in the Holy Ghost without knowing altogether what God's Word said about it. I just knew it was right to do it.

But as I looked back, I realized that before all of my greatest experiences in God—before the most spectacular healings, the most supernatural financial miracles, or the most outstanding experiences of casting out demons—I always seemed to be led to set aside time by myself to pray in tongues.

You see, the Lord knows what is ahead of you. You don't know what is out there, but He does.

I remember a particular example that happened on the first Saturday of May 1943, when my wife and I were pastors of a little Full Gospel church in the blacklands of northcentral Texas. Oretha and I had nothing planned that day except getting ready for the Sunday services. As was our custom, I washed the dishes and cleaned the kitchen while Oretha made the beds and cleaned the bedrooms.

As I went about my normal chores that morning, some way or another, I just couldn't get away from speaking with other tongues. I didn't pray loudly; I just stood washing dishes and praying quietly in other tongues.

Then I went over to the church next door to make sure everything was in order. We didn't have a paid janitor, so folks would volunteer to clean the church. Sometimes they didn't do a very thorough job, so I went over to check everything out and to clean what still needed to be cleaned. And while I did that, I kept on praying in tongues.

After I was satisfied that the church was ready for Sunday service, I stayed at the church another hour. I walked up and down the aisles of the church, praying in tongues. I knelt at the altar and prayed in tongues. I purposely stayed at the church longer than usual so I could put some extra time in, praying in other tongues.

Then I went to the post office to get our mail. Since it was springtime, I decided to walk through the city park to the post office, praying quietly in tongues all the way.

When I arrived at the post office, I had to wait in the lobby for a while until all the mail had been put in everyone's boxes. As I stood there waiting along with several other men, I continued to pray under my breath in tongues. (That's what's so wonderful about praying in other tongues. If you're around others, you don't have to pray loud at all. No matter how quietly you speak to the Lord, He hears you.) Finally, I got my mail. Then all the way back to the parsonage, I continued to pray in tongues.

I would say that from 8:00 in the morning until 2:30 in the afternoon, I was praying in other tongues 90 percent of the time—for almost six hours. But except for the extra hour I spent praying in church, I didn't stop doing the things I had to do.

As I prayed, it seemed like there was a great big spring on the inside of me—and the more I prayed in tongues, the tighter that spring wound up! I didn't know a whole lot about the purpose of tongues back then, but I sensed that I was building myself up. I was charging my spiritual battery.

I said to myself, *God must be getting me ready for the service tomorrow. I guess we're going to have a real "stem-winder" on Sunday!* (I meant that the service was going to be a good one!)

But then about 2:30 that afternoon, Oretha and I had unexpected visitors. A lady brought her sister to our home. These two were also accompanied by another woman.

This sister was an inmate of a Texas mental institution. She'd been there for two and a half years in solitary confinement because she had been violently insane, trying to kill herself, and she was considered dangerous to herself and others.

For more than two years, this poor woman had been locked in a padded cell—no exercise, no sunshine—until her general health had just deteriorated. So the authorities of the institution wrote to her mother and father: "We believe it would be good for your daughter to come home on furlough for a couple of weeks. She is no longer violently insane, but she is still insane, and she will always need institutional care. However, we are short on help. We don't have the necessary staff to take her outside for sunshine and fresh air.

"Could you come and take her to your home for a few weeks? Watch her closely, but go to the city park. Keep her out all day long in the sunshine. Do your best to walk with her and let her get some exercise, because if the change of environment doesn't improve her appetite, she isn't going to live much longer."

So this woman went to the institution, picked up her insane sister, and brought her home. A few days later, the woman brought her insane sister to our parsonage on that Saturday afternoon.

Well, I'd never dealt with an insane person before. People had been healed in my ministry, but I simply did not know how to deal with this kind of situation. Of course, I knew that a person could be sick in his head, just like he can be sick in his stomach. In that case, I knew to pray and anoint that person with oil so he could be healed.

Yet on the other hand, I knew that at times an evil spirit can get ahold of a person's mind. In that case, that evil spirit has to be cast out, which means the one ministering to the person has to depend on the Spirit of God to lead him in each situation.

So the two women and their lady friend came to our door that afternoon, and we invited them all in. The lady said to her insane sister, "This is Brother and Sister Hagin. This is the minister I told you about."

Immediately after the woman spoke those words, "This is the minister . . . ," her insane sister started quoting scriptures. Whole passages from the Word flowed out of this insane woman's mouth just like water out of a faucet!

Well, I didn't know *what* to do. How was a person supposed to act around people like that? Then I opened my mouth and said the wrong thing. (I'm going to let anyone who's never opened his mouth and said the wrong thing throw the first rock at me!)

I said, "Anyone who knows the Scriptures like that must really know God."

Immediately the woman reached up and started pulling her hair, her eyes flashing fire as she screamed, "Oh, no, no, no! I can't know God. No, no, I *can't* know God. I've committed the unpardonable sin!"

The other woman grabbed her insane sister's shoulders, shook her, and finally slapped her across the face. Later the lady shared with us, "I hated to do that, but that's what the doctor told me to do to bring my sister out of those fits."

After that the insane woman settled down, and we were able to get her seated in a living room chair. There she sat like a statue, never blinking an eye, looking straight ahead of her, never moving.

I realized we were going to need some help, so I said to the sister of the insane woman, "You stay right here. My wife and I will go get Sister Sylvia."

Sister Sylvia was a little red-headed woman in our church who could pray Heaven and earth together. Do you know what I mean by that? She knew how to really get ahold of God and change things! Not many folks can do that, but she was one of those who could. (I would to God that others would learn to do the same!)

So my wife and I went to Sister Sylvia's house, and I said to Oretha, "You go and tell Sister Sylvia why we need her. I'll just wait out here in the car."

While I sat there waiting, I took out my New Testament and read a little. Then I prayed, "Lord, I'll just have to depend on You."

After all, that's all any of us can do anyway! We have to depend on Him because in ourselves, we can do nothing. Thank God, the Holy Ghost who lives in us gets us ready for things to come. And one means by which He does this is when we pray in other tongues!

So I said to the Lord, "I know if this woman just needs healing, I can anoint her with oil, lay hands on her, and expect You to heal her. But if an evil spirit is involved here, *You'll* have to help me deal with that. I won't know what to do unless You show me."

My wife came back to the car with Sister Sylvia, and the three of us returned to the parsonage. The insane woman was still sitting in a straight chair in the center of the living room. She hadn't moved an inch since my wife and I had left. She just sat there like a statue, staring straight ahead.

My wife, Sister Sylvia, the insane woman's sister, and the other lady who had accompanied the two women all knelt across the room to the west. I knelt in the east corner of the room, and we all began to pray. I don't know exactly how long we prayed, but we prayed quite a while.

Then the Spirit of God said to me, "Go stand in front of her and say, 'Come out, thine unclean spirit, in the Name of Jesus!'"

I'd never done anything like that before in my life. To make a long story short, I argued a while with the Lord about what He'd asked me to do, but finally I obeyed. I walked over to the insane woman, stood in front of her, and said, "Come out, thine unclean spirit, in the Name of Jesus!"

You might ask, "What happened when you did that?" It didn't look like anything happened. The woman looked and acted just as insane as she had before!

But I knew this much: The anointing had come on me when I said those words. I *knew* that under the anointing, I'd spoken the word of faith.

So the insane woman's sister bundled her up and took her home. That was Saturday afternoon. On Monday afternoon, the other lady who had accompanied the insane woman and her sister that day came to our house all upset and said, "Brother and Sister Hagin, pray, pray, *pray!*"

I asked, "What for?"

"That insane woman is having another attack like she did when she first lost her mind!"

To my utter astonishment, I opened my mouth to say something else, but this came out of my mouth instead: "What of it? Didn't you ever read in the Bible what happened when Jesus told an evil spirit to leave the young lad? The Scripture says that before the spirit left, it threw the boy down and tore him" (Mark 9:17-29).

Then I declared, "That will be the last attack she will ever have! You see, I spoke the command of faith on Saturday afternoon for that evil spirit to leave. And it had to obey!"

And that is exactly what happened! The insane woman was perfectly delivered that day. The doctors ran all the tests, pronounced her well, and sent her home for good!

Nineteen years later, my wife and I were preaching in a certain city where the sister of this formerly insane woman lived, and we went out to lunch with her. We asked how her sister had fared over the past 19 years. The woman said, "Oh, my sister's just fine! Her mind is perfectly normal and has been all these 19 years. She works in a place of business, teaches a Sunday school class in church, and she's on fire for God!"

The point I wanted to make with this account is this: *The Holy Spirit got me ready for my encounter with this insane woman by prompting me to pray in tongues more than usual.* I really didn't understand what was happening at the time. But now I can look back and realize that He was preparing me for what was to come. The Holy Spirit knew what was coming, even if I didn't.

He knew I needed to utilize the divine means of spiritual edification He'd provided for me through praying in tongues!

As I said earlier, the greatest things that have ever happened to me in my walk with God—the greatest healing miracles, financial breakthroughs, and deliverances—came after I had spent a prolonged length of time praying in other tongues.

Thank God for the privilege of praying in the Spirit! Thank God for this supernatural means of building ourselves up on our most holy faith! Yes, we can be built up by reading the Bible. Yes, we can be greatly helped by praying other kinds of prayer too.[2] Yet this is one primary way God has given us to edify and build up our spirits, and nothing else will *ever* take its place!

Receiving Might in the Inner Man

We need the spiritual edification we receive from praying in tongues. The Apostle Paul also gave us a Holy Spirit prayer in Ephesians 3 so these believers could receive mighty strengthening power in their inner man to put them over in life.

EPHESIANS 3:14–16

14 For this cause I bow my knees unto the Father of our Lord Jesus Christ,

15 Of whom the whole family in heaven and earth is named,

16 That he would grant you, according to the riches of his glory, to be STRENGTHENED WITH MIGHT BY HIS SPIRIT IN THE INNER MAN.

I want to call your attention to the fact that Paul is writing to Spirit-filled believers here. Remember, we've already read in Acts 19 about certain believers in Ephesus, to whom Paul asked, *". . . Have ye received the Holy Ghost since ye believed? . . ."* (v. 2). Verse 6 goes on to say, *"And when Paul had laid his hands upon them, the Holy Ghost came on them; and they spake with tongues, and prophesied."*

So these believers in the Ephesian church had not only been born again and received the remission of sins in Jesus, but they'd also been baptized in the Holy Ghost. Nevertheless, Paul prayed for them in Ephesians 3:16 that they might be strengthened with might *by God's Spirit* in the inner man.

You see, just because you're born again and Spirit-baptized doesn't mean you've "arrived" and there's nothing else you need in your walk with God! You still need to receive might by God's Spirit in the inner man, your spirit man. And one of the primary ways you do that is by praying in other tongues.

It's true that you need to know the Word and to quote scriptures and make confessions in line with God's promises. All of these things are important. But you also need to be infused with mighty power in your inner man *by God's Spirit*. You need that strengthening in your spirit man, for the enemy never stops launching attacks against your faith and your life.

Thank God, the enemy can be repulsed when your inward man is strengthened with Holy Spirit might! As First John 4:4 says, *". . . Greater is he that is in you, than he that is in the world."* But how do you avail yourself of the mighty inward strength and spiritual edification that are yours? By praying much in other tongues!

[1]Stanley Howard Frodsham, *Smith Wigglesworth: Apostle of Faith* (Springfield, MO: Gospel Publishing House, 1948), 113.

[2]For a further study of the different kinds of prayer, please see Kenneth E. Hagin's book *Bible Prayer Study Course*.

CHAPTER 12

PRAYING IN LINE WITH GOD'S PERFECT WILL

Let's talk about another reason that tongues are of such value to the believer: *Praying in other tongues is praying in line with God's perfect will.* The Holy Ghost not only knows what God's will is, but He will also never lead us away from the Word. That means as we yield to the Holy Spirit and allow Him to help us pray, He will always lead us in line with what God has said.

Paul talks about this particular role of the Holy Spirit in our lives to help us pray out God's perfect will.

ROMANS 8:26-27

26 Likewise the Spirit also HELPETH OUR INFIRMITIES: for we know not what we should pray for as we ought: but the Spirit itself maketh intercession for us with groanings which cannot be uttered.

27 And he that searcheth the hearts knoweth what is the mind of the Spirit, because he maketh intercession for the saints ACCORDING TO THE WILL OF GOD.

Notice that phrase "helpeth our infirmities" in verse 26. Often people misunderstand the meaning of this word "infirmities," thinking that it always means physical sickness or disease. But the word "infirmities" in this case is used in connection with our *shortcomings*. And one of our infirmities is found in the next phrase: "for we know not what we should pray for as we ought." Our prayer "weakness" is that we don't always know what we should pray about!

Sometimes to understand what someone said, you first have to find out what he *didn't* say. Notice, Paul didn't say we don't know *how* to pray. We *do* know how to pray. How do we know? Well, we know we're to pray to the Father in the Name of Jesus because that's what Jesus Himself taught us.

JOHN 16:23

23 And in that day ye shall ask me nothing. Verily, verily, I say unto you, Whatsoever ye shall ask the Father in my name, he will give it you.

But just because we know *how* to pray doesn't mean we know *what* to pray for as we *ought*. Although we do know to some extent how to pray at times, we don't know how to pray *as we ought to know*.

Why not? Because there's no way in the world for us to know everything there is to know about a given situation. We can only observe circumstances from the natural standpoint. Even those people we pray for may not know exactly how to pray for their needs!

You don't even know how to pray for yourself the way you ought to know. Of course, if you're hungry, you know to pray for something to eat. If you're behind in paying your rent, you know to pray for your finances. But you don't know the future. Sometimes you don't even know underlying conditions that are causing your problems. And unless God shows you, you can't see into the spirit world and observe the activity of demons that may be trying to come against you.

EPHESIANS 6:12

12 For we wrestle not against flesh and blood, but against principalities, against powers, against the rulers of the darkness of this world, against spiritual wickedness in high places.

There are evil powers trying to work behind the scene against us. So in order to be effective, we have to deal with those unseen forces in prayer.

These are some of the reasons why we don't know what to pray for as we *ought* to know. For example, we may know something about a trial a fellow Christian is going through, and we may know to pray that God would bless and help that person. Beyond that, however, we may not really know exactly how to pray about the matter according to God's perfect will. But, thank God, the Holy Ghost does!

Let me give you an example from my own life. I was holding a meeting down in South Carolina at the time of the Cuban missile crisis. It was also the time when my son Ken had just entered the military.

My wife and I were greatly concerned both about our son and the nation during this crisis. I remember kneeling on the platform of the church in South Carolina where I was holding my meetings and praying, "Now, Lord, I'm concerned about the Cuban crisis. Are we going to get into war? Spirit of God, I don't know how to pray about this, so please help me." Then I began to pray it out in other tongues.

It wasn't long before the Spirit of God spoke to my heart and said, "Don't bother about it. The crisis will be over in a day or two. Everything will be all right." And it did turn out all right, praise God!

So let's train ourselves to be sensitive to the Spirit of God! Then, when things arise that we're ignorant about, we can get on our knees and talk to the Holy Spirit. We can say, "Holy Spirit, I don't know what to pray for as I ought regarding this situation, but You do, so please help me pray." And He will be faithful to do just that!

The Holy Spirit Doesn't Do Our Praying for Us

Let's go again to Romans 8:26–27 and look further into how to pray about things we know nothing about.

ROMANS 8:26–27

26 . . . The Spirit itself [a better translation would be 'Himself'] maketh intercession for us with groanings which cannot be uttered.

27 And he that searcheth the hearts knoweth what is the mind of the Spirit, because he maketh intercession for the saints according to the will of God.

In the early days of my ministry, P.C. Nelson (we young ministers called him "Dad Nelson") was considered the number-one authority on the Greek language in America. I didn't go to Dad Nelson's Bible school, but I heard him preach a number of times, and I collected almost all the books he ever published. He had 12 years of higher education, and I once heard him say that he could speak and write *32* different languages. (That beats me by 31!)

When commenting on this verse, Dad Nelson said, "Actually, the Greek literally says, 'The Holy Spirit maketh intercession for us in groanings *that cannot be uttered in articulate speech.*'" He went on to explain that "articulate speech" refers to our regular kind of speech.

Dad Nelson went on to point out that these "groanings" also included praying in other tongues. Paul is talking about utterances or groanings in prayer that "cannot be uttered in articulate speech." Dad Nelson stressed that these groanings are not something the Holy Ghost does apart from you. Rather, the Holy Spirit helps *you* pray in groanings.

The *Amplified* version of First Corinthians 14:14 shows us more clearly our relationship with the Holy Spirit in prayer: "For if I pray in an [unknown] tongue, my spirit [by the Holy Spirit within me] prays. . . ." Again, when you pray in tongues, it is your spirit by the Holy Spirit within you praying. The Holy Spirit within gives you the utterance, and you speak it out of your spirit. You do the talking—He gives the utterance.

By this method, then, the Holy Spirit helps you to pray according to the perfect will of God—and to pray out the perfect will of God. This is the way things *should* be prayed for!

ROMANS 8:27

27 And he that searcheth the hearts knoweth what is the mind of the Spirit, because he maketh intercession for the saints ACCORDING TO THE WILL OF GOD.

Praying in the Spirit in groanings *is also something the Holy Spirit does not do apart from you.* Those groanings are prompted by the Holy Ghost, coming from deep inside you. But *you* allow them to escape your lips as you open your mouth and pray.

Years ago, during a seminar we were holding in the early days of RHEMA Bible Training Center, a woman came over to speak to me as I walked off the platform at the end of the service. She was a denominational lady who'd just recently been filled with the Holy Spirit. She said, "You know, Brother Hagin, since I found out Romans 8:26 and 27 says that the Holy Ghost does my praying for me, I don't pray much anymore."

Like this woman, some folks try to build a doctrine on this one isolated text in Romans 8 and make it say something it doesn't say. "Well, if the Holy Ghost is praying for me," they say, "He knows how to get the job done, so there is no use for me to pray."

But you can readily see that this statement is unscriptural because the Bible constantly exhorts us to pray. Second, Romans 8:26 is not saying that the Holy Ghost does our praying for us. He helps us pray out in groanings according to the perfect will of God.

ROMANS 8:26

26 LIKEWISE THE SPIRIT ALSO HELPETH OUR INFIRMITIES: for we know not what we

should pray for as we ought: but the Spirit
itself [Himself] maketh intercession for us with
groanings which cannot be uttered.

Paul starts off by saying that the Holy Spirit *helps* us to
pray. Then Paul shows one way the Holy Ghost helps us—in
groanings!

The Spirit of God will alert you to pray, but you must respond.
He won't make you do something. He won't make you pray just
like He won't do your praying for you. That would make Him
responsible for your prayer life, and He isn't responsible—*you*
are. He's been sent to dwell in you as your Intercessor and your
Helper in prayer. Now it's up to you to cooperate with Him and
do the praying!

Responding to a Burden to Pray

I remember a testimony that illustrates this point about
the Holy Spirit as our divine Helper in prayer. It was told by a
denominational minister who had gotten filled with the Holy
Ghost and come over to Pentecostal circles. We were both
guest speakers at several different Full Gospel Businessmen's
conventions.

One day this minister said to me, "Brother Hagin, I saw
something while you were teaching on speaking with tongues
that I hadn't understood before. My wife and I are still relatively
new in this Spirit-filled life. But right after we both got filled with
the Holy Ghost and spoke in other tongues, one of the young
ladies in our church—the mother of three little children—
needed a heart operation."

Serious operations like that weren't always as successful back then as they are today. So in the course of this operation, some way or another, this young woman's heart stopped. The doctors finally got her heart started again, but the woman remained unconscious.

The minister related, "Finally, the doctors told us that this woman's brain had been deprived of oxygen too long. They said that even if she regained consciousness, she would be nothing more than a vegetable and wouldn't know anything; it would be better to just let her die."

That night, this minister was awakened by the sound of groaning. He reached over to the other side of the bed and realized that his wife wasn't there. Finally, he figured out that it was the sound of *her* groaning coming from the living room.

At first the minister thought his wife was sick. So he got out of bed and went into the living room. "Honey, what's the matter? Are you sick?" he asked.

"Oh, no," she said. "I just have such a heaviness, such a burden to pray for this young mother and her three children. She's not old enough to die! Those children need their mother."

The minister continued, "All my wife could do was go back to groaning and praying in other tongues. I didn't understand it; I had never seen anyone pray that way. I'd gotten filled with the Holy Ghost and I spoke with tongues, but that was different than what my wife was experiencing in prayer that night. When I got filled with the Spirit, there was a sense of joy and gladness in me. But this night my wife was feeling such a heaviness, such a strong burden in her spirit to pray, so much so that she was groaning deeply in prayer. So I decided, *Well, since I don't understand what's going on, I'll just leave her alone.*

"Brother Hagin, I really didn't understand what happened to my wife that night until you taught on it in the meeting today," the minister said. "But my wife kept on praying that way for about an hour and a half. Finally, she got up and came to bed. She told me, 'Well, the burden is gone. It's lifted.' And when we went to visit the young woman the next morning, she was sitting up in bed, laughing and completely healed! It's been several years now, and the young woman is still well and attending church with her family."

You see, the Holy Ghost helped this minister's wife to pray effectively that night. She knew what to pray for, but she didn't know how to pray as she ought. But the Holy Ghost came to her rescue to help her get the job done! She prayed out God's perfect will in the situation with groanings and utterance in other tongues.

The Holy Ghost is our Intercessor. He helps us in prayer, just as He helps us in every area of our lives.

The Holy Spirit Is Our Helper

Jesus promised He would send the Holy Ghost to be your Helper. The "Helper" is Someone Who helps you get the job done!

JOHN 14:16

16 And I will pray the Father, and HE SHALL GIVE YOU ANOTHER COMFORTER, that he may abide with you for ever.

That word "Comforter" is the Greek word "paraclete." The *Amplified* version gives us the sevenfold meaning of the word "paraclete," which defines the role of the Holy Ghost in our lives. The word "paraclete" means He's been sent to be our *Comforter, Counselor, Helper, Intercessor, Advocate, Strengthener,* and *Standby.* The Holy Spirit is *all* of that, and He is dwelling inside us!

The Holy Ghost was sent to be our *Paraclete* or our Helper in the area of prayer. That means He's going to help *us* pray through to victory as we pray in tongues. He'll do the job *through* us, but He won't do the job *for* us.

The truth is, nowhere in the Bible do you ever find that the Holy Ghost comes to do *anything* for you apart from *you.* Regardless what area of life you're talking about, He comes only to *help* you do it.

Never do you read in the Acts of the Apostles that the Holy Ghost meets someone on the street and saves him. It's always people, assisted by the Holy Ghost, who get people saved.

For instance, you can read in Acts 8 where an angel told Philip to go down to Gaza. When Philip obeyed, he came upon an Ethiopian eunuch in a chariot who was reading the Book of Isaiah. It was Philip who led the man to salvation, not the Holy Ghost, nor the angel. It was the Holy Ghost who instructed Philip to go up to the man's chariot and talk to him (see Acts 8:26–39). Philip was led and aided *by* the Holy Ghost to get this man saved.

If the Holy Ghost saved men, it wouldn't be necessary to send missionaries to the mission field. We could just send the Holy Ghost and let Him work on the unsaved, preach the Gospel to them, and get them saved. But Jesus told *God's people* to go into all the world and preach the Gospel to every creature (Matt. 28:19). He did not tell the Holy Ghost to do it!

You also never read anywhere in the Acts of the Apostles where the Holy Ghost met someone on the street and healed him. But you *will* read where people got healed through the ministry of Spirit-filled believers who allowed the Holy Ghost to work through them!

, And, finally, you never read in the Bible where the Holy Ghost went anywhere and filled believers with His Spirit all on His own. But you *will* read where men, full of the Holy Ghost, preached the Gospel and the Holy Ghost fell on the people. And you'll read where others laid their hands on believers and the Holy Ghost filled them.

God works in line with His spiritual laws, and when we understand those laws, we can work with Him. That's what the Bible calls us—joint heirs or co-laborers with Christ (Rom. 8:17). We are workers together *with* God (2 Cor. 6:1).

Jesus told us one way we co-labor with Him: *"And they* [Jesus' disciples] *went forth, and preached every where, the Lord working with them, and confirming the word with signs following"* (Mark 16:20). The disciples went preaching, and the Lord worked *with* them and confirmed what they said with accompanying signs.

We're workers together with Him, and He works together with us! This is true in every area of our lives—most assuredly in the arena of prayer!

Taking Hold Together With Us in Prayer

Dr. T.J. McCrossan, author of *Bodily Healing and the Atonement*, was a noted Greek scholar and university professor. He pointed out that the word "helpeth" in the phrase "likewise the Spirit also *helpeth* our infirmities" actually comes from three different Greek root words. One root word means *to take hold together*; the second means *with*; and the third means *against*. So this phrase could literally read: "likewise the Spirit also *taketh hold together with us against*." That means the Holy Spirit takes hold together with us in prayer against the obstacles and hindrances we encounter in life.

Let me give you an example in the natural to illustrate the scriptural word "helpeth." Suppose I were standing on a church platform, and after the service I wanted the piano to be moved off the platform onto the sanctuary floor. I might tell the congregation, "I'd like eight of you men to please stay after we dismiss and help us move this piano down on the floor."

What would I mean by the word "help" in this case? I'd mean, "We want you eight men to *take hold together with us against* the weight of that piano and set it down there on the floor."

That's what this word "helpeth" means in verse 26. The Holy Spirit helps us in our infirmities or our shortcomings in prayer. So if we don't pray—if we don't take hold first by starting to pray—the Holy Spirit doesn't have anything to *take hold together with us against*, because His role is to *help* us move obstacles!

Years ago in the early days of RHEMA Bible Training Center, I asked the students to come for a special prayer meeting one night. We were going to pray for someone who was in the hospital and in critical condition. I'd just visited this person in the Intensive Care Unit, and I felt that unless we were able to pray sufficiently for him, he was going to die.

So that night we all prayed at length for this person. The next day, we announced to another class that we would be holding a second special prayer meeting, and that night a big group of students came. Then we held a third prayer meeting the next night, and an even larger crowd of several hundred people attended.

On the third night, I was kneeling on the platform, praying in other tongues just as I had the previous two nights. But as I prayed in tongues, I said inwardly, "Holy Spirit, You're not taking hold with me against this matter."

Then on the inside of me, I heard the still, small voice of the Holy Spirit say this just as plain as anything: "No, and I'm not going to either."

I replied, "But why won't You take hold with me against sickness and death on behalf of this person?"

The Holy Spirit said, "Because he's going to die."

Of course, I didn't know all the details about that man's situation, but the Holy Spirit did. Perhaps this person had set something into motion long ago that could not be reversed at this point. But regardless what the situation was, I'd learned early in my ministry to let the secret things belong to the Lord (Deut. 29:29). And in this case since the Holy Spirit wasn't going to take hold together with me against the problem, that meant I had no good reason to keep praying about it!

I rose to my feet and said, "Let's all lift our hands and praise God." I didn't take time to explain. Many people wouldn't have understood anyway, and it probably would only have created more confusion. So we all went home, and the next day the person went home to be with the Lord.

But thank God for all those times the Holy Spirit does take hold together with us against a problem! His divine aid and assistance makes all the difference!

Praying in Tongues Eliminates Selfishness in Prayer

If Christians took the time to analyze the prayers they pray with their understanding, they'd realize a large majority of those prayers are selfish. Too often their prayers are like the old farmer who always prayed, "God, bless me and my wife, my son John and his wife—us four and no more!"

Christians may not use those exact words, but if they would examine the sum of their prayers, they may see that the old farmer's prayer represents the extent of their "praying with the understanding." In other words, most of their prayer time is devoted to praying about matters that concern only themselves and their loved ones.

This leads us to another benefit or value of praying in tongues according to God's perfect will. Since praying in tongues is Spirit-directed prayer, *it eliminates the possibility of selfishness entering into our prayers.*

When you pray out of your own mind, it is possible that your prayer may be unscriptural or selfish. And I don't know if you realize this or not, but it is possible for you to pray out of your own natural way of thinking and actually change things that are not the will of God and not His best plan for you.

The Bible says there is a *good*, an *acceptable*, and a *perfect* will of God.

ROMANS 12:2

2 And be not conformed to this world: but be ye transformed by the renewing of your mind, that ye may prove what is that GOOD, and ACCEPTABLE, and PERFECT, will of God.

If you persist in praying selfishly out of your own carnal thinking, you may find yourself asking for only the acceptable will of God, not His perfect will. On the other hand, we've seen that when you pray in the Spirit, you pray out the *perfect* will of God.

If God's people pray and ask for things to be a certain way—even if it is not God's best for them, nor His perfect will—God will often permit it. I want to prove that to you from the Bible, because a lot of folks doubt that statement. They claim, "But if God granted something, it has to be His perfect will."

I'll give you an illustration from the Scriptures to show you that God sometimes answers prayer that isn't His perfect will. It's found in First Samuel 8.

God didn't want the Israelites to have a king like all the surrounding nations. *God* wanted to be their King, but the children of Israel wanted to be like all the rest of the nations, and they kept persisting in their petition for a king. Finally, God said, "All right, go ahead. You have My permission to have a king." But from that point on, the Israelites were never in the perfect will of God again, even though God blessed them and helped them as much as He could.

This is where a lot of people have missed it. Many times God has dealt with them and told them what His will is for their lives. But they keep after Him, praying out of their natural understanding for something *they* want. Finally, God says, "All right, if you want it that way, go ahead."

But I'd rather be in God's perfect will than in His permissive will, wouldn't you? It's just so much better!

I remember a dear young lady who made the same mistake the Israelites did when they asked for something that wasn't God's perfect will. She suffered greatly for that mistake. This young woman was one of my church members when I pastored in Texas. She was a beautiful singer with a wonderful ability to speak to youth about God.

But this young woman was dating a fellow who wasn't even saved. He'd go to church occasionally and he claimed to be a Christian, but it was quite obvious that he was not. She finally got engaged to this young man, even though she knew all the time it wasn't the will of God.

One night when we were all around the altar praying, this young lady came down to the altar and prayed through about the matter. God spoke clearly to her, telling her not to marry that man. Afterward, she got up and hugged all the ladies and shook hands with the men. "Well, that's settled," she declared. "I'm going to break up with him!"

The young woman did break up with this fellow. However, over the process of time, she got back with him and wound up marrying him! You might ask, "*Why* would she do that?" Because she kept praying about it until the Lord finally told her, "Go ahead and marry him if that's what you want to do."

You see, if you just keep hounding God like the Israelites did and like this young woman did, He'll eventually give you permission to do what you want to do, even though it isn't His perfect will for your life. That's why when God tells you to do something—whether His instruction comes from the Bible or the Holy Spirit speaks directly to your heart—you don't need to pray about it. You just need to *do* it!

Since God really did tell that young woman not to marry that man, she shouldn't have prayed about it any further. She should have just obeyed God. But she kept praying and praying and praying about it until finally the Lord told her, "Go ahead and marry him if that's what you want to do."

Notice that the Lord *didn't* tell her, "It's My will for you to marry him" or "Go ahead and marry him—it's fine with Me!"

So the young lady married this man—and soon she became the most miserable person in town! We didn't see her for months at a time. She didn't even come to church, yet she lived right there in town.

Finally, this woman wrote a letter to one of the older ladies in the congregation who'd been like a mother to her. The older woman called me and said, "Brother Kenneth, I have to read this to you!"

In the letter, the young woman wrote, "I've been locked up for five months. My husband is so jealous of me that when he goes to work, he locks me in the house. I don't have a key, and I don't dare go out alone. I don't go anywhere without him. He got jealous of me and my guitar and had a mad fit and broke the guitar to smithereens. Then he got jealous of me and my piano, and he broke that up too."

No wonder God told this young woman not to marry that man!

The letter continued, "I've been a prisoner for five months in my own house." She finally found a way to smuggle this letter out of her house and asked a friend to mail it for her. What a miserable situation!

This young woman might have thought, *Why did God ever put me in this mess?* But God isn't the One who got her in that mess. It's true He said, "If that's what you want, go ahead and do it," because she kept persisting, asking and asking Him for it. But He never told the woman, "That is My will. Walk in it, and be blessed." No, He said, "Okay! Okay! If that's what you want, go ahead."

That's the reason you have to get the Word of God in you *first* before you pray. Make sure the Word is abiding in you! As Jesus said, "*If ye abide in me, and MY WORDS ABIDE IN YOU, ye shall ask what ye will, and it shall be done unto you*" (John 15:7). Then make sure you are setting aside time to pray every day in other tongues. When God's Word abides in you and you're built up in your spirit by praying in other tongues, you will know you're praying in line with God's will about every situation!

Never let yourself get outside of God's Word when you pray. Build a strong foundation of the Word in your prayer life. If you don't have that foundation, you may go off after a desire that's not God's will for you. And eventually, God may answer you just as He answered Israel: "All right, go ahead. You can have it, if that's what you want."

It was not God's highest will for Israel to have a king—but they wanted one, so they got one. And from that point on, they were never again in the perfect will of God. That doesn't mean God didn't continue to bless them all He could, but He couldn't bless them to the fullest extent He wanted to.

I don't know about you, but I'm not satisfied with God's permissive will or with His second best—I'm going after God's *best*! That's why I value so highly the gift of praying with other tongues. When I pray in tongues, I am fully assured that I've left behind all possibility of selfish praying. Thank God for the ability to pray out the perfect will of God!

CHAPTER 13

MORE SCRIPTURAL PURPOSES FOR SPEAKING WITH OTHER TONGUES

So far we have focused on three primary purposes of speaking with other tongues. One, tongues provide a divine, supernatural means of communicating with God. Two, tongues provide personal and spiritual building up or edification to the spirit of man. And three, by praying in tongues, we know we are praying out God's perfect will.

However, many more marvelous benefits await us as we yield ourselves to the Holy Ghost and allow Him to give us supernatural utterance. Let's look at several more benefits that demonstrate the great value of tongues.

Tongues: A Means of Magnifying God

Acts 10 gives us another scriptural purpose for speaking with other tongues: *It is a means by which we can magnify God.*

Let's read what happened when Cornelius and his household received this supernatural experience.

> **ACTS 10:45–46**
>
> **45** And they of the circumcision which believed were astonished, as many as came with Peter, because that on the Gentiles also was poured out the GIFT OF THE HOLY GHOST.
>
> **46** For they heard them SPEAK WITH TONGUES, and MAGNIFY GOD.

Notice that phrase in verse 46: "speak with tongues, and magnify God." We know that the word "magnify" means to make something bigger. But can God be made any bigger than what He already is? From His standpoint, of course, the answer is *no*. But from our standpoint, God *can* be magnified or made larger in our estimation, and speaking with tongues is one means whereby He becomes bigger to *us*.

I noticed this particular purpose of speaking in tongues early on in my ministry. Before I was filled with the Spirit, I was still a teenager between the ages of 18 and 20, yet I was already a pastor of a small denominational church. And, of course, I had all the tests and temptations of any young person.

But I noticed a change after I was filled with the Holy Ghost, spoke with other tongues, and began to pray in tongues every day. When I'd face those same tests and temptations, I had an added power to pass the tests and resist the temptations. Before I received the Holy Ghost and began to pray every day in tongues, I'd sometimes just "skim by." But afterward, it became much easier to live as an overcomer in those areas. Why? Because I was magnifying God, He became bigger in my life.

If you remember, I told you earlier what happened after I received the Holy Ghost in the little community church where I pastored. For two years, I never even mentioned to anyone (except privately to Mr. Cox) that I had received the Holy Ghost or that I spoke with other tongues. But after a while, people in my congregation began to say to me, "Something has happened to you. You have more power than you used to have. When you preach now, your words are so powerful, it almost knocks us off the pew!"

You see, after I received the Holy Ghost and started speaking with other tongues, Jesus was magnified in my preaching. He became bigger in my life!

People should say the same thing about you when they look at *your* life. Just determine to pray every day in other tongues, and let God be magnified more and more in your life. As a result, you'll begin to walk in His power to an extent you have not yet seen. People will begin to notice the difference, and they'll want what you have!

Speaking in Tongues Helps Us Stay Conscious of the Holy Spirit's Presence

Here is an important fact about the value of speaking with tongues: although speaking with tongues is the initial sign or evidence of the Holy Spirit's infilling, *continuing to pray and worship God in tongues helps us to be ever conscious of His indwelling Presence.* This one benefit alone is bound to affect the way we live.

In John 14, Jesus talked about the Holy Spirit's abiding Presence in the lives of believers.

JOHN 14:16-17

16 And I will pray the Father, and he shall give you another Comforter, that he may ABIDE WITH YOU for ever;

17 Even the Spirit of truth; whom the world cannot receive, because it seeth him not, neither knoweth him: but ye know him; for he dwelleth WITH you, and shall be IN you.

It would behoove us to stay conscious of the Holy Spirit's divine, holy Presence in our lives, for He is ever abiding *with* us and living *within* us.

I heard an evangelist give a testimonial along this line a number of years ago that was very helpful. It helped me understand this particular benefit of praying in tongues, so I've used it as an illustration ever since.

The evangelist related an incident that happened when he was staying with a pastor and his family in the parsonage while holding a meeting in their church. The evangelist said, "I usually took a one-hour walk after the noon meal to get a little exercise. Then I'd come back and get ready for the evening service. But on this particular day, I had some letters I needed to write and mail, so I went to my room first. My plan was to take the letters to mail when I went for a walk later."

The pastor and his wife had only one child, a 12-year-old daughter. This daughter didn't know their guest was still in the house; she thought he was out taking his afternoon walk as he normally did. So when something happened to make her angry with her mother, the young girl threw a temper tantrum and talked ugly to her mother.

Just about that time, the evangelist came out of the bedroom and into the living room. When the daughter looked up and saw their guest standing there listening to her tantrum, she turned white and started to cry. She wept, "Oh, forgive me, forgive me! I'm so sorry you saw me act this way and heard me speak like this!"

The evangelist took the young girl by the hand and led her over to a chair to kneel down. Then he said, "Well, I forgive you. But there is a Greater One on the inside of you Who also heard you. And if you'll repent, the Lord will forgive you too."

So the girl repented and began to weep and pray, "Lord, please forgive me."

After a while, the girl started praying and worshiping God in other tongues and got over into the Spirit. Then the evangelist asked her, "Do you often pray in other tongues and worship God like that?"

"No, not often," she answered.

"Well, I want you to promise me something. I want you to pray in other tongues every day from this day forward. I'm not talking about rattling off a few words in tongues. I want you to take time to wait before God and pray in other tongues for at least 30 minutes a day.

"If you'll do that, it will help you become more conscious of the Holy Spirit's Presence on the inside of you, and it will affect the way you live. When you're conscious of His indwelling Presence, you're not going to fly off the handle and lose your temper anymore." The young girl tearfully agreed to pray in tongues every day.

Of course, we all know born-again, Spirit-filled people who lose their temper and say a lot of things they shouldn't. But that doesn't need to happen. Believers act in the flesh because they're not conscious of the Holy Spirit's abiding Presence within them.

About two and a half years later, the evangelist returned to this church to hold another meeting. The young lady was now about 15 years old. After the service, she took the evangelist aside and asked, "Do you remember what you said to me when you were here a few years ago?"

"Yes, I do."

"Well, I've done what you told me to do," the girl said. "Every single day I pray at least 30 minutes in other tongues. And I want you to know that I haven't talked ugly or lost my temper one single time since then—not with Momma or anyone else!"

Praying in tongues on a daily basis helped this young girl become more conscious of the Holy Spirit's indwelling Presence, and it affected the way she lived.

The same thing can happen to us when we make a daily practice of praying in tongues. There are many things we wouldn't say or do if we were more conscious of the Holy Spirit's Presence in us.

Tongues Aid You in Worshiping God

Speaking with other tongues will not only make you more aware of the Holy Spirit's Presence in your life, but *it will also aid you in worshiping God.* In the process, your spirit will become more sensitive to the things of God, and your taste for natural things will be affected—even things that aren't necessarily bad in themselves.

Let me give you an illustration. For instance, in the years I was a pastor, we only had a radio; there was no television in those days. Our parsonage was next door to the church, and I remember coming into our home many times after spending time at the church, worshiping God in the Spirit and praying with other tongues. Sometimes when I walked in the door, music would be playing on the radio, and I remember how it affected me.

My wife and I never listened to a bunch of junk on the radio, nor did we watch junk on TV later on, as far as that is concerned (and certainly there's a lot of junk on both radio and television!). But I discovered something during those years about the effect praying and worshiping God in other tongues had on me.

Sometimes after a time of intimate fellowship with God, I'd come back home so conscious of His Presence, and my wife would be cleaning the house, playing so-called Gospel music on the radio in the background. It wasn't that the music was bad. That kind of music is good, clean entertainment. But to me, it sounded like someone was beating on the lid of a bucket! Some of the songs weren't even scriptural. I couldn't even listen to that music because I'd just been in the holy, hallowed Presence of the Holy Spirit, and I was highly conscious of His Presence within me.

Please understand—I didn't say that this kind of entertainment is wrong. I just wanted to get the thought over to you that speaking with other tongues is a devotional gift, given to help you worship and praise God. Worshiping God in tongues will make you more conscious of the Holy Spirit's indwelling Presence. It will make you hungrier for God and less drawn to things of this natural realm.

Howard Carter was a pioneer of the Pentecostal Movement and the general supervisor of the Assemblies of God in Great Britain for many years. He was also the founder of the oldest Pentecostal Bible school in the world and was recognized in Full Gospel circles worldwide as an outstanding teacher.

Carter once made a statement about this purpose of speaking in other tongues that I never forgot. He said: "We must not forget that speaking with other tongues is not only the initial evidence of the Holy Spirit's infilling, but it is a continual experience for the rest of one's life to assist us in the worship of God." Then he went on to say this: "Speaking in tongues is a flowing stream that should never dry up and that will enrich one's life spiritually."

Those of us who continually pray and worship God in other tongues experience the spiritual enrichment provided by this supernatural gift!

Tongues Stimulate Faith

You'll also find that *praying in tongues stimulates faith.*

We already looked at Jude 20. It says, *"But ye, beloved, BUILDING UP YOURSELVES ON YOUR MOST HOLY FAITH, praying in the Holy Ghost."* And we've established the fact that praying in the Holy Ghost or praying in the Spirit refers, at least in part, to praying in other tongues.

We can conclude, then, that as we pray in tongues, we stimulate our own faith. However, tongues will not *give* us faith. As Romans 10:17 says, *"Faith cometh by hearing, and hearing by the word of God."*

If you're a believer, you already have faith. But now you must build yourself up *on* your most holy faith. Charge yourself up in faith! How do you do that? By praying in the Holy Ghost.

When we pray in the Spirit, the Holy Ghost supernaturally directs the words we speak. You see, we must exercise our faith in order to speak in other tongues. We don't know what the next word will be, so we just have to keep trusting the Holy Spirit to give it to us. Well, trusting God in one area is going to help us trust Him in other areas—and that's going to stimulate our faith.

Some people have heard faith teaching for years and years. They try to believe God to meet their needs, and they receive some results. However, many times they don't receive the results they ought to because they're not taking the time to build themselves up on their most holy faith—stimulating the faith they already have—praying in the Holy Ghost.

You see, when you want to keep your body physically fit, you exercise it, and as a result, your body becomes more keen and alert. In the same way, if you want to keep your spirit keen and alert, you need to exercise it as well. And praying in other tongues is one of the greatest spiritual exercises there is, along with feeding your spirit on God's Word.

Since praying in tongues stimulates faith, it also helps you learn to trust God more fully in every area.

When I first began in the ministry and pastored that little country church I told you about, one of the women who went to the church suffered from severe ulcers of the stomach. She and her husband had a denominational church background.

This woman's husband told me, "I didn't tell my wife yet, but the doctors told me that my wife has stomach cancer and there is nothing further they can do. I have already spent more than $10,000 trying to get her healed."

That doesn't sound like much these days. But back in the 1930s, $10,000 was *a lot* of money. After all, you could buy a Cadillac with all the bells and whistles for $875. You could rent a three-bedroom house for 10 dollars a month. Your monthly electric bill was only about one dollar. Your monthly gas bill was about 50 cents, and a loaf of bread cost a nickel!

Back during Depression days, men worked 30 days for 30 dollars, and a dollar a day was considered good pay. So for this husband to spend $10,000 to try to cure his wife's illness constituted a real *fortune*!

The husband continued, "We'd just about paid for our home, but I had to sell it and use the equity to pay my wife's medical bills. I also sold my automobile and all of our furniture to pay for her medical expenses. Now we live in a little furnished apartment."

This dear lady cooked meals for her family but couldn't eat the food herself because she just couldn't keep any food on her stomach. She'd eat a little baby food, but even that she would often vomit up. The woman looked like skin and bones.

Then the family began to attend the Full Gospel Tabernacle, and I didn't see them for a while. One day I decided I'd go visit them, but I didn't expect what I saw when I walked into their house. There was this very woman, eating greasy foods, and I could tell she was enjoying it immensely!

My eyes got as big as saucers. The woman looked up and smiled. She said, "Yes, this is me! I'm eating anything I want. In fact, last night I had chili for the first time in nearly 10 years! It didn't bother me a bit, and I don't have any symptoms. My stomach is perfectly healed!"

I'd laid hands on this woman and prayed for her healing, and I knew other ministers had as well. I'd tried to teach her faith to the extent that I knew it at that time. But remember, I was just a boy preacher when this happened. Nothing seemed to help her.

I asked the woman, "How did you receive your healing?"

"I got baptized with the Holy Ghost down at the Full Gospel church!" she exclaimed. "I was praying and seeking the Holy Ghost at the altar when the power of God came on me. I didn't exactly fall, but it was easier for me just to lie down under that power than it was to stay upright. So with my eyes shut I just lay down between the altar and platform and kept praising God in English."

The woman continued, "Even though my eyes were shut, I suddenly saw a beam of light about the width of a pencil come down through the ceiling and strike me in the forehead. Then I began to speak in this unknown tongue—and ever since then, I've been well!"

I saw the woman again a year later, and she was still perfectly healed!

I kept hearing testimonies like this woman's. Then later I got baptized in the Holy Ghost and spoke in other tongues myself. In the years that followed, I saw this kind of healing happen again and again. I don't mean just one or two cases. I mean physical healing at the same time a person got baptized in the Spirit was a frequent occurrence!

I met folks who, like this woman, had been seeking healing without success for a long time. Many had asked every healing evangelist who came to town to lay hands on them, yet for some reason, they couldn't seem to get healed. But when they got baptized with the Holy Ghost, these same people were *instantly* healed!

I just couldn't figure it out, but I was determined to try. I'm just that way. It may take me days, weeks, or months to find an answer to something I don't understand, but eventually, I *will* find the answer!

So I kept studying and meditating and asking questions. Finally, I got a revelation about what Jude 20 says: "... *building up yourselves on your most holy faith, praying in the Holy Ghost.*"

Speaking with tongues stimulates a person's faith, and believing God in one area helps that person believe God in another area. That's what happened to these people who needed healing. When they got filled with the Holy Spirit and started speaking in tongues, it stimulated their faith—or stirred up the faith they already had—and helped them receive the healing they were unable to receive before.

Gives Spiritual Refreshing

Here's another value we derive from praying in tongues: *Speaking with other tongues gives us spiritual refreshing.* We find this scriptural purpose for tongues in Isaiah 28.

> **ISAIAH 28:11–12**
> **11** For with STAMMERING LIPS and ANOTHER TONGUE will he speak to this people.
> **12** To whom he said, This is the rest wherewith ye may cause the weary to REST; and this is the REFRESHING. . . .

Notice those two words "rest" and "refreshing." That sounds good, doesn't it? But what *is* the rest and the refreshing this passage of Scripture refers to? There's a hint of the answer in the words "stammering lips" and "another tongue" in verse 11. But the answer is *fully* revealed in the New Testament. We experience God's rest and refreshing when *we get filled with the Spirit* and *speak with other tongues* (Acts 2:4).

In some cases, a doctor will recommend a rest cure to someone under his care. People sometimes go on a vacation for their rest cure, but when they return home, they often need to rest from their vacation before they go back to work!

However, I know the best rest cure in the world. We can take this rest cure every day, and it doesn't cost us anything! "With stammering lips and another tongue"—*this* is the rest wherewith you may cause the weary to rest!

And I'll go so far as to say this: Anyone who takes advantage of God's rest cure on a daily basis will never have a nervous breakdown. You can say what you want to—that's absolutely true!

I'll tell you, in these days of turmoil, perplexity, and anxiety, we need spiritual rest and refreshing as never before. And God has provided a means for us to receive the refreshing we need by speaking in other tongues. We need rest and refreshing! And, thank God, we can enjoy this spiritual rest cure every day of our lives. Whenever we want to, we can rest and be refreshed by speaking in the Holy Ghost!

The Best Way to Give Thanks

Paul gives us another reason we should pray in tongues. *Tongues provide the best way to give thanks.*

1 CORINTHIANS 14:14–17

14 For if I pray in an unknown tongue, my spirit prayeth, but my understanding is unfruitful.

15 What is it then? I will pray in the spirit, and I will pray with the understanding also: I will sing with the spirit, and I will sing with the understanding also.

16 Else when thou shalt bless with the spirit, how shall he that occupieth the room of the

unlearned say Amen at thy giving of thanks,
seeing he understandeth not what thou sayest?

17 FOR THOU VERILY GIVEST THANKS WELL,
but the other is not edified.

Notice that Paul said, "he that occupieth the room of the unlearned" rather than "the room of the unsaved." What did he mean by that word "unlearned"? He meant *those people who are unlearned in spiritual things.* Paul was saying that if you give thanks in other tongues, someone who is unlearned in spiritual things can't join in with you.

For instance, suppose I accept your invitation to come to your house for dinner and you invite several others to come as well. At the dinner table, you ask me to bless the food, and I give thanks with my spirit by praying in other tongues.

However, the other people who came to dinner are unlearned when it comes to the baptism with the Holy Ghost and speaking with other tongues. Because of their lack of understanding about these matters, they wouldn't be able to say "Amen" to my prayer of thanks. Why not? Because they wouldn't understand a thing I said! That's why it would be better in this setting to give thanks with my understanding. Then those sitting around me at the table can understand my prayer of thanksgiving and agree in their hearts with what I say.

Of course, it's still good for us to give thanks to God by praying in tongues. In fact, verse 17 says, *"For thou verily givest thanks WELL. . . ."* Paul is saying here that giving thanks in tongues *provides the most perfect way to pray and to give thanks, especially when we are by ourselves.*

Now, folks who are learned in spiritual things will understand if we give thanks in other tongues. They may not understand what we're saying, but they can still say "Amen" because they understand spiritual things. They know we're giving thanks *well* with our spirits!

However, in the presence of people who are unlearned in spiritual things, it would be best to give thanks with our understanding in our own vernacular. That way others can understand what we say and be edified. As Christians, we are commanded to walk in love, and love always considers the other person and looks for ways to edify others.

Praying in the Spirit Brings Your Tongue Under Subjection

While we're discussing the many reasons why we should speak with tongues, let me include an important one here: *Speaking with tongues helps bring the tongue under subjection.* And I think we would all agree that our tongues *need* to be brought under subjection!

JAMES 3:8

8 But the tongue CAN NO MAN TAME; it is an unruly evil, full of deadly poison.

So what does speaking in tongues have to do with this verse? According to this scripture, the tongue is the most difficult member of our bodies to control. Notice it says no *man* can tame the tongue. But *God* can!

So when you yield your tongue to the Holy Spirit and speak with other tongues, you take a giant step toward fully yielding *all* your members to God. If you can yield the most unruly member to God, you can yield *any* member of your body to Him!

Think about it—the Bible calls the tongue an "unruly evil" and a "deadly poison"! Many Christians assume that the sexual members of the body are the hardest to control. And they may even condemn other Christians who fail to control their sexual appetites while they sin just as grievously or worse themselves because of their uncontrolled tongue!

Some people are always running around talking about fellow Christians and running them down. For instance, some preacher may fall into immorality, and everyone in the church starts talking about it. "Did you hear what the preacher did? Well, let me tell you all the terrible details!"

But putting out the other fellow's candle doesn't light yours! Criticizing and gossiping about others is a grievous sin too. The Bible says the sins of the tongue are an abomination to God.

PROVERBS 6:16,19

16 These six things doth the Lord HATE: yea, seven are an ABOMINATION unto him. . . .

19 A false witness that speaketh lies, and he that soweth discord among brethren.

The bottom line is this: You have the potential to do more damage and more sinning with your tongue than with any other member of your body. But the more you pray in tongues, the

. more you will learn to yield your tongue to the Holy Ghost—
and the easier it will become to speak only words that edify
others in every situation.

Praying in Tongues Protects You From
the Contamination of the World

Here is another reason why every Christian ought to
speak with tongues: *It's a means of keeping us free from the
contamination of the world*—the ungodly, the profane, and all
the vulgar talk that surrounds us, whether on the job or in
different public settings.

How can praying in tongues keep us spiritually clean from
worldly contamination? Well, let's first go back to what Paul
said about the proper use of praying in tongues in the public
assembly. A believer is to "*. . . keep silence in the church; and let
him speak to himself, and to God*" (1 Cor. 14:28).

The same principle can be applied to any public setting. You
are speaking to yourself and to God when you speak in tongues.
So just as you can speak to yourself and to God in a church
service, you can also do so in other public settings because
you're not speaking out loud—you are "keeping silence."

You can pray this way on the job. You can pray in the Spirit
riding on a subway, in a bus, or on an airplane. You won't disturb
anyone because you're speaking quietly to yourself and to God,
building yourself up and at the same time keeping yourself clean
from worldly contamination.

Years ago when I was a young pastor, I'd have to go to the
barbershop to get my hair cut, and sometimes I'd have to sit

and wait for my turn. Meanwhile, the barbershop would be full of men engaged in all kinds of conversations, many of which included vulgar jokes and profane language. But I'd just sit there and speak under my breath to myself and to God in tongues while I waited, and I didn't stop speaking in tongues even when I was in the barber chair. As a result, all that carnality and vulgar talk that surrounded me never registered on my spirit. I stayed free of the contamination of the world as I prayed in tongues.

You can do the same thing. Throughout the day, wherever you go, you can speak quietly in tongues to yourself and to God. As you do, you will be strengthened by the Holy Spirit's power in your spirit man to keep you free from all worldly contamination!

Praying in Tongues Is the Introduction to the Gifts of the Spirit

To be filled with the Holy Ghost and to speak with other tongues is also *the introduction to the gifts of the Spirit* (1 Cor. 12:1–11). I often say it this way: *Speaking with other tongues is the doorway into the supernatural realm of God.* In other words, the infilling with the Holy Ghost and the practice of praying in other tongues on a regular basis is the doorway to all the other benefits and spiritual equipment that are ours.

Before we go on, however, I need to clarify something. Tongues are *not* the doorway into the *fruit* of the spirit in a believer's life (Gal. 5:22–23). I need to point this out because many times, people have said to me, "I know a lot of Full Gospel folks who speak with tongues but don't have the fruit of the spirit the way they ought to."

Others have said, "I know wonderful Christians who don't speak with tongues, and they marvelously exhibit the fruit of the spirit!"

Certainly, both statements are true. But let me call your attention to the fact that the fruit of the spirit talked about in Galatians 5:22–23 are *not* the fruit of the Holy Spirit. The Holy Spirit doesn't produce fruit.

Jesus said, "I am the Vine, and you are the branches" (see John 15:1–8). Fruit grow on the branches, and *we* are the branches. Therefore, the fruit of the spirit refers to the fruit that grows in our lives because of the life of Christ within!

GALATIANS 5:22–23

22 But THE FRUIT OF THE SPIRIT is love, joy, peace, longsuffering, gentleness, goodness, faith,

23 Meekness, temperance: against such there is no law.

Someone might say, "Yes, but in the *King James* Bible of Galatians 5:22, the word *Spirit* is capitalized, so it must refer to the Holy Spirit."

But there is only one Greek word for *spirit*, so if the word "Holy" isn't in front of the word *spirit*, you have to determine by the text whether it refers to the human spirit or to the Holy Spirit. Paul is primarily talking about the *human spirit* here.

Paul is drawing a distinction between the fruit of the flesh and the fruit of the spirit, that is, the recreated human spirit.

The fruit of the spirit should be developed in the life of every Christian. But remember, the fruit of the spirit has nothing to do with the baptism in the Holy Ghost or the gifts of the Spirit.

I can prove that by the Scriptures. For instance, the first fruit of the spirit listed is *love*. First John 3:14 states, *"We know that we have passed from death unto life, because we love the brethren."* Love is the first evidence of a person being born again. Another fruit of the spirit is *peace*. Romans 5:1 says, *"Therefore being justified by faith, we have peace. . . ."* This verse tells us that peace is the result or the fruit of being justified so we can stand righteous before God.

I could go down the list of the nine fruit of the spirit and find chapter and verse to prove that each of these fruit is the fruit of the recreated human spirit. Fruit grows on branches. Believers are the branches, and Jesus is the Vine. Branches produce fruit as they draw their life from the Vine (John 15:1–7). The fruit is given for the purpose of *holiness* and *character*. Gifts are given for the purpose of *power*.

You can be holy and not be powerful, and you can be powerful and not be holy. Of course, God's ideal is for you to be both holy and powerful!

This is what Paul was saying to the Corinthians about walking in love: *"Though I speak with the tongues of men and of angels, and have not charity, I am become as sounding brass, or a tinkling cymbal"* (1 Cor. 13:1). Paul was saying in essence, *"You have spiritual gifts, but the gifts are for power and the fruit is for holiness and character."*

I know some wonderful saints of God—consecrated, dedicated Christians—who have the fruit of the spirit in abundance but no power in their lives whatsoever. I've never seen any supernatural gifts in manifestation in their lives whatsoever. On the other hand, I know people who are powerhouses for God and have marvelous manifestations of spiritual gifts. But they failed to grow up spiritually, and it's very obvious that they need to grow more fruit of the spirit in their lives.

You see, spiritual babes can have spiritual gifts. A person doesn't have to be a mature Christian for the Holy Spirit to operate through him in the gifts of the Spirit. I can easily prove this by the Scriptures as well. Paul told the Corinthian believers that they came behind in no gift (1 Cor. 1:7). Yet later Paul called these same Christians spiritual babes (1 Cor. 3:1).

Think about it: We don't expect baby trees to produce fruit. We know that it takes time for a tree to mature enough to bear fruit on its branches.

Well, the same is true for baby Christians. It takes awhile for baby Christians to start exhibiting the fruit of the spirit to any great measure. Yet baby Christians can be filled with the Holy Ghost and have divine power operating in their lives!

If we would be honest, I believe we would all have to admit that we are not fully mature in the fruit of the spirit, no matter how long we've been walking with the Lord. We may have been good, Spirit-filled, tongue-talking Christians for many years. But just about the time we think, *Man! I'm doing really well! I've just about got my flesh under control!*—some less-than-desirable circumstance arises, and we find out we're not nearly as sanctified as we thought! Those are the times we realize all over again that we are still living in the flesh and we still have the body to contend with.

1 CORINTHIANS 9:27

27 But I KEEP UNDER MY BODY, AND BRING IT INTO SUBJECTION: lest that by any means, when I have preached to others, I myself should be a castaway.

You see, sanctification is a process, and we have to learn to keep the body under. When Paul said, *"But I keep under my body . . . ,"* he was referring to keeping his body under subjection to the inward man. In other words, Paul was saying, "Instead of letting my flesh dominate me, *my spirit* must dominate my flesh."

On the other hand, carnal Christians who *don't* allow their spirits to dominate their flesh can still be filled with the Holy Spirit. And to tell the truth, they need to be filled with the Spirit more than anyone!

You see, tongues are the beginning of it all—the entryway into a new realm of power in your walk with God. But once you go through that door into God's supernatural power, are you going to develop in the things of the Spirit? Or are you just going to stop on the other side of the door and stop your spiritual growth, as so many people do?

Personally, over the years I've found in my own life and ministry that the more I pray and worship God in tongues, the more manifestation of the other spiritual gifts I experience in my life. And I've found that the opposite is true as well: The less

I speak in tongues, the fewer manifestations of spiritual gifts I experience.

Paul teaches believers to be desirous of spiritual gifts and to covet earnestly the best gifts (1 Cor. 12:31). But remember—those words were written to people who already spoke with tongues!

In conclusion, let me repeat. *Speaking with tongues is the entrance into all the spiritual gifts and the supernatural equipment God has for you.* But don't just stop at the entrance! Go on to develop yourself fully in God's mighty spiritual equipment as you press ever deeper in prayer!

The Inestimable Value of Speaking With Tongues

In light of all these purposes for speaking with other tongues that are set forth in the Scriptures, we can readily see that each one is designed for our benefit and our gain. Therefore, it is amazing to me that people ask, "What good does a person get out of speaking with other tongues?"

Is there any value in talking to God supernaturally? Emphatically yes! There must be, or God wouldn't have provided the means to do so!

If God says tongues are a supernatural means of communication with Him, then we emphatically need this supernatural means of communication with Him!

If God says tongues edify the one who speaks, then the one who speaks needs this supernatural ability to empower him in the Holy Ghost. No matter what a believer feels or does *not* feel, when he speaks in tongues, he is being built up!

And if God says tongues are of value, then they are of great and marvelous value—beyond the scope of anything we have yet imagined or experienced in Him!

THE SCOPE OF SPEAKING
WITH TONGUES

PART 3

CHAPTER 14

FIVE COMMON MISCONCEPTIONS ABOUT SPEAKING IN TONGUES

At the beginning of this book, I stated that even believers who are filled with the Spirit and speak with tongues are often ignorant concerning not only the *value*, but also the *scope* of tongues. Some believers don't know what God's Word says about speaking with tongues. As a result, they are robbed of all the benefits God intends for them to enjoy through this supernatural gift.

In the following chapters, I want to help you understand the *true* scope of speaking with tongues, both as it is presented in the Word and as it has been proven out in the powerful prayer lives of godly men and women through the years. But first, I believe we need to clear up some misconceptions and unscriptural excesses that many believers have embraced as truth over the years concerning this subject of tongues. We'll deal with misconceptions first.

Misconception #1: 'You aren't saved unless you're baptized in the Holy Spirit and speak with tongues.'

In the Church world as a whole, there are those who say no one is really saved unless he or she is baptized with the Holy Ghost and speaks with other tongues. These folks also usually put great emphasis on the belief that a person must be baptized by a certain baptismal formula.

But according to the words of Jesus in John 14, that doesn't bear up under scriptural examination. In fact, if people aren't saved until they receive the Holy Ghost and speak with other tongues, then Jesus told a lie in this passage because He emphatically declared the unsaved could *not* receive the Holy Spirit!

> **JOHN 14:16–17**
>
> **16** And I will pray the Father, and he shall give you another COMFORTER, that he may abide with you for ever.
>
> **17** Even THE SPIRIT OF TRUTH; WHOM THE WORLD CANNOT RECEIVE, because it seeth him not, neither knoweth him: but ye know him for he dwelleth with you, and shall be in you.

Jesus said the world or unsaved people cannot receive the Comforter, the Spirit of Truth—the Holy Spirit in His fullness. Why can't the world receive the Holy Ghost? *"Because it [the world] seeth him not, neither knoweth him. . . ."* You see, an unsaved person is recreated by the Holy Spirit in the New Birth when he accepts Jesus. But the world—those who are unsaved—*cannot* receive the Holy Ghost because they don't know Jesus.

If an unsaved person prays to receive the infilling of the Holy Spirit without accepting Jesus first, he may receive any kind of spirit, because there is more than one spirit in the spirit realm. There are evil spirits as well!

One of the most dangerous things in the world is to convince sinners to start seeking the baptism in the Holy Ghost. Sinners don't know one spirit from another. And by violating the Word of God and not accepting Jesus first, they may yield to a *wrong* spirit.

Over the years, I've witnessed this happen to several people. Since they didn't first accept Jesus and get born again, they actually received an evil spirit, and I had to cast that evil spirit out of them. Afterward, I led them to the Lord, they were born again, and *then* they were filled with the Holy Spirit!

For instance, I remember one meeting where several people came forward to be filled with the Holy Spirit. However, I sensed in my spirit that a certain woman in the prayer line had an evil spirit in her. As I laid hands on her, I asked her, "Are you a Christian?"

She said, "I am. Why, I even have the Holy Ghost. Do you want to hear me speak in tongues?" Before I could say anything, she started rattling off something, but it was just gibberish. I knew it wasn't tongues.

You know, it scares some people to talk about demons or evil spirits. But believers don't have to be afraid; they just need to read their Bible! The Bible tells us how to identify evil spirits: *"And every spirit that confesseth not that Jesus Christ is come in the flesh is not of God: and this is that spirit of antichrist . . ."* (1 John 4:3). Thank God, He doesn't leave us in the dark about which spirits are not of God!

If I had dealt with this woman when the evil spirit wasn't in manifestation, she could have said from her mind, "Christ has come in the flesh." That's why I knew I had to deal with it right then, while the evil spirit was in manifestation.

So I said to her, "Say this prayer after me, Sister." I prayed, "Heavenly Father." She followed me and said, "Heavenly Father."

Then I said, "I acknowledge that You are God."

She repeated after me, "I acknowledge that You are God."

Then I said, "And that the Lord Jesus Christ is Your Son, and He has come in the flesh."

The woman said, "Jesus Christ is not your Son, and He has not come in the flesh." Notice she *didn't* say "the *Lord* Jesus Christ." She could not confess that Jesus Christ is God's Son, that He is Lord, and that He had come in the flesh.

It was quite obvious that this woman hadn't received the right spirit. She had associated with those who say a person isn't really saved unless he is filled with the Holy Ghost and speaks with tongues. These people led this woman, still a sinner, into seeking the baptism in the Holy Ghost, and instead she received the wrong spirit!

Finally this woman said to me, "Something here on the inside of me won't let me say what you said."

I said, "I know it. Do you want to be free?"

She said, "I do." So I cast that evil spirit out of her, and before the service was over, she was born again and speaking with other tongues as the Holy Spirit gave her utterance!

Let me say this one more time: It is dangerous for sinners to seek to be filled with the Holy Spirit. They need to be made new creatures in Christ Jesus first. Only then can they be filled with the Holy Ghost.

On the other hand, as I said earlier, when you know the Lord Jesus as your Savior, and God becomes your Father in the New Birth, you don't have to be concerned at all about asking the Lord for the infilling of the Holy Spirit. You can know beyond any doubt that when you ask, you absolutely *cannot* receive the wrong spirit!

A Confirming Dream

I was holding a meeting in a large church and had a sermon all ready to preach for the Sunday morning service. But just before I awoke that Sunday morning, I had a dream that changed my message.

I saw myself standing in the pulpit, and I heard myself say, "You know, some people say you're not born again unless you're full of the Holy Spirit and speak with other tongues. But that isn't right."

Then I heard myself quote John 14:16–17. I said, "You see, the Bible says, *'Even the Spirit of truth; whom the world cannot receive. . . .'* God does have a gift for the world. According to John 3:16, that gift is eternal life. But for His children, God's gift is the baptism in the Holy Spirit" (Acts 1:5). Then in the dream, I quoted Luke 11:13: *"If ye then, being evil, know how to give good gifts unto your children: how much more shall your heavenly Father give the Holy Spirit to them that ask him?"*

That's all I saw in my dream. When I woke up, I thought, *Well, that wasn't what I was going to preach about, but it wouldn't hurt for me to talk about what I said in my dream.*

So when it was time for me to preach that morning, I told the congregation, "I have a sermon I'm going to preach, but I want to tell you what I heard myself say from the pulpit in a dream I had last night. It might help someone." Then I related what I said in the dream.

After the service, my wife and I went out to eat with the pastor, and he said, "Brother Hagin, what you told the congregation about your dream was of God! This morning a young man in our congregation came over to talk to me before the service. He's a fine young man, a husband and father of three, who got saved and filled with the Holy Spirit here at the church five years ago and has been a part of our congregation ever since.

"This morning this man said to me, 'Pastor, this will be my last Sunday here. I will be going to another church, but I wanted to be fair about it and let you know, so I came this morning. My mother is a member of Such-and-such church, and she has convinced me that no one is really saved unless he or she is filled with the Holy Ghost and speaks with other tongues.'"

The pastor continued, "But after the service, that same young man came to me and said, 'Pastor, my family and I are *not* leaving! Brother Hagin's dream was evidently for me, and I see what God is trying to tell me.'

"Then the young man told me, 'After Brother Hagin said what he did, I starting thinking, *Why, I got saved right there at that altar, and it was months later before I was filled with the Spirit!*

When I got baptized in the Holy Ghost, I KNEW I was already saved. I had the witness of the Holy Spirit all that time. Pastor, I know that my mother is a good woman and that she's saved. But even though she's right in her heart, she is wrong in her head!' "

That young man was exactly right. There *is* a big difference between God's gift to the world—the gift of eternal life by accepting Jesus Christ—and the infilling of the Holy Ghost, which is His gift to His children!

Misconception #2: 'Tongues aren't for everyone.'

Another misconception is the idea that believers can receive the baptism in the Holy Ghost without the evidence of speaking in tongues.

Speaking with tongues is not the infilling of the Holy Ghost, and the infilling of the Holy Ghost is not speaking with tongues— *but they go hand in hand.* You are not receiving tongues when you get filled with the Spirit. You are receiving the fullness of the Third Person of the Godhead, the Holy Spirit.

Some people erroneously say, "You can have the infilling of the Holy Ghost with or without tongues." But that's not biblical! We saw earlier the biblical pattern for receiving the baptism in the Holy Spirit in the Book of Acts. Those believers were filled with the Holy Spirit and spoke in tongues (Acts 2:1–4). And if *you* receive the infilling of the Holy Ghost, you can and should expect to also have the Bible evidence that goes along with it!

Receiving the Holy Ghost *with* the evidence of speaking in tongues is kind of like the tongue in a man's shoe. If I bought a pair of shoes, I wouldn't buy a pair without any tongues in them. But at the same time, I'd never buy just the tongues of the shoes either! I'd buy *shoes*, but I certainly wouldn't accept them without the *tongues* in them—even if they were the most expensive pair of shoes in the store!

Other people say, "Well, I believe in *speaking* in tongues, but tongues aren't for everyone." Then they point to First Corinthians 12:29–30 for their supposed scriptural proof:

1 CORINTHIANS 12:29–30

29 Are all apostles? are all prophets? are all teachers? are all workers of miracles?

30 Have all the gifts of healing? do all speak with tongues? do all interpret?

Since the implied answer to all the other questions in verses 29 and 30 is *no*, these people conclude, "Since all are not apostles, prophets, teachers, or workers of miracles, then it is also true that all do not speak with tongues. Therefore, tongues are not for everyone."

But you can take one verse or a part of a verse out of context and put it with another verse in the Bible to prove anything in the world you may want to prove.

So let's read the *whole* context of these verses and see what Paul is actually talking about.

1 CORINTHIANS 12:27–30

27 Now ye are the body of Christ, and members in particular.

28 And God hath set some in the church, first apostles, secondarily prophets, thirdly teachers,

> after that miracles, then gifts of healings, helps,
> governments, diversities of tongues.
>
> **29** Are all apostles? are all prophets? are all
> teachers? are all workers of miracles?
>
> **30** Have all the gifts of healing? do all speak
> with tongues? do all interpret?

Someone might say, "See? Paul is saying that not everyone speaks with tongues!"

But Paul isn't talking about spiritual gifts here. He already talked about that in First Corinthians 12:1–11. He's talking about *ministry* gifts, *not* gifts of the Spirit. Ministry gifts are people who are called to the fivefold ministry and *equipped* with gifts of the Spirit (Eph. 4:11–12). For example, an *apostle* is a ministry gift. A *prophet* is a ministry gift. *Evangelists, pastors,* and *teachers* are ministry gifts. People who are called and equipped to stand in a ministry gift office carry a specific calling upon their lives whereby they can minister and bless others.

Paul then goes on to say, "*. . . After that miracles, then gifts of healings . . .*" (1 Cor. 12:28). Now, Paul doesn't change his mind and start talking about something else in the middle of this verse. He isn't illogical. This phrase "miracles, then gifts of healings" is really referring to the office of the *evangelist*.

We can see the office of the evangelist in Philip's ministry in the city of Samaria.

ACTS 8:5–7

5 Then Philip went down to the city of Samaria, and PREACHED CHRIST unto them.

6 And the people with one accord gave heed unto those things which Philip spake, hearing and seeing the MIRACLES which he did.

> **7** For unclean spirits, crying with loud voice, came out of many that were possessed with them: and many taken with palsies, and that were lame, WERE HEALED.

The evangelist's ministry consists of preaching Christ to the people for their salvation; working of miracles; and gifts of healings in operation.

Next comes the *helps* ministry. The ministry of helps includes those people called by God to assist ministers called to the fivefold ministry. The ministry of *governments* refers to the pastoral office, because the pastoral office leads the government of the local church. Finally, Paul mentions another ministry— *diversities of tongues.*

So in this passage in First Corinthians 12:27–30, Paul is *not* talking about being filled with the Holy Ghost and speaking with other tongues as the Holy Spirit gives utterance. He is also *not* talking about a person magnifying the Lord in tongues and speaking divine mysteries to Him. He is also *not* referring to a layman who occasionally gives a message in tongues in the public assembly to edify the church.

Thank God for each one of these applications and uses of the gift of speaking in tongues, but Paul isn't talking about any of them in this passage. Notice that "diversity of tongues" is listed along with the rest of the ministry offices, because it is also a ministry gift! Paul is saying that God set *some*—that is, specific people—in the Church who have a *ministry* of diversities of tongues.

The ministry gift of diversity of tongues approximates the office of the prophet. It refers to one who is called to minister in the public assembly in tongues and interpretation.

Paul goes on to ask, "Are all apostles?" No. "Are all prophets?" No. "Are all teachers?" No. "Are all workers of miracles? Have all the gifts of healings?" In other words, "are all evangelists?" No. "Do all speak with tongues? Do all interpret?" In other words, "Do all stand in the prophet's office with the ministry of diversity of tongues?" Well, of course, the answer is no!

So don't take that question out of its scriptural context and conclude, "It is readily apparent from this verse that not everyone will speak in tongues." This passage isn't talking about spiritual gifts such as speaking in tongues given to individual people. No, it's talking about ministry gifts given to the *Church.* And in First Corinthians 12:30, it's talking about people called to the prophet's office as ministry gifts through the diversity of tongues and interpretation.

The first people I ever saw ministering in diversity of tongues and interpretation were Brother and Sister Goodwin. The Goodwins were two of the dearest friends and fellow ministers my wife and I've ever had the honor of knowing. They had a remarkable ministry in this area of tongues and interpretation.

For instance, I remember the time my wife and I held a meeting in a south Texas city. In times past, we had fellowshipped with a certain family that lived in that city, but I noticed that the husband never came to any of the church services.

That man's wife asked to go to lunch with us one day. During our time together, she told us, "I don't mean to run my husband down because he's a fine man. But something happened at the church that offended him, and he stopped going. He refuses to go there anymore."

Well, when a person gets out of church, he gets out of fellowship with God, because a believer who doesn't fellowship with other believers isn't walking in the light of God's Word (1 John 1:7). This man needed prayer, and, of course, we prayed for him with his wife that day.

We closed that meeting and traveled a hundred miles away to minister in another town. Brother and Sister Goodwin were in attendance at this meeting.

This time the man showed up, along with his wife and three carloads of people. He wouldn't come to the local meetings, but he drove a hundred miles to get to these other services!

At one of these meetings, the Lord said to me, "Minister to that man and his wife," so I called them forward. Suddenly I had what I call a mini-vision flash in front of me. I saw the couple walking along, and the wife was looking down.

In the vision, the husband asked, "What's wrong?"

The wife answered, "Well, now, I know Brother Hagin said all that to me prophetically, but he knew part of the situation because I told him."

Then the Lord said to me, "You could minister to this husband and wife, but it will be better if Brother and Sister Goodwin came and ministered to them. Then the devil won't be able to take advantage of them because they know the Goodwins don't know anything about them."

So while the worship leader led the congregation in singing, I asked the Goodwins to come up and minister to them. Sister

Goodwin spoke in tongues to this couple and Brother Goodwin interpreted. You would have thought I'd told the Goodwins all about their exact situation! Brother and Sister Goodwin told this husband and wife word for word what the wife had told Oretha and me at lunch that day. The Goodwins told the couple what their problem was and where they had missed it with one another. Then they gave the couple God's answer for their situation.

I saw the Goodwins minister like that over and over again through the years. You see, when laymen give a message in tongues in the public assembly, the number is to be limited to at least two or three people (1 Cor. 14:27). But in the ministry of diversities of tongues mentioned in First Corinthians 12:30, there is no end to its operation as the minister is led and anointed by the Holy Spirit.

Many times in my own meetings people would come forward to be ministered to, and the Lord would say, "Have Brother and Sister Goodwin minister to them." Then the Goodwins would minister to every one of them in tongues and interpretation. They wouldn't know anything about the people, but they would tell each one exactly what was wrong and give the person God's exact answer from Heaven.

So there are those who are called to minister in diversity of tongues and interpretation in the public assembly. Everyone isn't called to that ministry; *God* is the One who chooses and sets people into this ministry gift office.

However, *every* believer *should*, *could*, and *ought to* be filled with the Holy Ghost and speak with other tongues as the Spirit of God gives him or her utterance. These tongues are not for public interpretation in the church; rather, they are to be used in the believer's private devotional life before God.

Misconception #3: 'You can't pray in tongues at will.'

As a young denominational boy preacher, I received the baptism with the Holy Ghost on the eighth day of April (which was a Thursday) at 6:08 p.m. in the parsonage of the Full Gospel Tabernacle at 309 North Chestnut Street in McKinney, Texas. From that day on, I made it a habit to get alone and wait before God, praying and singing in tongues as I worshiped and fellowshipped with the Lord.

As I said earlier, the Pentecostals didn't teach me to do that. In fact, people had little or no teaching on what they were supposed to do with the prayer language they received in the baptism in the Holy Spirit. So I really didn't know whether praying in tongues on a regular basis was right or not.

I'd hear the Pentecostal folks say, "You can't speak in tongues at will. You have to wait for a spirit of ecstasy. You have to get all worked up!" But that wasn't *my* experience. When I got alone with God to pray and sing in tongues, I didn't get all worked up. There was no one there but me. Besides, I couldn't find that anywhere in the Bible.

So I always had this nagging doubt in the back of my mind: *Is it right to pray in tongues whenever I want to?* I continued to struggle for several years with this issue.

(I believe that's one reason God led me to start RHEMA Bible Training Center in the mid-1970s. God wants these biblical truths to be taught to young men and women who are called to the ministry so they don't have to struggle with some of these same issues the way many of us did for so many years. Now our students can study and start at the level of unction and anointing many of us older ministers reached after *years* in the ministry!)

Because no one taught the scriptural use of tongues and I didn't know the Bible on the subject, the devil harassed my mind with accusing thoughts. He'd whisper to my mind, *"You're out of step with all those other people! They can't pray in tongues unless they're in a spirit of ecstasy, but you just pray at will. You're wrong! In fact, you have a wrong spirit! You don't have the same spirit they have."*

I didn't stop praying privately in tongues, but I was still bothered when Pentecostal folks told me, "We can't pray in tongues at will. We can only pray in tongues on special occasions when the spirit of ecstasy lifts us to a higher realm in the Spirit." So I kept asking myself whether or not I was right. For the next several years, I wavered in my prayer life whenever I waited before the Lord, praying and singing in other tongues.

I don't know why we're like that, bless our darling hearts and stupid heads, but sometimes we are. We seek the opinion of man and try to find out what this one or that one has to say about an issue, and everyone offers a different opinion. Why don't we just go to God's Word in the first place to find our answer!

Then finally in February 1943, I found my answer. I had been Spirit-filled for six years and was the pastor of a little Full Gospel church in Greggton, an east Texas town. One day I was studying at my desk, and I decided, *I'm just going to settle this question with the Word. I'm going to just forget what everyone else says about praying in tongues at will and find out what GOD says!*

So I opened my Bible to First Corinthians 14. I read where Paul said: *"For he that speaketh in an unknown tongue. . . ."* The first thing I noticed was that Paul did *not* say, "For he that the Holy Ghost speaketh *through* in an unknown tongue . . ."!

1 CORINTHIANS 14:2

2 For HE THAT SPEAKETH IN AN UNKNOWN TONGUE speaketh not unto men, but unto God: for no man understandeth him; howbeit in the spirit he speaketh mysteries.

I looked up this verse in the *Moffat* translation and saw that it translated the word "mysteries" as "divine secrets." Then I read verse 4, which begins, *"He that speaketh. . . ."* Once again, I noticed that it is the *person* who speaks, not the Holy Ghost. The verse goes on to say, *"He that speaketh in an unknown tongue edifieth HIMSELF. . . ."* That immediately got my attention. The person who speaks in an unknown tongue edifies *himself!*

Next, I read First Corinthians 14:14–15. This passage was the clincher for me!

1 CORINTHIANS 14:14–15

14 For if I pray in an unknown tongue, MY SPIRIT PRAYETH, but my understanding is unfruitful.

15 What is it then? I WILL pray with the spirit, and I will pray with the understanding also: I WILL sing with the spirit, and I will sing with the understanding also.

Who prays? Does the Holy Ghost pray? No! Does the Holy Ghost pray through me? No! He *helps* me pray.

Verse 15 helped me. Paul says, *"I will pray with the spirit, and I will pray with the understanding also. . . ."* So I said to myself, "Wait a minute! Paul said, 'I will pray with my understanding.' Can I pray with my mind—my understanding—anytime I want to pray? Yes!

I concluded, "Anytime I want to I can say, 'Now I'm going to pray for 10 minutes and just start out praying with my understanding: Dear Father, I bow before You in the Name of Jesus. I lift my voice to Thee, the Father of our Lord Jesus Christ, the Father of glory. I thank You for Your great plan of redemption. . . .' I could keep on praying to God for that entire time—just because I willed to do so!"

Then I read the beginning of verse 15 again. Paul said, "I *will* pray with the spirit." In other words, he was saying, "I can *will* to pray with my spirit just as much as I can *will* to pray with my understanding!" I never saw that in the Bible before that day, but I realized then that I'd been right all along to pray in the Spirit anytime I wanted to.

So I said, "I know what I'm going to do. I'm going to kneel down right here and pray an hour in other tongues. I'm going to *will* to do it. I *will* pray with my spirit!"

Now, here's what you have to understand about praying in other tongues: *The devil will fight you.* He doesn't want you to enter this realm of praying in tongues in the Spirit whenever you want to. Let me tell you—he'll *fight* you! How does he do it? He does it in a number of different ways. But since this kind of praying is separate from your mind, one of the devil's favorite strategies is to cause discouraging thoughts to come to your mind to get you off track.

That's what happened to me the moment I started to kneel down to pray an hour in tongues. The thought came to my mind (and I knew it was the devil), *"What if someone were to come in and ask what you're doing? You'd have to say, 'I don't know.'"*

"Wait a minute, Mr. Devil," I said. I grabbed my Bible and opened it to First Corinthians 14. "If someone comes in and hears me praying in other tongues and asks, 'What are you doing?' I'll just say, 'I'm talking to the Father and edifying myself!'"

Immediately the next thought from the enemy came. *"Do you even know what you're saying?"*

"No, I'm talking divine secrets!"

"But do you feel any different than you did before you started praying?"

"I don't walk by feelings, Mr. Devil. I walk by what the Bible says! And besides, it's *spiritual* edification, not physical edification. So in case you can't read, I'll just read these scriptures to you." Then I read to him various verses that answered all the devil's accusations. When I finished, I said, "Now, then, Mr. Devil, you might as well go your way, because I'm going to pray an hour in other tongues!"

Then I shut my eyes and started to pray and pray and *pray* in other tongues. There was no unction or anointing to my prayer; I was just praying with my spirit.

After a while, I just *knew* I'd been praying for more than an hour. It seemed like it had been a *very* long time! So I opened my eyes and looked at my watch, and I'd only been praying for 10 minutes!

So I went after it again and just kept on plowing through, praying in tongues. Time slowly passed, and after a while, I just *knew* I'd prayed in tongues for an hour—probably for even an hour and a half! I looked at my watch. Only 20 minutes had passed. Oh, dear Lord!

I plowed on. It seemed like I would *never* get through that hour of praying in tongues. I had no idea one hour could seem so long!

Somehow I struggled through that hour. As I got up and sat down in my chair, a voice from the outside said to my mind, *"Well, you just wasted an hour! You could have been working on your Sunday sermon. You could have been out visiting people. But instead, you just wasted a whole hour. That's what you've done!"*

I said, "Mr. Devil, I have not wasted an hour. Let me read it to you again." My Bible was still open to First Corinthians 14. I said, "I've been talking secrets with my Father. You're mad because you can't get in on the secrets!"

"But you don't even know what you're saying!"

"No," I said, "but I wasn't praying to myself. I was talking to God! He understood everything I was saying, and that's all that's necessary. Besides, I was building up my spirit.

"Just for that, Mr. Devil, I'm going to get back down on my knees and pray *two more hours* in tongues. And if you say anything else to me when I get through with those two hours, I'm going to *double* the time. I'll make it *four hours* the next time!"

So I got down on my knees again and started praying in tongues. This time it was a little easier, and I made it through the next two hours without ever saying a word in English. I never felt the least bit of unction or anointing, but I still put in my two extra hours of praying in tongues. When I got up and sat down in the chair again, I'd prayed in tongues for three hours. I'd never prayed in the Spirit that long before.

Once again, a voice from the outside said to my mind, "*Well, you've just wasted two more hours now—three hours altogether. What good did that do you? Do you feel any better than you did before you started?*"

I said, "I don't walk by feelings or sight. I walk by faith."

"*Yes, but do you know anything you said?*"

"No," I said. "But I wasn't praying to me; I was speaking mysteries to *God.*"

"*What good did it do for you to pray in tongues if you don't know what you said?*"

"I've been edifying myself—building myself up on my most holy faith."

"*Yes, but you could have used that time to finish your sermons. Now the time is gone, and you haven't accomplished anything.*"

I said, "Mr. Devil, I warned you, didn't I? I told you that if you said anything to me, I was going to double my time praying in tongues. So I'm going to get back down on my knees and pray another four hours in tongues!"

So I knelt down and went after it again in tongues. I had prayed for another hour and 45 minutes when suddenly *I hit a gusher!* That is the best way I know how to describe it. In other words, I began to pray both with my spirit and with my understanding under the anointing. Revelation just came rolling out of me as the Holy Ghost showed me things to come (John 16:13). (Later we'll talk more about what He showed me during this time of prayer.)

Until that moment, I was speaking in tongues with no unction or anointing, building myself up on my most holy faith. But when I hit that gusher, revelation just started rolling out of me. It didn't seem like I had a thing in the world to do with it. *But if I hadn't started praying in tongues as an act of my own will, that "gusher" never would have come!*

Praying in tongues like that is just like drilling an oil well. If the oilman never put forth the effort to drill the well, all that oil would just stay in the ground. The potential of hitting a gusher would still exist, but unless the oilman drilled for oil, no one would ever see the evidence of it.

You may ask, "Was it right for you to pray in tongues for those four hours and 45 minutes with no unction or anointing?"

Absolutely. Countless times over the years, I've prayed in tongues just because I wanted to. But it is important to understand that there is a difference between praying with tongues as an act of your will and praying with the anointing.

When we get over into that deeper realm of prayer, praying by the anointing of the Holy Ghost, that's when miracles happen and revelation comes! Thank God for praying in the Spirit!

That day it took me almost five hours to get into that deeper realm of prayer. But as I kept on praying every day in other tongues, I came to the place where I could get into that place in the Spirit in 10 minutes.

If you'll start doing the same thing—praying in tongues every day for extended periods of time—you will also learn how to quickly enter that deeper realm of prayer.

I remember a time when I was holding a meeting in Houston, Texas, and a spirit of prayer suddenly fell upon everyone in the auditorium. By the time my knees hit the floor, I was praying like a buzz saw in other tongues! I could hardly catch my breath as I prayed that way for an hour and 45 minutes. Then the Holy Spirit gave me the interpretation of what I was praying (not everything I was praying about, because I didn't need to know all of it).

In that interpretation, God told me what outreaches my future ministry should include. After that time of prayer, I changed my ministry completely and immediately began to head in a different direction. Step by step, I did what the Lord instructed me to do that day. And each time I broke into another one of those areas of ministry, everything worked so well, it seemed like Someone behind the scenes guided the whole operation— and He did!

So keep on praying in tongues every day in your private prayer time. But don't stop there. Keep praying until you begin to pray under the anointing of the Holy Ghost—until that supernatural language begins to flow out of you like a mighty river!

Misconception #4: 'All tongues are prayer.'

At times you may hear someone in Full Gospel circles say that all tongues are a form of prayer. They say, "When a person speaks with tongues, he's really praying. Then when someone interprets the tongues, he's really prophesying."

But all tongues are *not* prayer, and all tongues are *not* given for the purpose of prayer. I know better than that because I've spoken in tongues in public assembly many times, and several times people came up to me afterward who knew the language I was speaking and understood exactly what I said.

I spoke in German one time, and I don't know German. I've also spoken in Spanish and in Arabic. Several times people in the congregation came to me who understood the language I spoke. And sometimes when I asked them if I was praying, they said, "No, you were addressing the congregation."

For instance, one time a man came up to me after a service and said, "I wondered what you were going to do when it came to translating what you said."

I asked, "Why is that?"

He replied, "You made a statement in Arabic."

Well, I had no idea I had been speaking in Arabic!

Then this man said, "Arabic is my mother tongue. You made a statement in Arabic that a person would normally never hear, and I wondered what you were going to do when you translated it." (This man was not a Christian and didn't understand anything about the gifts of the Spirit. He thought I knew how to speak Arabic and was translating what I said in English!)

I said, "How did I do?"

"Oh, excellently!" he said.

"Well, that's good," I said. "Praise the Lord! I'm sure glad I did all right, because I don't know Arabic."

The man looked at me, dumbfounded, and said, "What! Do you mean to tell me that you've never spoken Arabic before?"

I said, "That's right."

The man stared at me in disbelief. He said, "You can't speak Arabic?" Then he said something in Arabic to me. I recognized I'd said those same words, but the man could see by the look on my face I didn't know what he was saying.

Then the man asked, "How could you speak perfect Arabic without knowing what you said?" So I opened my Bible to First Corinthians 12 and 14 and explained the gifts of tongues and interpretation to him.

Now, when this man had first entered the sanctuary that night, he did not believe that Jesus Christ is the Messiah. But by the time we finished talking after the service, something had changed in him. He said to me, "You know, Christ could be the Messiah!"

I replied, "Thank God, He is!"

When I was speaking in Arabic, the Holy Ghost talked to this man about Jesus being the Messiah! I wasn't praying. I was speaking a specific message from God to this man that he needed to hear. I've had this happen a number of times in my ministry.

So not all tongues are prayer. Some are; some are not. Remember, all tongues are the same in *essence*, but they can be different in *purpose* and in *use*. That's one reason God calls it "*divers* kinds of tongues."

Misconception #5: 'Tongues are just the ability to speak in a foreign language.'

As I said, sometimes when you speak publicly in tongues, someone may understand you. But when you speak mysteries in other tongues to God, *no* man can understand it (1 Cor. 14:2). And I want to add something else: Satan can't understand you either! That's why the devil hates tongues so much and fights it so hard—because he doesn't know what you're praying. You're speaking divine secrets with the Father, and Satan's completely in the dark concerning what you two are talking about!

Years ago at a Full Gospel Business Men's Fellowship convention, we invited ministerial students to a banquet. Students from 14 different universities attended the banquet, as well as many denominational ministers.

During the banquet, we conducted a panel discussion. Several of us ministers were on the panel, as well as a psychiatrist and a medical doctor. I answered the questions on tongues that the audience presented. Brother Oral Roberts answered the questions on healing. And some of the other ministers answered questions on other topics. The questions about tongues accounted for nearly 70 percent of all the questions submitted.

Some of the seminary students were preparing for the mission field, and they asked this question: "Why must we attend school to learn the native language of the country God called us to? Couldn't He just give us their foreign language through the gift of tongues!"

These students misunderstood the scriptural use of tongues. They wrongly assumed speaking in tongues is always speaking in someone's native language.

But that's not the scriptural purpose for tongues at all. Tongues are not a substitute for missionaries learning foreign languages. Tongues are a supernatural language given to us by the Holy Spirit so we can talk to God!

Now, it's true that at times the Holy Spirit may give you an unknown language in tongues to speak. That is, it's an unknown language to *you*.

1 CORINTHIANS 14:14

14 For if I pray in an unknown tongue, my spirit prayeth, but MY UNDERSTANDING IS UNFRUITFUL.

That word *unknown* is italicized in the *King James Version* of the Bible. This means it wasn't in the original Scriptures. The translators added it for clarity. The original manuscript said, "For if I pray in a tongue, my spirit prayeth. . . ." The translators added the word *unknown* to clarify that some tongues you speak may not be unknown to others, but it is unknown to *you*.

Paul specifically refers to tongues of men, which can mean foreign languages. He says, "*Though I speak with the tongues of men and of angels . . .*"(1 Cor. 13:1). Most often we speak in heavenly languages when we speak divine secrets to God. But it is also possible to speak in the tongues of men.

I remember the time a Foursquare pastor told me about a memorable experience he'd had along this line. Years earlier, he'd traveled down to a Foursquare mission station in Mexico to bring provisions. During his weeklong stay, this pastor preached every day. After he preached, the people came around the altar and prayed.

"During a time of prayer around the altar," the pastor told me, "I witnessed one of the most glorious sights I've ever seen! A dear little old Mexican woman who didn't have a tooth in her head got filled with the Holy Ghost. Her face lit up like a neon sign in the dark, and she began to praise God fluently in English!

"At first when I heard the old woman speak in fluent English, I thought she knew the language. But then I learned that she'd never been to school a day in her life! It was such a thrill to listen to her magnify, worship, and praise God in a language known to me but completely unknown to her!"

Several American missionaries have told me similar testimonies. For example, sometimes in ministering the baptism in the Holy Spirit to people on the mission field, they'd hear them speak in English as their "unknown tongue."

As I said, I've personally spoken a number of different languages of men as I was praying or giving a message in tongues. I didn't know I was doing so at the time, but someone else understood what I said and told me afterward.

For instance, in 1954 I was holding a meeting in New Jersey for A. A. Swift, an old-time Pentecostal minister. Brother Swift was 72 years old at the time. He and his wife had gone to China in 1911 as missionaries. I ministered frequently in Brother Swift's church, and whenever I spoke a message in tongues, he'd interpret.

Brother Swift had developed the gift of interpretation of tongues beyond anyone I've ever seen. In all my years of ministry, his interpretation of tongues was the most beautiful display of that gift I've ever witnessed.

You see, spiritual gifts can be developed through use. Certainly a person can develop his ministry as he learns to wait before God and yield to the Holy Spirit. And so it is with the gifts of the Spirit.

You can learn to be more yielded to the Spirit of God in the operation of spiritual gifts.

During that service at Brother Swift's church, I gave a message in tongues, and I knew I was speaking some kind of oriental language. After the service, we went next door to the parsonage to have a bite to eat. As we sat there, Brother Swift said to his wife, "Mother, did you understand what Brother Hagin said when he spoke in Chinese tonight?"

Sister Swift replied, "Yes, I did."

The couple sat there and talked back and forth to one another in Chinese for a few minutes. As I listened, I noticed a number of words I'd used when I spoke with tongues. Brother Swift said, "It's been many years since we were there, but you spoke in a dialect of a nearby region, not a dialect where we lived. I understood about 50 percent of what you said."

Well, I didn't know I was speaking a Chinese dialect. I just knew I was yielding to the Holy Ghost as He gave me supernatural utterance in tongues!

It doesn't make any difference whether you speak in a tongue that is a language of men or of angels. When you speak in other tongues, what matters is that you're speaking an inspired utterance.

Tongues Used as a Sign

So at times, people can speak in an unknown tongue that someone in the congregation understands because it's given in his native language. Or sometimes the message in tongues is directed specifically to a certain person in his known language, but unknown to the one giving a message. However, in these cases, the message in tongues is given *for a sign.*

Consider what happened on the Day of Pentecost when the Holy Ghost was poured out on the 120 in that upper room. I'm sure some of theose people weren't speaking in languages that could be understood by man. Nevertheless, various people who were present in that crowd *did* hear their own language spoken.

But notice that even when all those people gathered to see what was going on, not one got saved until Peter got up and preached! Not a single person got saved as a result of hearing folks speak with tongues!

The gifts of the Spirit, including the gift of tongues, don't save people. That isn't their purpose. No, the purpose of these supernatural gifts is to be a sign to get people's attention! Once God has someone's attention, that person is more open to the Gospel!

We've just looked at five common misconceptions about speaking in tongues. Now let's look at excesses that go *beyond* the limits of God's Word.

CHAPTER 15

COMMON EXCESSES REGARDING SPEAKING IN TONGUES

Spirit-filled believers often do not realize the true scope or value of speaking with other tongues. Throughout the years, many misuses and abuses of tongues have caused problems in the Body of Christ, as well as with those outside the Church. But doctrinal error about speaking in tongues doesn't do away with the reality. We just have to stay with what the Scriptures say.

Excess #1: Fighting the Devil in Tongues

For instance, you don't find anywhere in the Scriptures where anyone ever dealt with the devil in other tongues. Some people call this "tormenting" the devil in tongues. There is no scripture for that. Now, that doesn't rule out the possibility that when you're praying in the Spirit, you may deal with the devil. However, you should live by the principles presented in the Word of God and not form a doctrine out of a personal experience.

Since there is no scripture to stand on for fighting the devil in tongues, you need to be careful about building a doctrine on that practice or trying to encourage other people to do so as well. The Holy Ghost may give them an unction in prayer to deal with the devil, and then again He may not.

I don't like to do anything I don't have scriptural evidence for, especially if there's no scriptural example. When we get away from the Word, we put ourselves in a position where Satan can mislead us.

Remember what Paul says in First Corinthians 14:2: *"For he that speaketh in an unknown tongue speaketh not unto men. . . ."* Then to whom is the person talking? It goes on to say, *". . . unto God. . . ."* Of course, the believer may be talking to God about Satan's activities. That could very well be part of the mysteries he is speaking to God. But here is my point: Paul says here that God has given to the Church speaking in tongues as a divine supernatural means of communication with *Himself.* The Bible doesn't mention dealing with the devil in tongues.

We've already established that tongues are primarily a devotional gift—not a weapon to fight the devil with. Yet some folks are heavily into what they call "spiritual warfare" in tongues or "warring" tongues. They "fight the devil" at the top of their voices in other tongues, sometimes for several hours!

But you don't exert more power over the devil by shouting in tongues at an ear-deafening pitch. *Authority is not attached to the volume of one's voice.* The devil is not afraid of noise. You can see that just by listening to some worldly music!

I often use the illustration of a policeman who stands in the middle of the street and directs traffic. He doesn't even have to lift his voice. He just lifts up his hand, and cars stop because his uniform and badge show that he is authorized or has authority.

All you have to do is tell the devil, "That's as far as you go! Stop right there in the Name of Jesus." You don't even have to be loud about it. The devil recognizes authority.

The whole idea behind so-called "warring tongues" is that the heavens above us are filled with demon spirits and that some way or another we have to plow through them in tongues. But these people are using an unscriptural method in an effort to do a spiritual job.

I certainly believe in spiritual warfare, but only as it is in line with the Word. I once asked a leader of a so-called "warring tongues" prayer group, "Do you have any scripture for what you're doing?"

He had only one scripture he could offer me. He said, "Well, First Corinthians 12:10 does say there are divers kinds of tongues."

From that one scripture, this man and other Christians like him assume that there is a "warring" tongue to speak to the devil. But that scripture no more says divers tongues is addressing the devil than it says you're an astronaut and landed on Mars the day before yesterday! Besides, the Bible says, "... *In the mouth of two or three witnesses every word may be established*" (Matt. 18:16). This one verse (1 Cor. 12:10) was the only scripture the man had to justify his position.

Some people have a spiritual experience and then assume that everyone ought to have an experience just like theirs and base it as scriptural doctrine. As a result, much that goes on among Christians is in the flesh. It's fleshly to try to imitate other people's spiritual manifestations or to establish doctrine on a spiritual manifestation. And did you ever notice that those who do imitate others' manifestations wear themselves out quickly?

There is a tendency for people to get in a ditch by fighting the devil in tongues. Yet on the other hand, if folks aren't careful, they can get in a ditch on the other side and stop praying in tongues altogether or stop ministering the way God wants them to. I'll tell you what—let's just stay in the middle of the road and be blessed!

Excess #2: Praying Loudly in Tongues Brings More Power

Other folks get the idea that they're going to be heard by God because they get loud when they pray in tongues. But the most outstanding, spectacular experiences I ever had in the Lord came as I was praying in tongues quietly, speaking to myself and to God.

I've heard people tell others who were new at praying in tongues, "Holler louder so God will hear you." Well, if it were true that God can only hear loud prayers, a person should just get a microphone and turn it up as loud as he could every time he prayed! You see, that's all in the flesh. *God hears faith, not noise!* And besides, He isn't hard of hearing!

Now, don't misunderstand me—that doesn't mean you will never get loud as you pray. But if you do sense a leading to pray that way, you need to keep in mind that God doesn't hear you *because* you are loud!

Here is something else to consider: When Jesus was teaching on prayer, He said in effect, "Don't be as the hypocrites who like to pray out loud and in public so they can be heard. When you pray, go into your closet and pray in secret to the Father" (see Matt. 6:6). But Jesus wasn't saying that we are always supposed to pray in a closet. He was saying that we are not to pray *to be heard of men*. Certainly this principle also applies to praying in other tongues. We are to speak to ourselves and to God in church and in other public settings.

Excess #3: 'Travailing Prayer' in the Flesh

Several years ago, it was all the rage to attend what some people called "groaning meetings." It was nothing in the world but people getting together and trying to conjure up groanings in the flesh—there was no anointing to it.

If God wants to give birth to a move of His Spirit through people's prayers, they are going to know it. The Holy Spirit will take hold together with them as they pray in tongues, and they may very well go into groanings in prayer. But it's a bunch of nonsense for someone to announce, "Tonight we're going to give birth to the next move of God, so let's all start groaning!"

It's true that the Holy Ghost helps believers pray with groanings that cannot be uttered in articulate language. But that does *not* mean they can announce whenever they want to, "We're going to have a groaning meeting. Now on cue—everyone groan!" No, that isn't the way it works. *The Holy Ghost has to take hold with believers as they pray in the Spirit*; otherwise, their groanings are nothing more than a fleshly display.

Let's look at what the prophet Isaiah had to say about this subject of travail.

ISAIAH 66:8

8 Who hath heard such a thing? who hath seen such things? Shall the earth be made to bring forth in one day? or shall a nation be born at once? FOR AS SOON AS ZION TRAVAILED, SHE BROUGHT FORTH HER CHILDREN.

You will find that Old Testament prophecies often have multiple applications. First, there is the natural one. Second, there is the spiritual applications. In this case, verse 8 does talk about Israel as a nation being "born at once," so to speak, in these last days. I believe that happened in 1948 when Israel became a sovereign nation.

But when the Bible talks about Zion, it is not necessarily always talking about Israel. For example, in the following passage, what is God talking about when He refers to "Mount Sion"?

HEBREWS 12:22–23

22 But ye are come unto MOUNT SION, and unto the city of the living God, the heavenly Jerusalem, and to an innumerable company of angels,

23 TO THE GENERAL ASSEMBLY AND CHURCH OF THE FIRSTBORN, which are written in heaven, and to God the Judge of all, and to the spirits of just men made perfect.

Notice that phrase "to the general assembly and church of the firstborn." That refers to *us*—the Church! Under the New Covenant, *we* are Zion!

That puts a whole new perspective on Isaiah 66:8, where it says, "*. . . For as soon as Zion travailed, she brought forth her children.*" When the Church travails, she'll bring forth her spiritual children!

What else does the New Testament say about travail? Paul made a statement that will help clarify travail in the Spirit even more.

GALATIANS 4:19

19 My little children, OF WHOM I TRAVAIL in birth again until Christ be formed in you.

There is that word "travail" again. Paul was implying that he travailed in prayer for these believers when he first led them to the Lord but that they hadn't really grown up in Christ the way they should have. As a result, Paul said he continued to travail in prayer for them so they would develop fully in their spiritual walk.

The travail Paul talked about here is like the travail of a woman who is bringing forth a child in birth. In the natural, bringing forth a baby involves at least some discomfort for the mother. Something similar happens in the Spirit when the Holy Spirit takes hold with a person and gives him the unction to travail and intercede for the lost.

An intercessor is one who takes the place of another. So when believers stand in the gap and begin to travail in prayer for someone who is lost, sometimes they can feel lost as well.

I remember this happening to me more than once, but I'll share the most outstanding experience I've had along this line. In January 1939, I was holding a revival meeting in a Full Gospel church in the blacklands of northcentral Texas. We only had an evening service, but about ten o'clock every morning in the parsonage living room, the pastor and his wife would pray with me and my wife concerning the upcoming services.

On this particular morning, I was kneeling by the sofa and praying when suddenly a strong burden of intercession came over me. At this time, I had only been baptized in the Holy Ghost for 18 months, so the things of the Spirit were new to me. Not knowing what to do with this burden, I just yielded to the Holy Spirit's direct unction to groan and to pray in tongues. On the inside of me, in my inner man, I had the sensation of being lost and a sinner. I knew what that felt like because *I* had been lost only a few years before that!

I found myself crying out, "Lost! Lost! Lost! I'm lost! I'm lost!" Of course, I knew *I* wasn't lost, but I was taking the place of people who were lost. I felt just like they felt, and I was travailing in prayer for them. "I'm lost! Lost!" I cried out as I continued to pray in tongues. I don't know how long I prayed that way because I was taken up in the Spirit, and time has no meaning in that realm of prayer. I just know that this time of prayer lasted for quite some time.

Then that evening in the church service, I had only been preaching for 15 minutes when right in the middle of my sermon, the power of God fell. Every single sinner in the house got saved, and every backslider recommitted his life that night. Not a single one of them was left out!

That's what I had been praying about earlier that day. I had been interceding for those unsaved people.

Here is something we need to understand: Churches set up all sorts of programs to win the lost, but many times folks are not born again because there was no travail beforehand. Of course, people can get born again just by hearing and believing the Gospel. Yet too often people undergo a mental "conversion" that says, "Yes, I believe Jesus is the Son of God. Yes, I accept Jesus." But they're just saying it mentally, so a real commitment to Christ doesn't occur down in their spirits.

Over the years, I have found that this problem of "mental conversions" is greatly reduced by this higher level of intercession referred to in Isaiah 66:8: *"As soon as Zion travailed, she brought forth her children."* When the Holy Ghost takes hold with you to intercede in the Spirit for lost souls, mighty power is made available to you to bring forth fruit that lasts for God's Kingdom.

Remember—the closer we pattern our prayer life to the Word of God, the greater results we will experience in every area of life!

There won't be any children born into a home without some travail. In the same way, there won't be any children born into the family of God without some spiritual travail. *But you can't conjure up travail without the help of the Holy Spirit* any more than you can give birth to a child if you're not pregnant! In either case, you can groan and travail all you want to, but nothing will ever be birthed.

Scriptural Prayer Under the Anointing

Of course, you *can* pray and sing in tongues whenever you want to, fellowshipping with God as you communicate divine mysteries with Him (1 Cor. 14: 2). But you should come to the place where you can distinguish the difference between praying in tongues for your own personal edification and interceding for others in the Spirit as the Holy Ghost takes hold together with you in prayer.

Notice what the Apostle John says about the Holy Ghost Who lives in you.

> **1 JOHN 2:20,27**
>
> **20** But ye have an UNCTION from the Holy One, and ye know all things. . . .
>
> **27** But the ANOINTING which ye have received of him abideth in you. . . .

Here John says that you have an "unction" or an "anointing" from the Holy Ghost. He says that unction or anointing is *in* you.

When you get baptized and filled with the Holy Ghost, you begin to speak with tongues out of your own spirit. And just as a baby in the natural eventually learns to speak its mother language, you become more fluent in your supernatural language the more you practice speaking in tongues.

Many times I wake up in the night and begin to praise God and speak with tongues just because I want to. In those times, I'm not necessarily anointed; I'm just speaking to God out of my spirit.

But then there are other times when I speak with tongues under the direct anointing and leading of the Holy Spirit. When I enter that realm of prayer, tongues just flow out of me and I don't have anything to do with it. They just bubble out of my spirit by the unction or the anointing of the Holy Ghost within, and all I do is speak out the words.

Speaking by the unction of the Spirit with groanings is an experience in prayer many Spirit-filled believers are lacking. Too often believers get filled with the Spirit and speak in tongues but never develop further in the supernatural realm of the Spirit. So how can believers move up higher in God? They need to pray long enough in other tongues to get over in that realm of prayer where the anointing starts flowing by the unction of the Holy Ghost!

Let's talk about how praying in tongues under the anointing applies to intercession. Certainly you can begin by making the decision to pray in tongues about someone you know who needs prayer. Of course, you still don't know what to pray for that person as you ought because you don't know all the details regarding his situation.

Many times I just say to the Holy Ghost Who lives in me: "I don't know what to pray for as I ought in this situation, Holy Spirit. I'm going to begin to pray in tongues and trust You to give me the utterance to intercede for this." You see, you don't pray *to* the Holy Spirit. You don't make petition or supplication to Him. You pray *to* the Father *in* the Name of Jesus. But you can talk to the Holy Spirit because He is a divine Personality, and He is living in you. Then I begin to pray in other tongues, and sometimes it's almost a labor to pray. In a sense, I have to "push out" the utterance, making myself pray in tongues just as I would make a deliberate effort to talk to someone in my own language.

But then after a while, I "strike fire," so to speak, and begin to pray with the anointing. That's when tongues begin to roll out of me without effort. That's also when the victory comes!

Then again, sometimes a spirit of prayer will just fall upon you, and you'll sense a strong burden to pray in the Holy Ghost for someone or something. When that happens, the unction is present and so strong you feel impelled to pray! Of course, if you are around other people who don't understand the things of the Spirit, you should excuse yourself and find a place where you can be alone to pray out that burden. We'll talk more about that later.

Through the years, there have been times when I've sensed that strong burden to pray. The moment I knelt down, I was in the Spirit. It was as if I knelt down in a white cloud that immediately enveloped me. I had my eyes wide open, but I couldn't see any of my surroundings. Tongues began to flow out of me as I prayed with a *strong* Holy Ghost unction. During those times of prayer, it seemed like I didn't have a thing in the world to do with it—yet of course I did to begin with. The Holy

Ghost didn't just take me over. It was a matter of my yielding to Him to pray out His perfect will with that stronger anointing.

You see, the Holy Spirit isn't going to come upon you and flow through you without your permission. But as you yield to Him, you *give* Him permission to give you that stronger unction to pray. That's when you enter into that deeper realm of prayer where tongues just begin to roll out of you with power.

When that stronger anointing comes upon me, I pray in tongues as hard and fast as I can. I keep praying that way until the burden lifts and I sense a note of victory. As a result of yielding to the Holy Spirit to pray this way, I've seen many people born again and supernaturally healed, and I've witnessed countless needs miraculously met throughout the years.

Actually, when you get out into the realm of the Spirit like this, it may even seem like your spirit is somewhere else ministering to someone, or you see certain situations God wants you to see. It isn't a matter of God physically translating your body to another physical location, although physical translation by the power of the Spirit is also a scriptural experience. After all, Philip was caught away by the Spirit and bodily found himself in another place (Acts 8:39–40). But that isn't what I'm talking about here.

You see, there is time and distance in this natural realm. But as you pray in tongues and you get over into the realm of the Spirit, there is no such thing as time or distance. That means the possibilities of what God can do through you in prayer are unlimited!

Excess #4: Doing What Does Not Edify in the Presence of the Unlearned

We briefly looked at First Corinthians 14:16–17 earlier, but I want to revisit these verses. We need to talk about a common mistake some believers make to the spiritual detriment of people around them.

1 CORINTHIANS 14:16-17

16 Else when thou shalt bless with the spirit, how shall he that occupieth the room of the unlearned say Amen at thy giving of thanks, seeing he understandeth not what thou sayest?

17 For thou verily givest thanks well, but the other is not edified.

As we discussed before, when Paul talked about "he that occupieth the room of the unlearned," he was referring to those who are unlearned in spiritual things. Unfortunately, this description applies to many believers in the Body of Christ. In some cases, much damage is done to the cause of Christ because people go into excess and error in this area of praying in tongues in front of the spiritually untrained. In other words, some believers don't take into account the fact that they're in the presence of the unlearned when they speak with other tongues. The situation is made even worse when a believer speaks in tongues before the unlearned in an especially distracting manner.

First Corinthians 14:15 tells us that we are to pray both with the spirit and with our understanding or minds. We are to pray both ways, but on the other hand, we need to know when to pray in tongues or when to pray with our minds. Verses 16–17 give us a vital factor we must consider: When we're in the presence of others, we want to do what *edifies them*!

I have always endeavored to obey that divine instruction. For instance, I remember years ago when I held an eight-week revival in Oklahoma and several of us were invited over to a local dentist's home for a meal. Everyone who came to dinner that night was Spirit-filled. In other words, I was *not* in the presence of the unlearned in spiritual things. So when they asked me to pray, I started in English—but before I knew it, I was praying in other tongues, and everyone else joined me!

We had a wonderful spiritual time praying together that night. However, if someone unlearned had been present, I would *not* have done that. I would have only spoken in English.

As the Bible says, ". . . *Let all things be done unto edifying*" (1 Cor. 14:26). You see, we speak in tongues by the inspiration of the Spirit, but we can choose to pray or not to pray. But if someone is present who won't be edified, it would be selfish on our part to speak with tongues because it would create confusion.

Another time I held a revival meeting in Arizona, and I stayed in the home of an older couple named Brother and Sister Fisher. One night after the evening service, the couple's three adult daughters and sons-in-law came over to eat a meal with us. The women were preparing the food, and we men were in the living room talking, when suddenly a burden—an exceptionally strong urge to pray—came over me.

Everyone present was Full Gospel, so they understood when I said to our host, "Brother Fisher, I have to pray, and I have to pray now!" Brother Fisher called the ladies into the living room and said, "Brother Hagin has to pray right now." So we all got on our knees and started praying in tongues.

Now, understand this: If there had been people present who were unlearned, I would not have prayed in tongues like that in front of them. I would have found a private place to pray out the burden by myself. We need to understand some of these things so we can keep from being a stumbling block to folks.

The moment my knees hit the floor, I was in the Spirit, praying up a storm in other tongues. I prayed as hard and fast as I could pray in other tongues for about an hour. It seemed as if I didn't have anything to do with it. What I mean by that is tongues just flowed out of me like a river. I knew from the way I was praying that I was travailing in the Spirit for someone who was lost.

At the end of our prayer, the burden lifted, and I experienced a spirit of lightness. I began to laugh and sing in tongues. Then I had a vision. This was on Friday night, and in the vision, I saw our upcoming Sunday night service. I saw myself in the pulpit and heard myself preaching. I finished my sermon and gave an invitation. Then I saw myself lean over the pulpit and point to an elderly man in the second pew.

In the vision, I told the man, "The Lord shows me that you're past 70 years of age and that you were raised by parents who did not believe there is a hell. But the Lord told me to tell you that you have one foot in hell and the other one is slipping in." Then I saw him come and kneel at the altar.

The moment I came into the church on Sunday night, I looked around, and sure enough, there sat the elderly man in the second pew, just as I'd seen in my vision.

So I preached my sermon (which was a brand-new message I'd never even thought of until I heard myself preach it in the vision!). Afterward, I spoke those words I'd heard myself say to the man in the vision. He came to the altar; then others came. After the service, the elderly man was talking to the pastor when I walked by. He stopped me and shook hands with me. Then he said to the pastor, "This preacher said I was raised to believe there is no hell. My parents were universalists, and they taught me there is no hell. This is the first time I've ever been inside a church building in my life."

The man went on to explain that he was a motel owner. Some of the motel guests who'd stayed for the revival finally convinced him to come with them on the last night of the meetings. The man thought, *I guess I'll go with these people this one time just to get them off my back.*

No one in the congregation that night knew to pray for this man. No one even knew he was unsaved. I certainly didn't know to pray for him—but the Holy Ghost did!

Then the man said to the pastor, "This man said I have one foot in hell and the other one is slipping in. I knew exactly what he meant. I've had a severe heart attack. In fact, the doctor said I could die at any minute." Then with tears of joy running down his cheeks, the man said, "Oh, I'm so glad I came tonight. I'm so glad I came."

There are two things to see in this account. First, the Holy Ghost knows who we should pray for. In this case, the Lord knew travail in prayer was necessary to bring this man to a place of repentance so he could be saved.

Second, *I would not have prayed in tongues that way if there had been unlearned people present.* For one thing, it would have done damage by causing confusion. Perhaps it could have driven them away from seeking the infilling of the Spirit, the very thing they needed to grow spiritually in their walk with God.

Let me give you an example of a woman who did *not* heed this scripture regarding the unlearned: *"... when thou shalt bless with the spirit, how shall he that occupieth the room of the unlearned say Amen at thy giving of thanks, seeing he understandeth not what thou sayest?"* (1 Cor. 14:16). As a result, this woman fell into excess that did damage to people because they didn't understand what was going on.

A Spirit-filled minister and his wife were invited by another Spirit-filled minister to take part in his relative's wedding ceremony. All three of them had a role in the ceremony. Most of the people present at the wedding were denominational people.

First, the minister who was a relative of the groom read his part of the ceremony, followed by the guest minister. Then the guest minister's wife, also a minister, was supposed to read *her* part. But instead, right in the middle of the wedding ceremony in front of all those saved and unsaved people, the woman suddenly fell to the floor, moaning and groaning and acting like she was giving birth to a baby. She was supposedly travailing in prayer for someone.

Now, as you remember, I travailed in the Spirit at the Fishers' house for that elderly man. But there's a huge difference between these two incidents. In my case, I was in a private home in the presence of Spirit-filled people who knew exactly what that kind of travailing prayer was all about. Also, I was in the Spirit. But this woman travailed with groanings in a public setting—and in the middle of someone's wedding no less! Besides that, she prayed like that in the presence of about 200 people who were "unlearned" in spiritual things. Plus, she was in the flesh!

The minister who had invited this couple to participate in the ceremony later told me, "I was so embarrassed. I didn't know what to do, so I just stood there."

Well, *I* would have known exactly what to do. I would have gotten this woman's attention and demanded, "Stand up and act like you have some maturity. What you're doing isn't scriptural! It's foolish! It isn't God—you're in the flesh!"

People started getting up and leaving the wedding by the droves, and you can understand why. They were scared because they were "unlearned" in spiritual things. And as the people left the wedding, they said, "I *knew* those ignoramuses who talk in tongues were crazy!"

Much damage has been done to the Body of Christ by people acting foolishly like that woman did. So many have been robbed of the blessings God wants them to have!

When someone acts foolishly in the presence of people uneducated in spiritual things like this woman did, someone in spiritual leadership may have to take a stand and speak out for what's right. The woman's actions weren't right because what she did didn't edify the congregation. Again, the Bible clearly says, *let all things be done unto edifying"* (1 Cor. 14:26). That means *edifying to everyone present,* not just to the person praying in tongues! Furthermore, the Bible also says, *"Let all things be done decently and in order"* (1 Cor. 14:40).

If you do get a burden to pray in tongues when you're with people who wouldn't understand, get up and excuse yourself! Go pray by yourself where you won't disrupt others. While the Holy Spirit might give someone an utterance or prompting to pray, that does not remove our scriptural responsibility to seek to edify others in an orderly and decent manner (1 Cor. 14:23).

At prayer meetings where everyone is praying out loud in the Spirit, it's all right to pray in tongues with everyone else. But no matter what the public setting, make sure you don't distract others. Don't pray in any way that would draw attention to yourself.

I once heard an account about a woman who seriously violated this principle. A fellow minister was preaching in a meeting, and right in the middle of his sermon, she got up and began prophesying. She declared, "The Lord told me to pray for you." She laid hands on the minister and started praying in other tongues. Then she pushed him down and lay on top of him, still praying in tongues!

Well, I guarantee you—that was *not* done decently and in order! People got up and left by droves. Of course, they were offended! Those who were unlearned in spiritual things didn't understand what was going on. Full Gospel people didn't even understand it. And the next night the crowd was greatly diminished.

If this woman's burden was really from the Lord, what should she have done? Interrupting the sermon wasn't doing things "decently and in order." She certainly drew attention to herself when she got up on the platform and prayed for the minister the way she did. She should have left the public meeting and found a place to pray in tongues by herself until the burden lifted.

But this woman wanted to be seen! She acted in the flesh and caused damage to the cause of Christ and everyone in attendance.

Misuse of tongues is really unedifying. But if people would always endeavor to walk in love, it would solve the problem! Love always puts others first (1 Cor. 13:4–8).

Therefore, to stay out of a ditch in this area of tongues, ask yourself this question in each situation: *I may edify myself, but is what I'm about to do going to edify the people around me?*

We've discussed just a few of the common "ditches" that believers can fall into regarding speaking in tongues. I've endeavored to show you the scriptural perspective on each of these excesses. Because the believers in these examples went beyond the scriptural scope of tongues, they got into error.

Now let's talk about the *scriptural* scope of speaking with tongues. For the most part, Full Gospel believers have only scratched the surface of what is possible to experience in this realm of prayer. But God is calling His people to *move up higher!* These are the last days, and there's so much to pray about according to His perfect will!

CHAPTER 16

THE SCRIPTURAL SCOPE OF PRAYING IN TONGUES

One reason many Christians don't grow further in spiritual things is that they are afraid to progress in spiritual gifts for fear of getting into error and excess. As a result, they don't attain what the Bible teaches about spiritual gifts. The Bible says, "*. . .desire spiritual gifts*" (1 Cor. 14:1). Believers can miss out on tremendous blessings because they interpret the Bible in light of what they *don't* see operating in their own churches, not what the Bible actually says.

Christians can also limit their spiritual growth by not doing their part to grow spiritually. For example, when the Holy Spirit prompts them to spend time praying in tongues, they often override that leading and go on about their daily lives. Therefore, they never learn to develop in the scriptural scope of speaking in other tongues as God intends.

What *is* your part in developing and growing spiritually? The truth is, the Bible plainly tells you to do some things that will absolutely impact your life in God. If you'll just obey God and do your part, you'll discover the depth, breadth, height, and scope of the supernatural power praying in tongues affords! Divine communication with God builds you up greatly in His Spirit!

Speaking to Yourselves in Psalms and Spiritual Songs

We've looked at length at First Corinthians 14:15, where Paul tells us that we can pray in tongues and we can pray with our minds.

1 CORINTHIANS 14:15

15 What is it then? I will pray with the spirit, and I will pray with the understanding also: I will sing with the spirit, and I will sing with the understanding also.

Paul also mentions another scriptural way to communicate with God in this verse. He talks about the importance of *singing* with the spirit.

You might say, "Well, I never get to the place where I can sing in tongues." Yet Paul said to sing both ways—with your spirit *and* with your understanding.

Colossians 3:16 gives us an added dimension about the value of singing in tongues:

COLOSSIANS 3:16

16 Let the word of Christ dwell in you richly in all

wisdom; teaching and admonishing one another
in psalms and hymns and spiritual songs, singing
with grace in your hearts TO THE LORD.

To whom do you sing? To the Lord. The problem with many churches is that much of the time people are not singing to the Lord, but to one another in the local congregation.

The following passage of Scripture tells us why we are to sing to the Lord.

EPHESIANS 5:18–19

18 And be not drunk with wine, wherein is
excess; but BE FILLED WITH THE SPIRIT;

19 SPEAKING to yourselves in psalms and
hymns and spiritual songs, SINGING and
making melody in your heart TO THE LORD.

Two key words immediately follow the phrase, "be filled with the Spirit"—*speaking* and *singing*. We get filled to overflowing with the Spirit by speaking and singing—to ourselves and to God. Then once we're filled with the Holy Ghost, we *stay* filled by continuing to speak or sing out of our spirits to the Lord!

An aspect of divine communication is to sing and make melody in our hearts by the Spirit to the Lord. We see the spiritual value of this practice in Acts 16.

ACTS 16:25

25 And at midnight Paul and Silas PRAYED, AND
SANG PRAISES unto God: and the prisoners
heard them.

Paul and Silas were in jail. Their backs were bleeding. Their feet were in stocks. But notice what they did at the midnight hour when all looked dark around them. Did they pray and sing praises to the prisoners? No, they prayed and sang praises unto *God* and brought mighty Holy Ghost power on the scene!

ACTS 16:26

26 And suddenly there was a great earthquake, so that the foundations of the prison were shaken: and immediately all the doors were opened, and every one's bands were loosed.

Much of our singing in our churches is not really patterned after Colossians 3:16 and Ephesians 5:19. We really know so little about speaking to ourselves in psalms, hymns, and spiritual songs. Yet the scriptural scope of speaking in tongues must include singing and making melody to the Lord by the inspiration of the Holy Ghost. This is true New Testament worship and should be a common, everyday occurrence in our lives and in our churches.

Now, some believers are more given to speaking than to singing psalms by the inspiration of the Holy Ghost. However, the end result is the same.

In my own personal walk with God, I speak with psalms quite frequently. I drive down the road in my car, speaking in psalms. I lie on my bed in the nighttime, speaking in psalms. Sometimes in services, the Holy Ghost inspires me to speak in psalms. Speaking or singing psalms by the Spirit in the public assembly is a demonstration of "... *teaching and admonishing ONE ANOTHER in psalms and hymns and spiritual songs*..." (Col. 3:16).

Over the years, I've also noticed another spiritual pattern in my own life: Whenever the "heat" was turned on—when the enemy was attacking and I was under a great amount of pressure—I'd speak *more* in psalms as inspired by the Holy Ghost. Some nights I'd go to sleep speaking in psalms and wake up speaking in psalms. Some nights I'd sleep very little. I'd just speak all night long in psalms one after another!

Speaking or singing in psalms by the inspiration of the Holy Spirit just builds up your spirit like nothing else can do. It lifts you above the clouds of natural circumstances right into the higher realms of supernatural peace and joy in the Holy Ghost!

You need to maintain this practice as a way of life—speaking and singing to yourself and to God in psalms, hymns, and spiritual songs by the inspiration of the Holy Spirit. Sing and praise God both with your spirit and with your understanding.

You may say, "But I've never done that." Well, determine to develop yourself in this wonderful means of spiritual edification. Keep on praying in other tongues until you get over into the Spirit. Then start singing in tongues and in psalms as you're inspired by the Holy Ghost!

The Pentecostals used to sing a little chorus that went like this: "It's bubbling, it's bubbling, it's bubbling in my soul. . . ." That's exactly what inspired utterance does in your spirit. If you'll just keep praying in tongues, inspired utterance will keep bubbling up until psalms, hymns, and spiritual songs flow freely from your spirit!

So keep praying until you get to that place of Holy Ghost-inspired utterance. Learn to obey the Holy Ghost within you.

Tap into your spirit! Sing or speak out what's on the inside of you!

Anytime you want, you can make the decision to speak or sing with tongues. But as you press into God in tongues, inspiration will come from the Holy Spirit. He will take hold with you, and the inspired utterance will just start rolling out of you. You'll think, *I didn't know I had that in my spirit! It just flowed out of me, and before I knew it, I was speaking it out!*

Supernatural utterance in psalms, hymns, and spiritual songs ought to be an everyday occurrence in your private devotional life. In certain settings, it is also scriptural to speak or sing in psalms and spiritual hymns publicly. So if you haven't developed yet in this area of supernatural utterance, just keep on praying much in other tongues. You'll soon come to that supernatural place in prayer where Holy Ghost-inspired utterance is a source of continual edification!

Continual Renewals of Your Spirit

Another key to developing ourselves spiritually is found in Second Corinthians 4:16.

2 CORINTHIANS 4:16

16 For which cause we faint not; but though our outward man perish, yet THE INWARD MAN IS RENEWED DAY BY DAY.

If you're fainting spiritually—getting tired and worn out in your spirit—you're not renewing your inner man!

You see, everything you received at the moment you were

born again came by the Spirit of God. Of course, you were not fully developed at the moment of your conversion. But the same Holy Spirit at work in the New Birth is the One Who helps you develop and grow spiritually. How does that spiritual development take place? It happens as you get your inward man renewed daily!

We are to seek God for constant renewals of our spirit man. In the following passage we are shown how to do this.

> **ISAIAH 40:28-31**
>
> **28** Hast thou not known? hast thou not heard, that the everlasting God, the Lord, the Creator of the ends of the earth, fainteth not, neither is weary? there is no searching of his understanding.
>
> **29** He giveth POWER TO THE FAINT; AND TO THEM THAT HAVE NO MIGHT HE INCREASETH STRENGTH.
>
> **30** Even the youths shall faint and be weary, and the young men shall utterly fall:
>
> **31** But THEY THAT WAIT UPON THE LORD SHALL RENEW THEIR STRENGTH; they shall mount up with wings as eagles; they shall run, and not be weary; and they shall walk, and not faint.

Continual renewals of your spirit come by spending time before God in prayer. When you wait before God, praying in the Spirit, you'll not only be refreshed and renewed in your inner man, but that spiritual renewal will also affect your mind and your physical being.

However, notice that this kind of renewal comes about by

waiting before God. Actually, the word "wait" carries the idea of being *intertwined* with the Lord.

I believe in waiting meetings, whether it involves waiting before God in one's private devotions or waiting before Him collectively as a body of believers. But these kinds of meetings have become rare in the modern-day Church, even among Pentecostals and Charismatics.

Those of us in the "faith camp" have emphasized faith based on God's Word, and rightly so. However, many folks have wrongly come to the conclusion, *Well, I'm walking by faith and maintaining the right confessions, so that's all that is necessary.*

It is right to feed on God's Word and to maintain one's confession according to the Word. But as important as these are, they will not take the place of waiting before the Lord. We need all of them. The Bible says that *those who wait upon the Lord* shall renew their strength!

There was a great amount of blessing and truth in the old-time Pentecostal tarrying, or waiting, meetings. However, they missed it in one important area: they were waiting on the wrong thing! They thought they had to tarry to be filled with the Spirit according to Jesus' command to His disciples: *". . . tarry ye in the city of Jerusalem, until ye be endued with power from on high"* (Luke 24:49). But as we've seen, since the initial outpouring on the Day of Pentecost, believers don't have to tarry for the baptism in the Holy Spirit. They can receive by faith!

The problem with many old-time Pentecostal folks was that once they received the Holy Ghost for whom they had been tarrying, they quit tarrying! But the truth is, believers ought to first be endued with power from on High; *then* they can start tarrying or waiting before God in prayer, exercising their supernatural means of communication with Him!

Much blessing came out of those tarrying meetings—and to tell you the truth about it, we need to get back to those kinds of waiting meetings. We need to spend time waiting before the Lord—not so we can be baptized in the Holy Ghost, but so we can renew our strength in our inner man *after* we have been filled with the Spirit (Isa. 40:31)!

This idea of continual spiritual renewals can also be found in Paul's prayer for the Ephesian church:

> **EPHESIANS 3:16**
>
> **16** That he [God] would grant you, according to the riches of his glory, TO BE STRENGTHENED WITH MIGHT BY HIS SPIRIT IN THE INNER MAN.

Through times of waiting before the Lord praying in tongues, our inward man is renewed and strengthened by the power of the Holy Ghost. Oh, yes, we need waiting meetings in our day!

Times of Refreshing

Waiting before God in prayer will not only renew your strength, but it will also bring a great refreshing to your spirit. In fact, the words "renew" and "refreshing" are similar in meaning. Peter uses the word "refreshing" to describe what occurs in the Presence of the Lord.

> **ACTS 3:19**
>
> **19** Repent ye therefore, and be converted, that

your sins may be blotted out, when the TIMES
OF REFRESHING SHALL COME FROM THE
PRESENCE OF THE LORD.

Notice that expression "times of refreshing." We don't get
just *one* time of refreshing in our walk with God. We can have
continual *times* of refreshing as we set aside time to spend in
God's Presence, praying and worshiping Him in the Spirit.
We must need these times of refreshing and renewal, or God
wouldn't have provided them for us!

Years ago I was praying in tongues on the platform of the
RHEMA auditorium during one of our Monday night prayer
meetings. At that time, the students and staff were meeting twice
a week at these evening prayer meetings for the very purpose of
experiencing times of refreshing that come from the Presence
of the Lord.

As I knelt by a chair and prayed in other tongues, the Lord
began to speak to my spirit. (As people pray together in unity,
they create the kind of atmosphere where the Holy Ghost likes
to speak.) The Holy Ghost said to me, "I want you to close down
the RHEMA Counseling Center. I never told you to get into
counseling anyway. You just sort of 'fell into' it. All I told you to
establish was a Prayer and Healing School."

Then the Lord said to me, "Most Christians don't need
counseling anyway. What they need to do is *pray through*."

I remember what one Pentecostal pastor once said to me.
This man was the pastor of one of the largest churches in his
denomination and had been in the Pentecostal Movement all
his life. He said, "On Monday, our church schedules counseling
sessions to try to help people. We *were* hoping these sessions
would take the place of the altar services we used to have—but

they won't. If those folks would only come to the altar and wait on God, they wouldn't need any counseling!"

The pastor was right. After all, the Word of God tells us that the Holy Ghost is our Counselor—and He dwells within us! We just need the time to wait before Him, praying and worshiping Him in tongues and with our understanding. As we do, He will answer the cry of our hearts and grant us continual renewals—spirit, soul, and body!

Too many Christians are running around looking for someone to counsel them and tell them what to do. But for most people, all they really need to do is get on their knees and pray through! If they will take time to wait before God, their inner man will be renewed, and they will receive the wisdom from On High they need.

I've often thought that if I ever pastored another church, I would have regular prayer "waiting" meetings. Then I'd tell all the people who wanted counseling, "You all come on Thursday night, and we'll wait before God in prayer from eight o'clock until midnight!" Of course, not many of them would show up because most people are looking for something easy!

Unfortunately, some who seek counsel are actually looking for someone to condone their sin and tell them that they are right when they are wrong. For instance, one fellow came to our Counseling Center—saved, baptized in the Holy Ghost, and a husband and father of three children—claiming that the Lord had told him to leave his wife and start living with another young woman! The man said the Holy Ghost was leading him to do it but that he wanted someone to counsel him about the situation.

That man didn't need to be counseled—he needed to get right with God! He needed to heed Peter's words in Acts 3:19 and *repent!*

The Lord also said this to me during that time of waiting on Him and praying in the Holy Ghost: "If folks need counseling, they need to go to their own sheepfold and their own pastor for help. You just tend to your own sheepfold" (which to me, meant taking care of the students at our training center).

How were we going to help the rest of the people who wanted someone to counsel them? By teaching them to pray and to wait before God in His Presence! We couldn't have taught them that with a little counseling session. If our counselors had said to these people, "Let's get down on our knees and pray in the Spirit for an hour," most would have answered, "Oh, no! I want to get some answers from *you.*" The trouble is, many believers want a counselor to do the work of hearing from God for them instead of taking time to pray to hear for themselves.

But for the most part, counseling isn't the way God wants believers to receive the answers they need. They will find their answers as they wait before Him and enjoy times of refreshing in His Presence!

I almost get aggravated with Christians who are always looking for someone to counsel with them. After all, the whole time they're looking for someone, they're carrying the true Counselor around on the inside of them! The Holy Spirit is not just a spiritual hitchhiker. He's their divine Teacher and Guide! If they'd just get down on their knees and pray through in other tongues, they'd receive wisdom from the Counselor within, which would provide the direction for solving their problems. Now, I don't say this in an egotistical way, but I never went to anyone for counseling in my entire life. I always got down on my knees and prayed in tongues to my Heavenly Father. And as I looked to the Counselor on the inside of me, He always gave me direction.

You see, *there are simply no shortcuts to waiting before God in prayer.*

I think many believers are waiting for God to have a "99-cent sale" on answered prayer. These people want their answers, but they want them cheaply and fast.

No, getting your answer may require waiting all night before God. It may mean missing a few meals. It may even mean turning off that "one-eyed monster" in your living room for a while!

Get alone with God, and pray in the Spirit for your personal edification. Get some things straightened out on the inside of you. Find out what your priorities are and what God wants you to do.

Thank God for the help of the Holy Ghost! He is our Helper and our Intercessor in time of need!

Learning the Voice of Your Guide Within

Another benefit of waiting on the Lord is that you will begin to discern the Voice of the Spirit more and more. As you wait in the Presence of God, praying in other tongues, He will speak to your spirit and let you know how to stay in His perfect will in every area.

The Holy Ghost, the Spirit of truth, is a Guide, and He is in you. Your Heavenly Guide will speak a sure word for you to follow.

ISAIAH 30:21

21 And THINE EARS SHALL HEAR A WORD behind thee, saying, This is the way, walk ye in it, when ye turn to the right hand, and when ye turn to the left.

People often say to me, "I need you to tell me how I can know the Voice of the Holy Spirit."

This is my answer: "I can't do that. You'll have to learn the Voice of the Holy Spirit for yourself—which you *can* do because He dwells in you. But if you're not going to take the time to wait in the Lord's Presence to learn to listen to Him, all I or anyone else could teach you would be in vain."

"But how can I tell if it's really the Holy Spirit talking to me?"

The fact that a person asks me that question lets me know he hasn't become acquainted with the One Who lives in him. He doesn't know His Voice. That person just needs to spend time waiting before God. If he will stay in God's Presence long enough, he won't have to ask anyone to tell him how to discern the Holy Spirit's Voice!

But if a person refuses to spend time in God's Presence on a daily basis, it wouldn't do me a bit of good to tell that person everything I know about the subject. He would still miss what the Holy Spirit is trying to tell him!

Praying Out the Plan of God for Your Life

As for me, I have the Guide within me, and I'm *not* going to miss what He's endeavoring to tell me because I listen to Him. He knows what's out in front of me, and He's faithful to show me things to come (John 16:13).

Sometimes our staff gets aggravated with me when they have deadlines to meet and they're waiting for an answer from me. But I don't move until I get the answer from God in my spirit. I live by Psalm 127:1: *"Except the Lord build the house, they labour in vain that build it. . . ."* We may build the house, but it is all in vain if the Lord isn't building it. That's why I don't move until I get the Holy Spirit's direction clear in my spirit.

You see, you can do a lot of good things—even *right* things—that are not what God wants you to do, and, as a result, you can get into trouble. Even if what you did is good and helps humanity, it may not be what God wanted *you* to do. You have to find out what His plan is for *you*. Then you have to follow what He tells you to do!

You might ask, "But *how* am I going to find out God's plan for me?" The Holy Spirit will lead you as you wait before God, praying in other tongues. As Jesus promised us, *". . . He* [the Holy Spirit] *will shew you things to come"* (John 16:13). Besides, God promised us that *". . . as many as are led by the Spirit of God, they are the sons of God"* (Rom. 8:14). That means *you* can be led!

You know, I have always been very studious, but almost everything I know about the things of God and His Word, I didn't get from studying books. Now, please don't misunderstand me. Although I didn't go to Bible school, I purchased books used by several different Bible schools and studied them diligently. In fact, on many occasions, I read those textbooks all night long.

But do you know the primary way I learned the Bible? *On my knees, praying in other tongues.* That's how the revelation of the Bible came to me. Sometimes as I prayed in tongues, the Spirit of God would take me through several chapters of the Bible and in the process change me and change my ministry! I'd get revelation from the Counselor within that would cause me to start moving in another direction.

In addition, with every new direction I've ever taken through the years in the ministry—radio ministry, publication ministry, RHEMA Bible Training Center, and so forth—I received divine guidance for that specific direction while I was praying in tongues.

That's the reason a lot of people never receive any revelation about God's plan for their lives. They simply don't spend enough time praying in tongues. They never get into the Spirit to obtain their answers from God. As a result, all their reasoning and planning is in the mental realm, and in the end their man-made plans fail.

That's why you need continual times of refreshing from the Presence of the Lord. Your part is to set aside time to wait before Him. Get into God's Presence and pray in the Holy Ghost, and you will receive all the answers you need. And as you wait on the

Lord, times of refreshing and divine guidance will come—both of which are absolutely necessary for correct spiritual growth.

So cultivate your spiritual life by feeding on God's Word. Spend time fellowshipping with the Father, praying much in other tongues. Learn to follow what your spirit is saying to you. Every day the Holy Spirit will use your spirit to enlighten you to God's will. Remember, God will direct you through your own spirit, for the Bible says, *"The spirit of man is the candle of the Lord . . ."* (Prov. 20:27).

Learn to walk in this new realm of Holy Ghost power. Everything starts by determining to get before the Lord every day, allowing Him to lead you, to teach you, and to continually renew your spiritual strength.

CHAPTER 17

HELP TO PRAY ABOUT
THE UNKNOWN

Why should believers pray with other tongues? Because it enables them to pray for the unknown concerning things their natural minds don't know about.

We touched on this benefit of speaking with tongues earlier in Chapter 12. But I want to go further in our discussion about praying for the unknown because it's so crucial to operating in the full scope of praying in the Spirit.

Praying in tongues provides a way to pray for things that you are not aware of and that you would never think to pray on your own. This is why praying in tongues is one of the most important ways for you to pray. You just don't know what to pray for as you ought (Rom. 8:26). Therefore, you need the Holy Spirit to help you pray out the perfect will of God concerning people and situations your natural mind knows nothing about.

The Unknown Becomes Known When You Receive the Interpretation

Let's look again at First Corinthians 14:15 for a moment.

1 CORINTHIANS 14:15

15 What is it then? I will pray with the spirit, and I will pray with the understanding also: I will sing with the spirit, and I will sing with the understanding also."

Personally, I think this verse has a twofold application. First, it literally means what it says: "I will pray both ways—with my understanding and also with my spirit." But I believe this verse has a further application as well. Of course, you don't need to know the meaning of everything you say when praying or singing in tongues. However, when it's necessary, the Holy Ghost will give you the interpretation of what you said in tongues. Then you will be able to pray by inspiration of the Holy Spirit with the spirit *and* with the understanding!

I've often received the interpretation as I prayed in tongues in the past, but it doesn't always happen. Many other times I've prayed at length in tongues without ever knowing one thing I prayed for. That's part of the rest and refreshing Isaiah 28:11–12 talks about. Sometimes it's refreshing and restful *not* to know— just to entrust the matter to God.

But sometimes when I pray in the Spirit, the Holy Ghost does give me the interpretation so I can know what I prayed about. One example particularly stands out in my mind. In 1956, my wife and I were holding a meeting in California. We'd driven out West pulling our large trailer and had brought with us our teenage son and daughter, Ken and Pat.

We were all sleeping soundly one night when I was suddenly awakened and sat straight up in bed. It was just like someone had nudged me in the ribs. I thought I heard a door slam. Then it sounded like someone came into the trailer. I got up and walked through the trailer. I checked the doors, but they were all closed and locked. No one could have come in. I listened at the bedroom door. Pat was breathing evenly, sound asleep. So was Ken, sleeping on the hideaway couch in the living room. I didn't want to disturb my wife, so I lay back down and prayed, "Lord, why was I awakened?"

I started putting up my spiritual antenna. (Do you know what I mean by that? I simply mean that, in my spirit, I began to reach out toward God.) Meanwhile, I kept asking the Lord, "What's wrong? What's wrong?" I felt a heaviness inside me; then revelation began to come. I asked, "What is this about, Lord?" As I got a little further into the realm of the Spirit, I realized it concerned some of my kinfolks.

I said, "It's one of my kinfolk. His life is in danger. He is near death. Lord, who is it?"

I couldn't get that part, so I said, "Holy Spirit, I don't know whose life is in danger, but You know. I could pray for each of my kinfolk, one by one, with my understanding, but I'm looking to You to give me utterance and to help me pray."

So I started praying in tongues the way Smith Wigglesworth once described it. He said, "I began in the flesh and wound up in the Spirit." In other words, I began to pray in tongues without any unction or anointing, and it wasn't very long before the tongues were just flowing out of me as I lay there in bed. Throughout all of this, I never disturbed my wife, who was sleeping next to me.

I must have prayed for an hour and a half in other tongues. I kept on praying until I'd prayed through.

How do you know when you've prayed through on a specific matter? The sense of heaviness lifts, and you have a note of victory in your spirit. You'll either laugh or sing in the Spirit. (If you never seem to get to the place where you have that note of victory in your spirit, perhaps you haven't prayed long enough in tongues!)

I began to sing very quietly to myself and to laugh in the Spirit. I thought, *Well, whatever it is or whoever it is, I got the answer! That person is all right.* Then I went to sleep.

What happened next doesn't happen with me very often, but it did that night. When I went to sleep, I had a spiritual dream.

Sometimes God will speak to you in a dream. But let me help you along that line. The minute I woke up from this dream, I knew exactly what it meant. If you have what you think is a spiritual dream, but you don't know what it meant, just forget it. God didn't speak to you through that dream. Don't try to come up with some meaning out of your head. This is a mistake many people make and, as a result, they go off on a tangent in their walk with God.

In my dream, I was in Shreveport, Louisiana. I was standing across the street, and I could see a hotel sign on the other side. I knew that my youngest brother, Pat, who had known God but was backslidden at the time, was staying at that hotel and had taken sick in the nighttime.

Then I saw my brother in his room. I saw him pick up the telephone and try to dial to get the hotel operator; then he passed out. As I stood there in my dream, I saw the flashing red light of the ambulance and watched the paramedics take my brother to the hospital. Then I was standing in the corridor of the hospital with my back up against the wall, looking across the hall at a closed door. I knew Pat was in the room behind that door.

As I stood there, a doctor came out. He pulled the door closed behind him and walked over to me. Without lifting his head or looking up at me, the doctor said, "He is gone."

I said, "No, doctor, he is not gone."

Then the doctor looked up and said, "Didn't you understand me? He's dead."

I said, "No, he isn't dead."

"What makes you say that?" the doctor asked.

"Jesus told me that he wasn't."

"Oh," he said. "You're one of them."

"Yes," I replied in the dream.

The doctor whirled around, opened the door, and said, "Come here. I'll just show you!"

So we walked into the room. There was a body lying there on a bed with a sheet pulled up over the head. The doctor jerked down the sheet and said to me, "Look!"

As we looked down at Pat, he opened his eyes and blinked a few times. The doctor looked at me; then he looked at my brother and said, "You must have known something I didn't know."

I said, "I told you I did."

Then I woke up, and I knew I'd been praying for my youngest brother. That was the month of May. In August, we returned to our home in Garland, Texas.

Ken and I started getting our trailer situated in the backyard. We hadn't been working on it for more than 15 minutes when Pat pulled in the driveway and walked back to talk to us.

After we had talked a little while, Pat said, "I almost died while you all were gone."

I answered, "Yes, I know. You were down in Shreveport. You took sick in the nighttime. The paramedics rushed you to the hospital. The doctor told you afterward that he didn't think you were going to make it."

"Yeah!" he exclaimed. "Who told you—Momma?"

"No," I replied. "We haven't seen Momma yet. We haven't been back here for more than 15 minutes." Then I told him about my experience in May.

Pat said, "Well, that's exactly the way it happened." Thank God for the Holy Ghost!

I could tell you experience after experience along this same line. Through the years when our extended family members were younger, I prayed nearly every one of them out of death at one time or another. (Of course, after a while, God expected them to use their own faith, so I couldn't carry them the way I had before.) Also, no crisis would happen to one of my family members without the Holy Spirit alerting me to pray ahead of time. Then as I yielded to that urge to pray, at times He would let me know what I was praying about in tongues so I could pray with my understanding as well.

Supplicating for *All* Saints as We Pray in the Spirit

There is a life in the Spirit and a realm of prayer in the Spirit—a realm of authority and supplication for all saints—that the majority of Christians know nothing about and the rest have barely touched. It is only in this realm of the Spirit that we can fulfill God's command: *"Praying always with all prayer and supplication in the Spirit, and watching thereunto with all perseverance and supplication for all saints"* (Eph. 6:18). We don't know all saints, so there is no way we could pray for all saints if we didn't pray in the Spirit or with other tongues.

So many outstanding examples of operating in this realm of prayer stand out to me, but I will mention just a few from my own life. One incident happened years ago when we had just started Prayer and Healing School on the RHEMA campus. One day as I was ministering the Word, I had a sudden, urgent burden to pray, but I didn't know what to pray about. I asked, "What is it, Lord? What is it?"

Then I realized that someone's life was in danger. Someone was near death—not because of sickness or disease, but because of some kind of accident.

So I got up and said to the crowd, "Folks, I have to pray, and I have to pray now. I'm inviting you to help me pray. I don't know who it is, but someone's life is in danger." I knelt down and began to pray. I prayed hard and fast in other tongues and in groanings for about 45 minutes. Then I had a note of victory that let me know I'd prayed through. I sang and laughed in the Spirit, and that heavy burden to pray lifted.

I said, "Well, I don't know who it is. Sometimes the Holy Spirit will show me the person or people I'm praying for. This time He didn't. But whoever it is, I got the answer, glory to God!"

That evening my wife and I invited our ministry singing group, Faith's Creation, over to our house so we could pray about certain matters. While we were praying, the telephone rang and my wife answered it. It was a young lady, a student at Oral Roberts University. She and her family were personal friends of ours.

The young woman said, "Momma just called from our home in Texas. She told me to call you and ask you to *pray!* There was an explosion this afternoon in the Texaco Refinery in Port Arthur, Texas!"

That was the division where the girl's stepfather worked. Due to the intensity of the fire, no one had been able to get into the refinery since the explosion, and quite a bit of time had passed. (We figured out later that I got the burden to pray in the Spirit for someone in danger just about the time the explosion occurred that afternoon.) There were 17 men trapped in the refinery, and the rescue workers didn't know how many were injured or possibly dead.

When Oretha related to the rest of us what the young woman had said, I told my wife, "Tell her that we've already gotten the answer. Her stepfather is all right. The Spirit of God alerted us this afternoon to pray. Tell her we prayed through about it, and he is safe."

You may ask, "How did you know that this man and his coworkers were the people you were praying for in tongues?"

The Holy Spirit simply let me know through the inward witness as soon as I heard what had happened.

So my wife and I and the members of Faith's Creation went on with our business of praying about other matters. When Oretha and I finally got to bed, it was after midnight. About 1:30, the phone rang. It was the same young lady calling again. She told us, "Momma just called and said, 'They finally got the fire put out—and when they went into the refinery, they discovered that not one person was hurt! They can't believe it! Every single person's life was spared! Daddy's fine!'"

Thank God, the Holy Ghost knows what we are to pray for, and He helps us pray for the unknown!

Later on, this young lady and her parents all graduated from RHEMA and are in the ministry today. These folks in Texas had been friends and supporters of this ministry for many years, and the moment they had an urgent need, the Holy Spirit alerted us to pray miles away in Tulsa. There is no distance in the Spirit. The Holy Spirit can help you pray about anyone, anywhere!

God Looks for Available Vessels to Use in Prayer

Here is something else to understand: The Holy Spirit will often alert you to pray about a specific need or situation in other tongues, as He did with me concerning this man and his 16 coworkers at the Texas refinery. But then once you yield yourself to Him and get over into the realm of the Spirit, He may give you other things to pray for.

This happened to me that afternoon in Prayer School when I prayed for someone whose life was in danger. I'd just gotten that note of victory after praying 45 minutes. Then as I kept praying, the face of a pastor I knew kept coming before me—a man who lived 1,200 miles away. I assumed I was praying for him at that moment.

In the midst of my praying in tongues, I heard myself say a few words in English over and over again: "Don't leave yet. Don't leave yet. Stay there a little while longer." Then I'd go right back to praying in tongues. In my mind, I thought, *Well, I guess this pastor is thinking about leaving his church.* However, I didn't know anything about the situation in the natural.

A few days later, I happened to go into a staff member's office while he was talking on the telephone to this particular pastor. I said, "Before you hang up, let me talk to him."

When I got on the phone, I said to this pastor, "I don't know whether this will mean anything to you or not. If it doesn't, just forget it."

You see, you should never accept a "word from the Lord" just because someone says it, because people can miss it. The Holy Ghost is perfect, but He is manifested through imperfect channels.

I continued, "I was praying the other day in the Spirit, and your face kept coming up before me. Then a few words in English came out of my mouth. I kept saying, 'Don't leave yet. Don't leave yet. Stay a little while longer.' "

The pastor said, "Well, yes, Brother Hagin, I've already given my resignation to the church board. I believe it's time for me to move on."

I replied, "But God seems to be telling you, 'Stay a little while longer.'"

"Well," the pastor said, "I'll pray about it, Brother Hagin."

I found out later that this pastor stayed three more months at that church. He met with the board again, and the board members agreed to delay his resignation.

Later that pastor came over to me at one of my crusade meetings and said, "Thank God for the Holy Ghost!"

The pastor continued: "When I resigned and told the board I was leaving, I was supposed to leave within the next two weeks. However, I didn't have a dime. I said to my wife, 'I don't know where we're going. We have to move out of the parsonage, and I don't know what we'll do with our furniture. I don't have enough money to store it.'

"But by staying three extra months," the pastor said, "I was able to save $3,750 by the time we left the church. I would have been $3,750 short if I hadn't stayed just a little while longer!"

I replied, "Well, that's good to know! I didn't know whether those words, 'Don't leave yet' meant anything or not." But the Holy Ghost knew, and He prompted me to pray about what was unknown to me for the benefit of that pastor.

You may try to figure out in your head what you should be praying about and how you should be praying—but you won't ever be able to do it! Thank God, the Holy Spirit knows the perfect will of God concerning every situation, and He will use you to bring about God's will in specific situations and in people's lives as you yield to Him, praying in other tongues.

Supernatural Deliverance on the Mission Field

I could talk to you all day long, giving you illustration after illustration of miracles that occurred as the Holy Spirit used me to pray in tongues for a situation unknown to me. But marvelous testimonies have also happened in the lives of others I know—many of whom were missionaries on the foreign field, thousands of miles away from home.

For instance, years ago a missionary friend of mine shared a testimony with me along this line. He and his wife Blanche were missionaries to Africa during the years leading up to World War I. Of course, they traveled over to Africa by boat and didn't have any means of quick communication the way we do now. It would take a month for their parents in America to receive a letter from them.

Blanche's father and mother had been old-time Pentecostal dairy farmers all their lives and at this time were in their 80s. Even though Blanche's father didn't operate the dairy any longer, he did still keep three cows, which he would milk every day and then sell the cream.

One morning, Blanche's elderly father got up at dawn, as he always did, and started out toward the barn to milk the cows. But halfway between the house and the barn, he was arrested in his spirit with a strong inner impression that something was *wrong*. Some way or another, the farmer knew it was about his daughter Blanche, so he set down the milk pails and returned to the house.

Blanche's mother had just started to make breakfast on the old wood stove. When her husband walked in the back door, she looked at him and exclaimed, "You look like you just saw a ghost! What is the matter?"

"I don't know," the farmer answered, "but something's wrong with Blanche. She's in trouble, near death. Her physical life is in danger. We have to pray!"

"How do you know?" his wife asked.

"I can't tell you how I know. I just know it on the inside of me." That was the Spirit of God letting this farmer know something about the unknown!

So the elderly father and mother got down on their knees right there on that kitchen floor, and the man said to the Holy Spirit, "I don't know what's wrong, but *something* is wrong with Blanche. And we don't know what to pray for as we ought, but *You* do, Holy Spirit. So please help us make intercession for our daughter." Then they began to pray with other tongues.

That was at about 5:30 in the morning. Hours passed. Noon came and went. The cows were lowing; they hadn't been milked. The hogs were squealing and the chickens were clucking; they hadn't been fed. But still the farmer and his wife prayed on in other tongues for their daughter.

Then at about two o'clock in the afternoon, the elderly man began to laugh and sing in tongues. He said to his wife, "Blanche is going to be all right!"

Now, let me stress this one more time: *Once you begin to pray this way, keep on praying until you get a note of victory.* Whatever it is you're praying about, you'll know in your spirit when you have your answer. You'll have an urge to laugh, to worship, or to sing in tongues, and you'll know you prayed that burden through.

It was nearly six weeks later that Blanche's parents received a letter from their son-in-law. In that letter to his in-laws, the missionary explained, "Several weeks ago, Blanche contracted one of the deadly fevers that are common over here. The people told us there was no cure for her."

Remember, this was between 1910 and 1920. Medical practices in this part of Africa were extremely primitive. Back in those days, once a person in Africa contracted this terrible fever, that person died—end of story!

The son-in-law wrote, "Blanche sunk to the edge of death. In fact, as far as we could tell, she died. We couldn't detect any life in her. But then all of a sudden, Blanche rose up well!"

The parents wrote back and asked, "What day and time did Blanche rise up well?" They didn't tell their daughter and her husband why they were asking. When they received a letter in response, they compared notes with the date and time of their urgent need to pray for Blanche. Her parents found out that the hours when she had sunk close to death were the very hours when they'd been praying for her. And when they figured in the difference in time zones, they realized that the moment their daughter rose up healed in Africa was the same moment—two o'clock their time—that her father was laughing in the Spirit and singing in tongues!

Those old-time Pentecostals knew something about praying through in the Holy Ghost! We'd do well to learn from them!

Over the years, I've read many testimonies in Pentecostal publications that were similar to the one I just related. Missionaries on the foreign field found themselves in a crisis, but someone at home obeyed a sudden urge to pray in other tongues. As a result, the missionary was delivered. Often the person who prayed didn't even know the missionary—but the Holy Spirit did!

For instance, I read about one British missionary to Africa who developed a serious case of cancer. This missionary was an older man who had pioneered the Pentecostal message in that area. His associates transported him to a modern hospital in South Africa to undergo surgery. But when the doctors opened him up, the cancer had spread throughout so much of his body that they just sewed him back up and rolled him out of surgery. The case was hopeless. The man was going to die; there was nothing any medical doctor could do about it.

But about this time, several thousand miles away in Australia, a dear old saint of God saw this man's picture in a Pentecostal publication where he was listed as a missionary from England. Suddenly this elderly woman sensed a strong burden to pray and spent the biggest part of the night praying in other tongues. Then in a vision, God showed this woman what she'd been praying about. She saw this fellow lying sick in bed. She knew who he was because she'd just seen his picture, and she knew he had cancer. In the vision, she saw him rise up well.

In the process of time, this missionary was a guest speaker in the city where this woman lived, so she attended the meeting and went up to the man after the service. The woman related her experience in prayer to the missionary. After they compared dates and took into account the time zone differences, the missionary said to her, "At that very moment, I lay dying on the hospital bed. The doctors had given up on me after the operation, and I was so far gone I couldn't do anything for myself. But then suddenly, I just rose up well! The doctors ran every kind of test they could think of on me, but all traces of the cancer had disappeared!"

I want to share two more testimonies of spectacular deliverance on the mission field that a missionary named Brother Boley experienced because of someone's obedience to pray. Brother Boley was a missionary in the African bush country back at the turn of the twentieth century. I was a young minister at that time, and I attended a meeting where Brother Boley related these two experiences.

On one occasion, a rival hostile tribe stole a little six-year-old girl from the village where Brother Boley was preaching and nearly everyone had gotten saved. Brother Boley said, "We knew from experience that if we didn't get the little girl back before nightfall, she would never be recovered."

These two tribes spoke different dialects, so Brother Boley left for the rival tribe's village with one of the natives—a Christian convert—who could speak their dialect. Boley hoped to barter with the chieftain, trading the child for beads and trinkets.

Miles before the two men reached the village, they smelled the odor of putrid, rotting meat. This particular tribe would select three or four women to prepare and cook an animal that would then be hung on a post just outside the village. The animal would hang there for days and even weeks, rotting in the sun. Everyone who came to the village had to cut off a chunk and eat it—including Brother Boley and his companion.

Brother Boley said, "You might think you believe God—but you really find out whether or not you believe Him when you go to some of those extreme areas on the mission field! In this case, each one of us had to cut off a big chunk of that rotting meat and eat it. But, thank God, it never did affect us!"

Brother Boley and his companion finally reached the chieftain and traded a bunch of trinkets and beads for the girl. At that point, however, nighttime overtook them, which was a problem because it was impossible to travel in the dense jungle at night.

The two men were led to the "guest quarters" of the village—a primitive, thatched-roof hut. Darkness fell, and they had nothing left to do but lay down on the hard ground and go to sleep. Hours later when it was near midnight, they woke up to the sound of drums rolling. Boley asked his companion, "What does the sound of those drums mean?"

His native companion replied, "That is the death sentence they have passed on us. It has finally dawned on the chief that he's already gotten our trinkets, so now he can kill us and still keep the girl! The drums are signaling the tribe's intention to come and kill us. They are coming with bolo knives that with one slice can cut off our heads!"

Brother Boley and the native interpreter could hear the approaching enemy rustling outside their thatched-roof hut. So Boley said to the other man, "Let's kneel down and commit ourselves into the hands of God. Then we won't wait for them to come in and get us. Let's go out first. I'll lead the way."

Brother Boley related what happened next: "After we prayed, I shut my eyes, pulled back the grass-thatch entrance covering, and stepped out of the hut. I stood in front of the hut for what seemed like a long time, although it was probably only a few seconds." (Of course, at a time like that, a few seconds would seem like a very long time!)

Brother Boley continued, "Suddenly I realized that no one had cut off my head! I could hear the sound of these warriors saying something, so I opened my eyes and looked around at the circle of tribal warriors surrounding me. They were all on their knees with their faces bowed to the ground and their bolo knives lying on the ground beside them!"

Just then the interpreter stepped out of the hut, and Boley asked him, "What are these warriors saying?"

"They are worshiping you as God!" he exclaimed.

Brother Boley asked his interpreter to find out what had happened. The village warriors told the interpreter, "When this foreigner stepped out of the hut, two giant men in shining white apparel—nine feet tall and with huge swords—stepped out on either side of him!"

Then the warriors fell down before the missionary and continued to worship him. Of course, Boley retrieved the little girl and took her back home and returned her safely to her parents and to her tribe.

Two weeks later, Brother Boley was planning another mission trip, and he found out that the staff at the mission station was short-handed. Someone told him, "We have a young lady at the mission station alone with no help. I check on her every couple of weeks to see how she's doing, but she always seems to be doing fine."

So Brother Boley went to see this young woman who was operating the mission station all by herself. While he was there, she asked him, "Brother Boley, did something happen to you sometime around midnight on Monday night? Was your life in danger?"

"Why do you ask?"

"Well, I work here by myself between 10 to 12 hours a day," she said. "One night I was very tired and went to sleep almost immediately after going to bed. Then at about 10:30 that night, I was awakened with a very heavy burden to pray. So I got out of bed, sunk to my knees, and began to pray in other tongues."

The woman continued to pray from 10:30 until midnight. "That whole time," she said, "it seemed like *your* face kept flashing before me as I prayed. Then I had a note of victory and began to sing in tongues and to laugh in the Holy Ghost!"

Brother Boley said, "Sister, just about the time you began to laugh is when I stepped out of my thatched-roof hut to meet a group of hostile warriors—and their attack was stopped by the two shining, gigantic men they saw on either side of me!"

Here is the question to seriously consider: *What if this young woman hadn't yielded to the Holy Spirit's leading to pray?*

Brother Boley shared one more amazing testimony that I want to share with you so you can see how great the scope of praying in tongues really is. (Of course, having served for so many years as a missionary in the primitive African bush country, he could have told us many more experiences of supernatural deliverance!)

Off the west coast of Africa was an island whose inhabitants had never yet been reached for Jesus. So Brother Boley leased a native sailboat and crew and took a Spirit-filled native interpreter with him to the island each week to preach the Gospel and minister to the people.

Then one Monday, a sudden storm arose late in the afternoon as Brother Boley and his companions were returning to the mainland after their weekly visit to the island. They'd been trying to get home before dark, since their boat had no lights or navigation instruments. But as the crew fought to stay afloat in the storm, nighttime overtook them and the situation became even more desperate.

Hours passed, and the storm continued to rage in the black darkness of night. Finally about midnight, the boat captain said to Boley, "I don't know where we are in relation to the harbor we have to enter. There is only one narrow space into the harbor that is safe. The rest is very dangerous because of hidden reefs. If we make a run for it, we'll probably be dashed to pieces on the rocks. But if we stay out here in the open ocean, we're going to sink and everyone's life will certainly be lost."

Brother Boley replied, "Well, I don't know anything about navigation. You're the captain. What do *you* think we should do?"

The captain answered, "Our only chance is to try to make a run for it."

Boley said, "Then before we do, let's pray."

The captain and his crew were not Christians, but when people are facing death, everyone gets reverent in a hurry! So they all got down on their knees with Brother Boley and the interpreter and committed their lives into the hands of God. Then Boley got up and said, "Well, just let the boat go!"

Relating his testimony, Brother Boley said, "As God is my witness—not to mention the witness of all those folks on the boat—the moment the captain pointed that sailboat toward the harbor and let it go, it just took off in the air like an airplane and sailed right over the reef, landing in the harbor where the water was calm and peaceful!"

Of course, there was abundant rejoicing going on in that boat over their miraculous deliverance!

A few days later, Brother Boley went to visit one of the mission stations he oversaw. At this time, one woman was staying at this mission station by herself. (This was a different woman than the one who prayed for Brother Boley in the first testimony he related.)

During Boley's visit, the woman asked him, "Brother Boley, did anything happen to you in particular last Monday night?"

"Well, now, what do you mean?" Boley asked. (Of course, he definitely remembered something happening that night!)

"Well" she said, "I went to bed early that night and had been asleep for several hours. About ten o'clock I was suddenly awakened and bolted upright in bed. I said, 'Lord what is it? Something is wrong here.'

"I began to pray just lying there in bed. But I'd worked so hard and was so tired that I kept drifting back to sleep. So I got out of bed and got down on my knees. I prayed, 'Lord, I don't know what it is. But whatever it is, the Holy Ghost knows. I'm going to trust Him to help me.'

"So I started praying in other tongues, and the Holy Ghost began to help me. I spent the next two hours—from 10 till midnight—praying in other tongues. I didn't know what I was praying about or whom I was praying for.

"But at the end of that time I knew that whatever it was, I'd gotten the victory because that heavy burden lifted and I felt a spirit of lightness. I began to sing and laugh in the Spirit. Right then your face flashed before me, so I thought maybe I was praying for you. Did anything happen to you last Monday night about midnight?"

"Sister, midnight on Monday night was the very moment we were miraculously delivered from certain death!" Boley exclaimed.

While that missionary woman was laughing and praising God in the Spirit, that sailboat just took off and sailed right over the reef, landing in the harbor with everyone on board safe and sound!

So why don't we have more supernatural testimonies like this happening? I'll tell you why—*because more folks are not praying in other tongues.* Now, they may pray a little in other tongues to keep themselves in basic fellowship with God. But they don't take an extended amount of time to wait in His Presence—an hour or two or even longer. That's when the Holy Ghost can take hold with them to pray through on matters that desperately need to be prayed about.

There's no doubt in my mind that the Holy Spirit is continually searching for those whom He can use in prayer. When He finds believers willing to yield to Him and to pray for as long as it takes in other tongues, He takes hold together with them, helping them pray out God's perfect will about matters they often know nothing about.

I've read many other such reports as the ones I just related, and I've personally heard many missionaries relate similar testimonies of supernatural deliverance as a result of someone praying in the Spirit. Even so, I believe that the large majority of Spirit-filled Christians haven't yet realized the profound effectiveness of this kind of praying. If they had, they would be doing much more of it!

The Holy Ghost knows what we should pray for as we ought—we don't. Yet so many times when we get a burden or an inward witness to pray in our spirits, we go right on about our daily business instead of stopping to pray. If we would only yield more to the Holy Ghost and make ourselves available to pray in other tongues, even when we have no idea what we are praying about, we'd see more victories in our own lives. We'd also see many more dramatic deliverances in the lives of those for whom we pray.

This is one of the greatest areas in which the Holy Spirit is a Helper to us—our prayer life. Of course, He helps us in all realms of life. But one of the most productive, most fruitful, most outstanding, and most miraculous areas He helps us in is praying out God's perfect will in other tongues for what is unknown to our natural minds.

CHAPTER 18

PRESSING INTO NEW DEPTHS OF PRAYER

God is calling us to a deeper realm of prayer in these last days. That means we need to train ourselves to be sensitive to the Spirit of God so we can learn to yield to Him. As we do, He will help us pray out God's will in situations that arise, even when we know nothing about the circumstances or the people who are involved. We can get on our knees and say, "Holy Spirit, I don't know what to pray for as I ought, but You do."

We won't know until we get to Heaven how many great miracles have been wrought and how many countless lives have been saved because believers have been willing to do just that. When they sensed a burden to pray, they obeyed. And as they prayed in other tongues, the Holy Ghost took hold together with them, giving them the unction and anointing to pray out unknown situations according to the will of God.

A Life Spared Through Someone's Obedience to Pray

I remember an outstanding example of this that happened to Brother and Sister Goodwin during the World War II years. At the time, they were pastors of an east Texas Pentecostal church. One Sunday night after Brother Goodwin had already gone to sleep, Sister Goodwin got a strong burden to pray. She tried not to disturb her husband as she prayed in tongues and in deep groanings, but her groanings became so loud that she awakened him.

When Brother Goodwin woke up and heard his wife groaning, he thought at first that she was sick. "What's the matter?" he asked her.

"I have a burden to pray," Sister Goodwin said. "Some of our church folks are in danger."

"Who is it?"

"I don't know," she said, "but someone's life is in danger."

The Goodwins tried to think of who it might be, but all they could come up with were the four families from church who were on vacation and driving all night long to get back home. So they prayed and claimed divine protection for all the families. Then Brother Goodwin fell back to sleep.

Sister Goodwin tried to go to sleep as well, but that burden to pray was still there. She started praying once more in tongues and in deep groanings. Finally, she woke up Brother Goodwin again.

Sister Goodwin told her husband, "That wasn't it—it's someone else in our congregation." She just had a spiritual discernment, a spiritual sense, that someone's life was in danger who attended their church.

So the Goodwins prayed together again and received some sense of relief in their spirits. Brother Goodwin went back to sleep, and Sister Goodwin tried to do the same. But she just couldn't shake that burden to pray. She started praying in tongues and groaning again, and after a while, she once more awakened her husband. This time he said, "Well, let's just get out of bed and pray."

As the Goodwins prayed together in other tongues, Sister Goodwin couldn't seem to get relief from that sense of heaviness in her spirit. Finally, Brother Goodwin said, "Let's just pray in agreement that the Lord will give the person, whoever it is, a dream or a vision that shows him the danger that's ahead."

So the Goodwins agreed in prayer and then prayed in the Spirit awhile longer. By the time they finally got back to bed, it was four o'clock in the morning. Consequently, they were still sleeping later that morning when the phone rang. It was one of the men in their church—their Sunday school superintendent—and he had quite a story to tell!

This man worked in the oil fields as a member of a gang of "roughnecks" (the name for workers employed on the oil wells). That morning when he showed up at work, the gang pusher, his foreman, told him that Bill, the man who worked the drilling tower, hadn't shown up that day. Then the gang pusher said to the Goodwins' Sunday school superintendent, "You work the tower today."

The man started to climb up the ladder to the tower—but after climbing up about 14 rungs, he reversed direction and climbed back down. On the ground again, the man told the gang pusher, "I'm not going to do it."

"Why not?" the gang pusher asked.

"Well, I'll tell you," the Sunday school superintendent said, "I had a dream at four o'clock this morning. I know the time because the dream woke me up and I went to the kitchen to get a drink of water and looked at the clock. In the dream, Bill didn't show up, and I climbed up there to work that tower. Then all of a sudden, a huge cable broke and cut off my head! I actually saw my head fall down to the ground in the dream—so I'm not going to climb up there today!"

Another worker on the gang was also present. He was a Christian man and a member of a nearby denominational church. This man laughed and said, "Well, I'm not superstitious. I'll do it."

The gang pusher agreed, and the man climbed up the ladder to the drilling tower. The gang started working, pulling one of the massive drill-rig pipes out of the ground. But the man hadn't been up on the tower for more than 10 minutes when a huge cable broke and cut off his head, just as the Pentecostal man had seen in his dream!

You might ask, "But the man who died was a Christian. Why didn't the Lord warn him too?"

Remember, dear friend, that when you get over into this realm of prayer through speaking with other tongues, you are in a different and deeper dimension of prayer. In this realm, you can pray out a matter you don't know how to pray for as you ought. The Holy Ghost helps you pray it through.

The church where this denominational man attended believed in prayer, but their way of praying went something like this: "Lord, help those who need help, and bless those who need blessing. Do what You can, Lord. Amen."

On the other hand, those who pray in other tongues can speak supernaturally to God and thus pray out those things that need to be prayed for. The Holy Ghost knows the will of God and helps believers pray according to God's will so that His plans and purposes can be brought forth on this earth.

That's what happened as Sister Goodwin prayed that night for someone in her church whose life was in danger. She didn't know what the situation was or who was involved. But the Holy Ghost knew, and He helped Sister Goodwin pray out the situation on behalf of her church member. In the end, the Sunday school superintendent's life was spared because Sister Goodwin made herself available to pray out that burden and because *the man* acted on the divine warning in his dream.

God Is Limited by Our Prayer Life

Many times when folks hear an account like the one I just related, they ask, "But why does it have to be that way? Why couldn't God save that Sunday school superintendent without someone praying? And what if Sister Goodwin *hadn't* prayed?"

If someone hadn't prayed in that situation, that man's life probably would have been lost.

Someone might ask, "But if God wanted to deliver that man, why didn't He just go ahead and do it anyway? After all, when Jesus was raised from the dead, didn't He say, 'All power and authority is given unto Me both in Heaven and on earth'?

Doesn't that mean the Head of the Church has authority on earth to do whatever He wants to do?"

First, as soon as Jesus said, *". . . All power* [or authority] *is given unto me in heaven and in earth,"* He immediately delegated that authority on earth to the Church when He said, *"Go YE therefore . . ."* (Matt. 28:18–19).

Again and again, the New Testament scriptures use the analogy of the human body to describe the relationship between Jesus and the Church. He is the Head, and we are His Body, and the Head doesn't act apart from the Body.

For example, consider your own body for a moment. Your head cannot exercise any authority except through your body. If you don't believe me, just try to tell your head to get up and walk out of the room without the rest of your body!

Often people will try to sound humble by saying something like this: "Well, the Lord doesn't need me, but I need Him."

That would be like saying, "My head doesn't need my body, but my body needs my head." No, the head and the body both need one another in order to function. The same thing is true regarding the Head of the Church and the Body of Christ. Jesus needs His Body in order to perform His will in this world, and the Body of Christ sure needs Jesus!

Second, I am reminded of a statement I read early on in my ministry from the writings of John Wesley, the founder of the Methodist Church. Wesley made this statement: "It seems that God is limited by our prayer life. He can do nothing for humanity unless someone asks Him to do it."

When I read that, I didn't know whether or not it was so. I examined the Scriptures but couldn't find an answer that satisfied me. Ten years later, I was reading another author on the subject of prayer and faith, and he made almost the same statement. This author said, "It seems that God is limited by our prayer life. He can do nothing for humanity unless someone asks Him." Then this author added this afterthought: "Why this is, we don't know."

That last statement bothered me. I thought, *Well, if what this author says is true, we ought to know why!*

I knew there was only one way I was going to find the answer: by getting in the Word. The answer had to be there. As I studied and prayed, the Lord spoke to my heart, "Go back to the Book of beginnings." I knew He meant the Book of Genesis.

So I started to study Genesis, and I saw that God made the world and the fullness thereof. Then He made His man Adam and said, "Adam, I give you dominion over all the work of My hands." You could say that Adam became, in a sense, "the god of this world." In other words, God put Adam in a position of ruling and having dominion over this natural world (Gen. 1:26–28; Ps. 8).

But then Adam committed high treason against God by disobeying Him and sold out to Satan. Adam didn't have a moral right to do that, but he had a *legal* right to do it. The Scriptures tell us that Satan then became the god of this world. In other words, Satan became the ruler of this fallen world system (2 Cor. 4:4).

Then in Ephesians 6:12, Paul describes Satan's fallen kingdom. Paul also lists Satan's hierarchy of demonic forces:

EPHESIANS 6:12

12 For we wrestle not against flesh and blood, but against principalities, against powers, against the RULERS OF THE DARKNESS OF THIS WORLD, against spiritual wickedness in high places.

Also, the Apostle John confirmed that Satan is the god of this world system: "... *The whole world lieth in wickedness*" (1 John 5:19). The devil has a right to stay here until Adam's lease runs out. And it's getting closer and closer to the time when that will happen!

The first Adam who sold us out to Satan's dominion was a man. Therefore, justice required that a *Man* pay the price of *man's* sin. That means God, Who is a spirit being, couldn't move in and run Satan out because Adam had given Satan legal dominion over the earth. That's why Satan could say to Jesus, "All the kingdoms of the world I'll give to You if You'll just bow down to me" (Matt. 4:8–9).

That's the reason God sent Jesus to be born as a Man—to redeem man back from Satan's captivity. Yes, Jesus is also the divine Son of God, but He laid aside His mighty power and glory to be born as a human being (Phil. 2:7). It was as a human being that Jesus defeated Satan and redeemed us from the hand of the enemy. Jesus was tempted in all points like as we are, yet without sin (Heb. 4:15). He died not as God, but as a Man. He never became a sinner, but He was *made to be sin* when our sin was laid on Him that we might be made the righteousness of God in Him (2 Cor. 5:21).

When the first Adam sinned, Satan legally took over Adam's lease on the earth, and therefore Satan has a right to be here. That means God can't just move in on him. If He did, Satan could accuse God of being unjust, and God has to stand as a just God before all the creation of three worlds—Heaven, earth, and hell. That's why He sent the Second Adam, Jesus Christ, to earth as a Man to purchase back the authority that the first Adam gave away!

Once redemption was complete through Jesus' death, burial, and resurrection, He delegated the authority He'd won back from Satan to His Body, the Church. Now as man prays and asks God in faith about matters pertaining to this life, God intervenes to perform His will on the earth.

Jesus Himself declared He'd given man such great authority: *"And I will give unto thee the keys of the kingdom of heaven: and whatsoever thou shalt bind on earth shall be bound in heaven: and whatsoever thou shalt loose on earth shall be loosed in heaven"* (Matt. 16:19). Notice that something is done about "whatsoever" on earth first before anything is done in Heaven! *Today's English Version* reads, "I will give you the keys of the Kingdom of heaven; what you prohibit on earth will be prohibited in heaven, and what you permit on earth will be permitted in heaven."

So Jesus is the Head, and we are His Body. His authority is through us, His Church, as we take *our* authority on this earth. Just as our head doesn't have an experience apart from our body, so Jesus, our Head, does not exercise His authority on this earth apart from His Body, the Church.

I'm well satisfied that we as the Church of the Lord Jesus Christ have never fully realized the extent of our authority. Once in a while we get a glimpse of it and by the Spirit step into a greater revelation of who we are in Christ, but not one of us has ever yet walked consistently in our full realm of authority. However, in these last days, God desires to raise up a company of believers who will do exactly that!

Plead Your Case With the Father

With this understanding of our authority in mind, let's look at a vital passage of Scripture in this discussion on praying in the Spirit. Learning to act on the following verses from the Book of Isaiah should be an integral part of our prayer life as we pray both with the spirit and with our understanding.

> **ISAIAH 43:25–26**
>
> **25** I, even I, am he that blotteth out thy transgressions for mine own sake, and will not remember thy sins.
>
> **26** PUT ME IN REMEMBRANCE: LET US PLEAD TOGETHER: declare thou, that thou mayest be justified.

What does God mean by that phrase "let us plead together"? We are to remind Him of what He said in regard to our sin. The devil will try to condemn us, but we can laugh at him. We can put both God *and* the devil in remembrance that God has forgiven our iniquities and will not remember our sins. Once we confess our sins and ask God's forgiveness, He doesn't remember that we have ever done anything wrong. With that confidence, we can come into God's Presence with great boldness and confidence.

That same principle is true regarding *anything* you may be praying about. Remind God in prayer what He's said in His Word about your need. Plead your case with Him, setting forth your cause that you may be justified.

Don't let those verses get by you without acting on them. Plant them in your heart and *use* them. They are there for your benefit. God said, "Let's plead together." God is the One Who invites you to do so. You plead your case with Him, and He will plead His case with you.

Of course, when you plead your case, you won't always be able to receive the answer you want. After you plead your side, God may plead His side. Remember, He said, "Let *us* plead together."

I remember one time in particular when I applied these scriptures to a difficult situation in my own life. I'll share this example with you because it shows the connection between praying in tongues and pleading our case with the Father using words that our minds understand. (Remember the "two-wheeled bicycle" analogy I shared with you earlier. We need both "wheels" in prayer to get where we need to go!).

My wife and I were preaching up in Oregon when my sister called to tell me that my mother, 68 years old, was in critical condition. My sister didn't know what to do. I called my mother's pastor, Brother Wood, to talk to him about the situation. He said to me, "Brother Hagin, Pat's Momma [that's what we all called my mother] is calling for you. If I were you, I believe I'd come home. The situation is serious."

I talked to the pastor of the church where I was holding the meeting, and he said, "It will be fine if you want to close the meeting and go home to be with your mother."

So I closed the meeting that night. But while the service was still going on, I spent some time in a youth hall beside the auditorium—walking up and down the room, praying in other tongues. I was building myself up on my most holy faith, preparing my heart to plead my mother's case with the Lord.

I realized from what Brother Wood said that Momma's condition was critical and that she could very easily die. So after praying for a while in tongues, I said, "Lord, I want to plead my case with You concerning Momma. I just can't give her up, Lord. Momma did so much for us back when I was only six and our daddy forsook us. She stayed with us and tried to make a living for all four of us children until she had a complete nervous, mental, and physical breakdown.

"Besides that, Lord, I'm closer to Momma than all the rest of her children, because I was sick and afflicted in my younger life and wasn't able to run and play like the others. And after Daddy left us, I only had her to focus all my love on as her son.

"Lord, Momma has done so much for me and the rest of her children, and I've finally gotten to the place where I can do something for her. I know it's selfish of me, Lord, but I can't give her up. She's only 68 years old, and You promised us at least 70 or 80 years. I just can't let her go."

As I kept praying in tongues, I got over in the realm of the Spirit. Then the Lord began to plead His case with me as the Holy Spirit permitted me to interpret what I'd prayed in tongues. Remember, God said, "Let us plead *together.*"

The Lord said to me, "Paul said, 'For me to die is gain' [Phil. 1:21] and 'I have a desire to depart and be with Christ, which is far better' [Phil. 1:23]. And in Second Corinthians 5:8, Paul said, *'We are confident, I say, and willing rather to be absent from the body, and to be present with the Lord.'*"

Then the Lord said, "Your mother will be better off if you'll let her come on home. She's never heard you preach, and she doesn't even have a glimpse of the faith message. She is a spiritual baby who doesn't know how to believe, and she will suffer a great deal. She would be better off if you would just let her come on home."

The Lord pled His side. Now it was my turn to plead my case again.

With tears, I said, "Lord, I realize it's selfish, but someway or another on the inside of me, I just can't do it. I love Momma so much, and You promised us at least 70 or 80 years. So if Momma dies now, I want You to know I'm not going to be mad at You, but I'm not going to feel good about it either. I'm going to keep serving You and doing Your will. But the longest day I live, every time I think of it, I'm going to remind You that You let Momma go home early. And when I get up to Heaven, every time I think of it, I'm going to remind You."

Do you know what the Lord said to me then? He said, *"All right. I'll do whatever you say."*

I said, "Give her at least 80 years."

"All right, I'll give her 80 years," the Lord answered.

Well, when Momma turned 80, she started dying. Within two weeks, she had gone home to be with the Lord. But she had lived long enough for us to see her get filled with the Holy Ghost and speak in other tongues, and she had a good homegoing!

Thank God for the authority of the believer! We're making headway in learning how to walk in that authority, but it starts with learning how to pray in the Spirit according to His Word!

Oh, there are depths in prayer that we know so little about! There is a place in prayer that so few have attained. But if we will listen to the Helper and follow Him, He will be faithful to lead us into that greater dimension of prayer.

I can tell you this: I'm not satisfied with where we are as a Body in this area of prayer. We are nowhere near where we ought to be. But, thank God, I believe many are making some giant steps! We're beginning to move on into that deeper realm of prayer and intercession with the help of the Holy Ghost within.

'God Never Uses Me'

As I said earlier, I could tell you a number of different experiences where I was led to pray in other tongues and, as a result, God was able to intervene supernaturally to perform a miracle in someone's life. But this type of experience isn't peculiar to me. It ought to be true concerning *every* believer's life. And it *would* be true if Christians would give more of their time to the Lord in prayer.

You might say, "God doesn't ever use me." First, if you're going to be used of God, you have to make yourself available to Him. Second, you must yield to the Holy Spirit when you sense His prompting to pray in the Spirit.

Or you may say, "I don't think God ever speaks to me." The Holy Spirit is continually communicating with your spirit, but you may not recognize His voice when He speaks. Maybe you aren't walking in close enough fellowship with the Lord to understand what He's saying. But as you get better acquainted with Him through the supernatural means of communication He's given you—praying in tongues—you will get better at hearing Him when He speaks!

You see, the Holy Spirit isn't going to force you to do anything. He'll give you a *burden*, a *prompting*, or an *inward urge* to pray. But if you keep overriding those inner promptings or urges, at some point you won't experience them any longer.

The trouble with a lot of Spirit-filled Christians is that they say a few words in tongues and then that's the end of it. They leave their place of prayer and go on about their day. But if believers are willing to pray long enough in tongues, God *will* be able to use them.

So spend some extra time just fellowshipping with the Lord—glorifying Him, magnifying Him, and worshiping Him with your spirit and with your understanding. As you do that, you will make yourself more and more available to God so He can use you. Then when He's looking for someone to pray about a particular person or situation, He'll choose you!

Revelation Comes *by the Spirit*

God has prepared so much wisdom for us to receive for our benefit and enlightenment—but we miss out on that divine wisdom unless we walk in the Spirit. How are we going to do that? The Bible tells us in First Corinthians 2.

1 CORINTHIANS 2:9

9 But as it is written, Eye hath not seen, nor ear heard, neither have entered into the heart of man, the things which God hath prepared for them that love him.

Often people take this scripture out of its context and give it a meaning that, although partially true, does a great injustice to its full meaning. They say, "See? When we all get to Heaven, it will be so wonderful! Eye has not seen, nor has ear heard what God has prepared for us who love Him!"

Yes, it's true that one day we'll enjoy what God has prepared for us up in Heaven. But that isn't what this text is talking about. We know that because of what the next verse says:

1 CORINTHIANS 2:10

10 But God hath revealed them unto us BY HIS SPIRIT: for the Spirit searcheth all things, yea, the deep things of God.

Paul is saying that we cannot know the things of God by our natural senses. Our natural eyes have not seen, nor have our natural ears heard what God has prepared for those of us who love Him.

But to those of us who will cultivate fellowship through prayer, the revelation of the deep things of God will be given to us by the Holy Spirit.

It was the Holy Ghost Who gave Paul revelation of the great plan of redemption. It was the Holy Ghost who revealed to Paul the mystery that was hidden and that has now been made manifest (see Eph. 3:3–6).

You see, you can study God's Word and receive head knowledge about what it says. But just because you can quote scriptures doesn't mean they have been made real to your spirit. In order for you to enter into the reality of a truth, you have to receive it by revelation of the Holy Spirit.

I know this from personal experience. At one time, I could quote three-quarters of the New Testament! I'd just rattle off scriptures as hard and fast as I could go when I first started preaching as a young denominational boy preacher. The congregation would say to me, "Slow down! We don't get half of what you say!"

After four years of preaching that way, I was baptized with the Holy Ghost and spoke with other tongues. Then the Holy Spirit slowed me down and began to talk to me. I started praying in other tongues on a daily basis.

As I prayed in other tongues and fellowshipped with the Father in prayer, almost immediately the Bible became like a new Book to me. Every page and every line seemed different. The revelation of the supernatural in the Word leapt off the pages as I read.

Paul shows us how the Holy Spirit searches the deep things of God so He can reveal truth to man:

1 CORINTHIANS 2:10–13

10 But God hath revealed them [what He has prepared for us] unto us by his Spirit: for the Spirit searcheth all things, yea, the deep things of God.

11 For what man knoweth the things of a man, save the spirit of man which is in him? even so the things of God knoweth no man, but the Spirit of God.

12 Now we have received, not the spirit of the world, but the spirit which is of God; that we might know the things that are freely given to us of God.

13 Which things also we speak, not in the words which man's wisdom teacheth, but which the Holy Ghost teacheth; comparing spiritual things with spiritual.

So many times this passage of Scripture was fulfilled in my own life. As I'd wait on the Lord and pray in other tongues, the Holy Spirit would take me through two or three chapters of the Bible, verse by verse. By the time I'd get up off my knees, I'd see those chapters in an entirely different light because of all the revelation the Holy Ghost revealed to me during that time.

I'll say it again—the primary knowledge I've gained from the Bible, I didn't get by reading someone's book. The deeper things of the Word of God I learned on my knees praying in other tongues. In fact, the greatest things that ever happened to me in my walk with God came as a result of praying with other tongues.

For instance, it was while I was praying in other tongues as a young single preacher that I received the revelation of being married. I also knew by the same inward revelation that I would have two children: The oldest would be a boy and the second child would be a girl.

Later when I met Oretha and we got married, I related to her what God had told me about our children. So when she was pregnant with our first child, we only picked out a boy's name. For the second child, we didn't pick out anything but a girl's name.

I kept telling family members, "This first child is a boy."

They'd say, "Oh, but what if the child *isn't* a boy? I mean, just supposing . . ."

I'd reply, "I'm not living on 'supposings.'"

You don't have to live on "supposings" either. Just stop trying to figure everything out in your head and start taking time to pray out God's plan for your life in tongues!

So I received the revelation about my future wife and children—part of God's plan for my life—as I prayed in other tongues. I'd never even conceived such a thought before that moment. I hadn't even found my wife-to-be yet!

That happened to me again and again over the years about various situations. The Holy Spirit would reveal different steps in God's plan for my life and ministry as I took the time to pray in the Spirit and fellowship with the Father.

Brother Oral Roberts and I have great respect for one another, and many times we've enjoyed great fellowship together. You talk about a fellow knowing how to pray—that definitely describes Oral Roberts! That man knows how to get in the Presence of God! I've been there with him more than once and have been blessed tremendously by those experiences.

During our times of fellowship, Brother Roberts and I would talk about any number of different subjects. When it came to this area of praying in other tongues, we discovered that we had a great deal in common. In comparing notes, we realized that the direction our ministries have taken over the years came to us identically the same way and by the same Spirit. We prayed in other tongues over a long period of time and then began to interpret by the Spirit what we were praying.

The revelation of God's Word also came to me as I prayed in the Spirit over an extended period of time. I'll share exactly how it happened.

I'd been a pastor for almost 12 years and was going along pretty well in my ministry, following and reading after other ministers I respected, just as all young ministers do. But something changed while I was at the last church I pastored in east Texas. I had every reason in the world to be satisfied at that church. We were living in the best parsonage we had ever lived in. We were more comfortable, well-fed, and well-clothed as a family than we had ever been.

During the time I was the pastor, that church was better off financially than it had ever been before. We had the biggest Sunday school attendance the church had ever had. On Sunday night, our sanctuary was filled up most of the time. From the natural standpoint, we had every reason in the world to be satisfied. We had no problems, and the congregation wanted me to stay and continue pastoring.

In those days, it was the custom for the church to vote on the pastor every year. But the congregation told me, "Brother Hagin, if you'd like, we'll just vote you in indefinitely. Stay as long as you want to." That was unheard of in those days!

But I couldn't get rid of a deep sense of dissatisfaction inside me. I thought to myself, *What is wrong with me? I have it so good. I ought to be rejoicing!* I'd pray, "Lord, what is the matter with me? Everything is so good here, yet I can't shake that feeling of dissatisfaction on the inside!"

Finally, I decided to wait on God in earnest about the matter. I said to my wife, "If church members stop by, tell them I don't want to be disturbed unless it's an emergency." Ken and Pat were in the first and second grades at the time, and they'd usually come over to the church study when it was dinnertime to tell me supper was ready. But I told Oretha, "I know when we eat. If I don't come home, don't send the children to get me. It will mean I'm going to skip that meal."

I did a lot of fasting during that time. Once in a while, I'd fast a whole day, but most of the time, I'd skip one or two meals a day and spend that extra time waiting on God.

I also spent a lot of time praying in the Spirit and praying Paul's prayers in Ephesians 1 and 3 for myself over and over again (see Ephesians 1:15–23; 3:14–21). I kept my Bible open on the altar all the time, and every time I'd walk into the church for any reason, the first thing I'd do is get on my knees and pray those two prayers, inserting my name in them. Then I'd wait in His presence, sometimes in silence, sometimes praying in other tongues—trying to identify that sense of dissatisfaction deep inside of me.

Sometimes it's difficult to explain spiritual things with natural words, but I will try. As I'd wait on God at that church altar, at times I would move over into the realm of the Spirit and almost lose consciousness of my natural surroundings. I'm not talking about falling into a trance, where a person's physical senses are temporarily suspended and he isn't even conscious he has a body. I simply mean that as I waited on God, I would get over in the realm of the Spirit, and it would seem as if I could see myself reaching deep down inside my inner man to pull things out and lay them on the altar before me.

Why am I not satisfied? I laid that question on the altar and reached down into my spirit again. Then the answer came. *The reason I'm not satisfied is that there is something else I should do.* I laid that revelation on the altar and reached down again. *What else should I do?* I pulled out that question and laid it on the altar.

As I continued to wait on God in prayer in the days and weeks that followed, it wasn't long before I had things lying on that altar from one end to the other!

Finally, it seemed like I had gotten down to the bottom of my spirit, and I pulled something up. It looked to me like an old, black shoe that had been rained on—all dark and wrinkled— except that it had tentacles sticking out of it like an octopus! I held it up and asked, "Dear Lord, what in the world is this thing?"

"Oh," said the Lord, "that's some of your old denominational tradition."

"Why, Lord!" I exclaimed. "I thought I got rid of that a long time ago!"

"Well," the Lord replied, "you didn't."

I didn't lay that thing on the altar—I threw it away! You see, there are some things you're supposed to lay on the altar in surrender to God—and other things you're supposed to get rid of forever!

Incidentally, that wasn't the only thing I had to throw away during those times of prayer. I also pulled something else out of my spirit that didn't look bad, yet it didn't look quite right. I asked God, "What in the world is that?"

"That," said the Lord, "is some of the Pentecostal tradition you've adopted as your own since you've been among the Pentecostals." Obviously, that was something else that had to go!

One day the Lord said to me as I was kneeling at the church altar praying in other tongues: *I'm going to take you on to revelations and visions.* I ran back in my study and wrote that down.

That was the winter of 1947 and 1948. In six months' time, revelation regarding God's Word began to come to my spirit in such waves that I finally said to my wife, "What in the world have I been preaching all these years? I've been so ignorant, it's a wonder to me that the deacons didn't have to come and tell me to get in out of the rain!"

By the end of 1948, I'd learned more about the Bible and the deeper things of God than I had learned in all the 14 years of ministry before that combined! Then in 1950, the visions began to come. Between 1950 and 1962, the Lord Jesus Himself appeared to me eight times. On two of those occasions, He talked to me for an hour and a half.

But all that didn't happen because I whiled away the hours, doing whatever my flesh wanted to do. The revelations and the visions came *by the Spirit* as I waited before God in prayer, hour after hour, hour after hour, hour after hour—fellowshipping with Him and praying in other tongues.

Yes, you will receive some revelation of the Word as you feed on it, and it's crucial that you do feed on the Word continually to get it planted deeply in your heart. But revelation of things to come, revelation of God's plan and purpose for your own life, and revelation of the deeper things of the Word all come by fellowshipping with God through the supernatural communication of praying in tongues.

Revelation Regarding a Future Move of God's Spirit

I found out early on in my ministry that by praying with other tongues, the Holy Spirit would prepare me for things to come. For instance, I made mention earlier about the time in 1943 when I was alone in my study in Greggton, Texas, and I made a decision to pray in tongues for an hour. Then because the devil kept telling me I was wasting my time, I determined to pray two more hours—and after that, another four hours! But as I neared my fifth hour of praying in tongues, I hit a *gusher* and started praying under a *strong* anointing in the Holy Ghost.

Most folks never pray in tongues long enough to hit a gusher. They drill down right below the surface and hope to hit "oil" with as little time and effort as possible!

When I hit that gusher in February 1943, revelation of things to come suddenly started flowing out of me. The Lord said, *"At the close of World War II, there will come a revival of divine healing to America."* I wrote those words down and dated the paper.

A year and a half later in September 1944, I was preaching at a Pentecostal youth rally in east Texas, and in the middle of my sermon, I saw that paper in my Bible where I had written down the words the Lord had spoken to me. So I said to the people, "Let me read to you something the Spirit of God said to me while I was praying awhile back." Then I read those words: "At the close of World War II, there will come a revival of divine healing to America."

As God is my witness, the moment I read those words, the power of God fell on that crowd! The Spirit of God moved in like a wind, and every minister in the room ran down the aisle and fell on the altar. Everyone else hit the floor, and everyone started praying in tongues.

I didn't tell them to do that—I was right in the middle of my sermon! But when I looked around and saw everyone on the floor, I just got down on the floor and prayed with them! We prayed up a storm for a good while. When we finally got through praying, I just picked up where I left off and finished my sermon!

We need more of those kinds of services, where God's power manifests while the preacher is preaching. If today's Spirit-filled believers would start believing God for the move of His Spirit and pray in the Holy Ghost the way Pentecostal believers did in those days, the same mighty power would be in manifestation today as it was then. That Holy Ghost power may fall like rain. It may move in like a cloud. Or it may blow through like a wind and sweep everyone off the pews and onto the floor, just like it did in that meeting in September 1944 when God confirmed the word He'd given me.

'Catching the Wave' of Divine Healing

The revival of divine healing began in 1947, sweeping the nation with the force of God's healing power and lasting through 1958.

You see, moves of God on this earth are like waves of the sea coming in to shore. And when those waves start coming in, blown by the wind of the Spirit, anyone can jump on them and ride!

For instance, one Pentecostal minister told me, "Before this revival started, my wife and I had ministered for 35 years together and had never prayed for the sick or had a healing ministry. We'd minister in song, and my wife would minister a short message from the Word. Then we'd exhort sinners to get saved and give an altar call, and people would get saved. But when that wave of divine healing came, we just got on the wave and rode it! We started praying for the sick, and to our utter astonishment, people started getting healed everywhere! One completely blind woman was instantly healed under our ministry. It was the easiest thing in the world to get people healed!"

Others told me the same thing. They got on the wave and rode it into shore! Now, it's fine to do that, but people need to be careful that they don't ride the wave when God's Spirit is moving while neglecting their own time of personal fellowship with the Father. If they do that, they will miss the Holy Spirit's cue when it's time to get off that wave and get on another one. And as a result, they'll be washed up on the shore and left there to sit and bellyache about how dry it is!

Personally, I determined never to make that mistake, and I knew how to make sure I didn't.

During that mighty move of God's healing power, an organization was formed among the healing evangelists called the "Voice of Healing," and I was one of the ministers in that organization. One day a fellow "Voice of Healing" minister asked me, "Kenneth, how did your ministry suddenly just blossom out? What did you do to make that happen?"

Some folks are always looking for something "they" can do to reach their goal or find success. But the answer isn't found in man's natural strength or reasoning powers.

I simply replied, "I'll tell you what I did. It was a matter of waiting on God and spending hours praying in the Holy Ghost. That's how I have received direction and revelation for every step and every stage of my ministry."

The Next Two Waves of God's Spirit

In 1958, I was preaching at a church in Dallas, when suddenly by revelation, I spoke out, *"The next revival is in the Church!"*

The congregation thought I meant in the Pentecostal church. But I didn't mean that at all. In fact, the next wave of God's Spirit almost missed the Pentecostal churches entirely. I meant the next revival would be in the *denominational church world.*

After that, it wasn't long before the Charismatic revival began. We rode that wonderful wave for quite a few years, and many church people's lives were dramatically changed as they received the infilling of the Holy Spirit. Then that revival ran its course and has virtually subsided, although there are certainly people in the denominational church world who continue to receive the Holy Ghost and speak in tongues.

Then we had a great revival of teaching God's Word—what some folks call the "faith message." I don't like that term. I simply call it "faith in the Word of God." We're not talking about trying to believe something that's way out in left field. We just accept and believe what God has said in His Word.

This teaching revival had its beginnings in the mandate the Lord gave me years ago when He said to me, "Go teach My people faith." As a result of sowing the Word into God's people, a great harvest has been reaped. I tried to be faithful with that message over the years, but the day came when the Lord said to me, "Today there are many other good teachers of faith in My Body." (For a long time, it seemed like I was the only voice out there!) *"Now you must go teach My people about the Holy Ghost!"*

The Lord went on to say, "Charismatic believers know how to praise Me, but there is a move of the Spirit they know little or nothing about. And should I tarry My coming, that understanding will be lost to future generations if you don't teach them."

Of course, we will never leave behind the teaching of God's Word. But God wants to combine a move of His Spirit with the solid foundation of Bible teaching that's been built over the past few decades in the Body of Christ. The combination will cause the next move of the Holy Ghost to be the biggest one yet!

The Next Wave of God's Spirit Is Coming

When you've preached as long as I have (almost seven decades!), you can start to see some things come in waves. And I can sense it in my spirit—there is another wave coming. Get ready for it. It isn't coming just because God said it's coming. We are going to have to enter into the deeper realm of prayer we have been talking about and give birth to that which God wants to do.

If you've ever gone down to the ocean and watched the waves come in, you know that before a wave ever breaks on the shore, it has its beginnings way out in the deeper waters of the ocean. The potential energy of the wave begins long before you ever see the final result washing up on the shore.

Well, that's what praying in tongues accomplishes in the spiritual realm. When you pray in tongues, you give impetus to the next move of God's Spirit before that spiritual "wave" is ever seen with your natural eyes!

When I talk to other ministers, I realize we all have the same thing in our spirits. We haven't necessarily communicated in the natural with one another. There is just something in our spirits that tells us another wave is coming!

So what do we do about it? Well, we determine that we're not going to stay with the old wave and ride it into the shore, only to be left high and dry on the sand! Instead, we turn around and start swimming back out to the deep part of the ocean so we can get on the next wave—the next mighty move of God's Spirit on this earth. And how do we swim back out to the deep? *By setting aside time and dedicating ourselves to fellowship with the Father and to pray in the Holy Ghost!*

But if we are going to usher in the next mighty move of God's Spirit in these last days, judgment must begin at the house of God. There is so much more God wants to do for His people. But He *can't* do what He wants to do until Christians humble themselves, forget their petty little differences, and come together in unity to enter the realm of the Spirit in prayer.

God is calling us to answer His call to *pray* in these last days. Jesus is coming soon—but before He comes, there is something He wants to do. And what He does on this earth, He will do through us, His Body.

The Body has no coordination when half of its members are going one way and the other half are going the other way. So God is getting us ready. He is calling us to a common goal— to yield to the prompting of the Holy Ghost to pray in other tongues! The next wave is about to burst upon us in all of its glory, and every one of us should be determined not to miss it!

We have seen the wave called the healing revival. We have seen the wave called the Charismatic Movement. We have seen the wave of faith and of the teaching of God's Word. But now another wave is coming! It's the wave of the Holy Ghost!

Oh, yes, we've seen the power of the Holy Ghost in a limited fashion, but a wave is coming that will bring His power on a higher level and in a far greater measure than we have ever seen heretofore. I can see that wave way out yonder in the deep waters. It's coming! The waves of Holy Ghost power are building higher!

Don't stay on the old wave of yesterday's move of the Spirit. Swim out to the deep waters of the Spirit realm by praying in the Holy Ghost, and get on the *next* wave of God's purposes for this hour. Then keep on praying so you can ride that new wave as it builds and builds in divine power and glory.

I'm convinced the wave that is coming will be twice as high as the healing wave, the Charismatic wave, or the faith wave. In fact, it will be twice as high as all of them put together! I believe it is going to be the wave that sweeps us right on in to the shores of the Glory World!

Answering God's Call to Prayer

The Lord told me that there is a depth of prayer and intercession in the Spirit that will be lost unless we who are experienced in prayer somehow get those truths over to this present generation of believers. I've known a few folks over the years who were great intercessors and who became experts in this deeper realm of praying in the Holy Ghost. But God wants *more* who can pray like those few. He *must* have more believers who know how to pray in that deeper realm, because there is a job to get done in these last days. If His plans and purposes are to be fulfilled in this late hour, more and more of His people must say no to their flesh and spend time praying out divine mysteries to God.

You know, several decades ago, we all got concerned when the Russians put the first Sputnik satellite up in space. We spent billions of dollars to get ahead of them in the space race and to put the first astronauts up there. However, when our first astronauts went up into space, they didn't get very far. They barely got out of the earth's atmosphere, entering only into the very edge of space. Why didn't they go farther? Why didn't they go to the moon on the first try? Because they hadn't been out there before. *They didn't know how to maneuver in space.*

In the same way, some of us have only gotten the edge of the Spirit realm in prayer. We don't know how to maneuver out there, so we have to take it a little at a time. Nevertheless, as we continue to make ourselves available to God, praying in other tongues, He will lead us further into that deeper realm of prayer where miracles are wrought and divine revelation is granted.

I'm going to be honest and make a confession about this: I've been so far out there a few times, I got scared! I don't mean I got scared the way you are scared of a tornado or a rattlesnake. I'm talking about a holy fear. For one thing, I was afraid I couldn't get back. I believe that may be what happened to Enoch. He got so far out in the realm of the Spirit that he couldn't get back!

There is a moving out beyond time and beyond space into the realm of the Spirit that is beyond my ability to describe. Some have walked out into that realm of prayer only far enough to get their feet wet. Like children wading in the water, they talk about what they experienced, saying, "That was so wonderful! It was the ultimate in praying in the Spirit!" But in reality, their experience in prayer was barely the beginning!

These people have only *touched* the realm of the Spirit. They need to wade on out into the deep waters of the Spirit until it isn't only knee deep or loin deep, but *so* deep they can't possibly touch the ocean bottom! Then they can swim on out and enjoy the fullness of what God has for them in prayer (see Ezekiel 47).

However, it is important to understand that these things will not always come easy. For one thing, the flesh will do everything possible to hold us back. That's the reason the Word of God teaches us to crucify the flesh. The mind will also hold us back, trying to make us focus on the realm of the physical senses and what can be seen. That's one reason God tells us to get our minds renewed with His Word (Rom. 12:1-2). Once our minds are renewed, we'll be able to move further into the realm of His Spirit through prayer.

But as more and more of us respond to God's call to pray, there will begin to be greater and greater manifestations of His power and glory on this earth. The manifestation and demonstration of God's Spirit will become as common and as real as everyday natural things are to us. This is what our hearts have longed for and what intercessors have prayed for so many years.

You see, the realm of the Spirit is actually the natural realm for us who are born of the Spirit. Of course, it is necessary that we walk in the natural realm to a certain extent because our bodies are natural and have natural functions. We must live in that realm. But on the other hand, we can let our spirits have the continual privilege of communicating with the Father of spirits. We can let our spirits move out beyond the natural on a daily basis.

So don't take up all your time with natural things. Some of those things are legitimate, and it's all right to take a certain amount of time pursuing them. But see to it that you give heed to your spirit.

Give your spirit opportunity to feed upon the Word and to commune with your Heavenly Father. Build yourself up on your most holy faith by making a practice of praying in other tongues. It doesn't take a lot of time. As you do that, your own life will be changed and empowered, and your prayer life will become a mighty force, helping to fulfill God's purposes in these last days.

God wants us to move out further in the Spirit and learn how to maneuver in that greater realm of prayer. As we are faithful to obey His call to pray, the day will come when we move beyond the edge of space—further on out into the Spirit—and reach the fullness of God's glory!

I'll tell you this much: Jesus *is* coming. There is no use splitting hairs about that truth, because it *will* happen, whether you believe it or not! So let us commit ourselves to praying in the Spirit so a great harvest of souls can be reaped in these last days. *People are dying, and the end is coming. The end of all things is at hand, and what we do, we must do quickly.*

The Lord is calling us to prayer, and I, for one, am determined to answer that call.

Do you want to go with me? Just declare, "Count me in!" Then walk through the doorway to the supernatural and enter a whole new realm of prayer in the Spirit. It's a realm where revelation, direction, and supernatural communication with God are continually provided to help you fulfill *all* He's called you to do in this hour.

Kenneth E. Hagin's
Prayer on Behalf of the Church

Forgive us, O Lord. We've fallen and come so far short of the prayer life You intended us to have. We have settled for such a low grade of fellowship with You, until the things of the Spirit are so unreal to us, while mental and physical things are so very real and dominate us.

May we do just what the Bible commands us to do: Present our bodies a living sacrifice, holy and acceptable unto You, which is our reasonable service. And may we not be conformed to this world, but be transformed by the renewing of our minds—until the things of the Spirit become more real to us, and until Thou, O Father, become just as real in our spirits as the clothes we wear and the automobiles we drive.

Then we will move out into the realm of the Spirit to pray, for Thou art the Father of all spirits—but especially of our spirits, for we have been born again and are born of You. And Thou hast given to us a means of supernatural communication whereby our spirits can be in direct contact with the Father of spirits, for as Paul said, "If I pray in an unknown tongue, my spirit prayeth."

But we have taken so little advantage of this means of prayer, and You have not been able to do what You wanted to do with us, and for us, and in us, and through us in the past. We weren't ready. We weren't in place.

Now we are ready to some extent, and You are able to move us forward. But may we not stop here, Lord. May we not be satisfied. May we be like Smith Wigglesworth of old who said, "I am satisfied only with the dissatisfaction that has to be satisfied again and again."

May we move on from glory to glory. May we understand what You're saying about these last days. May we, through intercession and travail, give birth to that wave and to that move of God in the earth that You desire. May we understand what You are saying to our spirits.

We sense the urgency of it. We sense the need of it. We sense the necessity of it.

May we respond unto it, O God, that Your holy will may be wrought in this hour and that we may rise up in faith and, in the power of the Spirit, be the giants in the earth You always intended us to be.

May we be sensitive to the Spirit. May we be sensitive to His touch when He arrests our attention. May we know what He wants. May we respond to His prompting that He may manifest Himself through us and demonstrate Himself among us through signs and wonders and through diverse miracles and distributions of the Holy Ghost.

May we respond in the crisis of the hour and in the crisis of the day. And so shall we be ready for whatever arises. We will flow with the Spirit, and out of our innermost being shall flow rivers of living water.

Then the dry places shall spring forth in beauty, and those who are thirsty shall find water to drink. The spiritually dead shall be raised and revived, and life shall be made manifest everywhere. And we shall rejoice and be glad and declare that You have done it. All praise and honor and glory will be given unto You, for You deserve it and You are worthy.

May we be so dead to the flesh, so dead to selfishness, but so yielded unto the Spirit as we do the works of righteousness and perform the works of God so that the acts of God are made manifest in us. For we are in the end times. We face the last days when armies shall gather at Armageddon.

That day will come. But there will also come a sweeping harvest that sweeps across the world and around the globe because we prayed—because we dared to stand in that place of prayer. We dared to stand in the gap, to make up the hedge, and to intercede for the land.

Thus, the work of God shall be accomplished, and that which the Lord desires for the last days shall come to pass. And the harvest shall be reaped, the angels shall rejoice, men shall be blessed, and the glory of the Lord shall shine round about us brighter than the noonday sun. In the Name of Jesus, amen.

Why should you consider attending
RHEMA
Bible Training Center?

Here are a few good reasons:

- Training at one of the top Spirit-filled Bible schools anywhere
- Teaching based on steadfast faith in God's Word
- Growth in your spiritual walk coupled with practical training in effective ministry
- Specialization in the area of your choosing: Youth or Children's Ministry, Evangelism, Pastoral Care, Missions, Biblical Studies, or Supportive Ministry
- Optional intensive third-year programs: School of Worship, School of Pastoral Ministry, School of World Missions, and General Extended Studies
- Worldwide ministry opportunities—while you're in school
- An established network of churches and ministries around the world who depend on RHEMA to supply full-time staff and support ministers
- A two-year evening school taught entirely in Spanish is also available. Log on to **www.cebrhema.org** for more information.

Call today for information or application material.
1-888-28-FAITH (1-888-283-2484)
www.rbtc.org

RHEMA Bible Training Center admits students of any race, color, or ethnic origin.

OFFER CODE—BKORD:PRMDRBTC

Always on.

For the latest news and information on products, media, podcasts, study resources, and special offers, visit us online 24 hours a day.

www.rhema.org